D1053367

Beyond Blue
Economic Horizons

Beyond Blue Economic Horizons

U.S. Trade
Performance
and International
Competitiveness
in the 1990s

ALLEN J. LENZ

FOREWORD BY
PETER G. PETERSON

PRAEGER

New York
Westport, Connecticut
London

Library of Congress Cataloging-in-Publication Data

Lenz, Allen J.
    Beyond blue economic horizons : U.S. trade performance and
international competitiveness in the 1990s / Allen J. Lenz ; foreword
by Peter G. Peterson.
      p. cm.
    Includes bibliographical references.
    ISBN 0–275–93624–4
    1. Balance of trade—United States.   2. United States—Commercial
policy.   3. United States—Foreign economic relations.
4. Competition, International. I. Title.
HF3031.L38   1991
382′.17′0973—dc20   90–7625

Library of Congress Catalog Card Number: 90–7625
ISBN: 0–275–93624–4

First published in 1991

Praeger Publishers, One Madison Avenue, New York, NY 10010
An imprint of Greenwood Publishing Group, Inc.

Printed in the United States of America

The paper used in this book complies with the Permanent
Paper Standard issued by the National Information Standards
Organization (Z39.48—1984).

10 9 8 7 6 5 4 3 2 1

Copyright Acknowledgment

Chapter 8, "Trimming the U.S. Trade and Current Account Deficits," is taken from Allen J.
Lenz, "Slimming the U.S. Trade and Current Account Deficits," in *International Economics and
Financial Markets: The AMEX Bank Review Prize Essays*, edited by Richard O'Brien and Tapan
Data (OUP 1989), © The AMEX Bank Review 1989, pp. 19–41. Reprinted by permission of
Oxford University Press.

Contents

Tables and Figures

FIGURES

Foreword

One's career always has its thresholds. Certainly one of mine came in 1971 when President Richard Nixon invited me to Washington as his Assistant for International Economic Affairs. Having run Bell and Howell, a manufacturer of photographic equipment, I had become "oriented" to foreign competition. I was uncomfortably aware—as were most of us in the "real world"—that American industry faced harsh, new challenges in world markets. The wind was no longer at our backs.

On arriving in Washington, I therefore expected that the government would inundate me with long and brilliant memoranda, analyzing the changed global posture of our economy and recommending coherent, new departures for public policy that dealt with the root causes of what later came to be known as our "competitiveness" problem.

This expectation was grotesquely naive. In Washington, policy seemed to have little to do with commercial reality. In those days, Washington responded instead to bureaucratic imperatives. Even statistics obeyed this imperative. Simply to take the pulse of global economy, I had to place my fingers on a half-dozen different departments and agencies—on the Federal Reserve Board (money supply), the Bureau of Labor Statistics (productivity), the Treasury (international money), the State (aid), Commerce (trade, investment, output, industrial production and the like), the Agriculture Department (agriculture, not surprisingly), the Interior Department (energy and resources), the Economic Research and Intelligence section of the CIA, and so on. Unfortunately, our global economic problem was a multidimensional one that did not respect these territorial imperatives.

In going from data collection to analysis, the bureaucratic obstacles became even more formidable. The government, like ancient Gaul, was divided into three parts.

First (at least in self-esteem) came the foreign policy establishment: State, Defense, and the NSC. Here, economics had led a shadowy existence. Problems involving productivity, balance of payments deficits, trade barriers, investment flows, and currency crises were regarded as trivial and tiresome. This was work for technicians; it was not the stuff from which first-rate minds could mold brilliant careers. Those of us with acknowledged second-rate minds could worry about the second-rate subjects like trade, investment, currencies, and the like. Indeed, Henry Kissinger once chided me about being preoccupied with "minor commercial affairs." I retorted with surprise that he was being uncharacteristically redundant. In his world view of that earlier era, were there any *other* sorts of commercial affairs?

One had only to observe Kissinger to know that the "real" business of foreign policy was diplomatic nuance and nuclear negotiations. Did the United States face serious new international economic problems? "What problems?" senior officials in the State Department would ask me. The foreign policy elite, focused obsessively on Viet Nam or U.S.-Soviet relations, barely knew, or really cared. Even in the years thereafter, too many in our foreign policy establishments failed to perceive the profound relationship between the American slide economically and the inevitable slide politically in our relative world position. The Justice Department antitrust people implicitly joined the crowd, arguing perversely that foreign competition didn't really count.

Next, in second position, came the economic policy community—which was debating income policies and the merits of wage and price controls.

Accordingly, international economics usually received top priority attention only in the third bureaucratic community—made up of the "constituency" agencies of Commerce and Labor. Here, there was no complacency. The problem was, instead, something approaching hysteria. This community believed that more or less permanent and terminal competitive problems were caused by two forces—unfair competition by foreigners and a shift in the American economy from manufacturing to services. These forces, in turn, were inexorably eroding the position of the United States in world manufacturing markets. The favored "solution" was to protect our manufacturing industries with tariffs, quotas, and subsidies.

In short, it was no one's vocation to see the problem whole. With the enthusiasm of an amateur (and the naiveté of a noneconomist), my approach was hardly sophisticated. With the help of Allen Lenz and other members of my White House staff, we gathered data and information from every conceivable source, governmental and private, and then quickly arranged it on color slides in the form of simple charts, tables, and graphs. The first audience for what became known as "The Peterson Slide Show" was the Council on International Economic Policy, chaired by Richard Nixon. But we also tried to show it to any group of legislators, businessmen, labor leaders, or journalists that agreed to sit still for an hour or so. Notwithstanding its amateur status, this presentation became a best-seller, at least by U.S. Government Printing Office standards.

There was no sophisticated theory behind the charts. Nor were there any blinding insights—nor even any original information. Rather the response was simply symptomatic of the need—in this increasingly competitive and interdependent world—to understand the connectedness of the forces that increasingly determined our economic and political future.

By the later seventies, the mild befuddlement earlier in the decade had deepened into a conviction that our economy might be in more fundamental long-term trouble. Economic woes began to dominate our political discourse and a great deal of our dinner-table conversation. The warning signs are now even more obvious and enduring. In five short years, the world's largest creditor nation has become the world's largest debtor nation; the world's strongest and most resilient economy has become far more vulnerable to foreign I.O.U.s; the world's leading industrial power, the nation which once set the standard for product quality and productivity growth is being eclipsed by other nations; and the free world's principal defender has set its government down a path of severe fiscal imbalances and finds itself in the awkward posture of attempting to stand tall while on bended knees.

The story that emerged from the original 1971 slide show (and from the much more sophisticated and coherent tables and analyses included in this book) is one of deep and self-inflicted wounds. To be sure, there were "unfair" trade practices then, as now. But the overall message was and is that our economic problems were neither made in Japan nor smuggled here in OPEC's oil barrels. Nor were they caused primarily by the misguided policies of any particular domestic group of conspirators or extremists on either the left or the right.

The international economic challenges of the United States that were evident to some in 1971, are now painfully obvious to all. Likewise, it should be equally obvious that international economic power will increasingly displace military power in shaping world leadership and events in the decades ahead. Certainly, by now, the high priority of first-rate minds should have turned to identifying and resolving our international economic problems.

But we have done too little about these problems. We have become adept at wringing our hands—but more adept, it seems, at avoiding resolute action. Perhaps that is because most of us are seeing only unconnected bits and pieces of the problem. Recalling my Washington experience, it is profoundly difficult for any one of us to sift through the tons of data that cross our desks to form a coherent understanding of the real issues and what is at stake. Perhaps if we understand better the connected, systemic, structural aspects of our competitiveness—as any reader of this book certainly will—we will take action.

Peter G. Peterson
June 1990

Preface

The objective of this book is to provide an understanding of important international economic issues the United States must deal with during the next several years. It focuses primarily on two critical problems—the unprecedentedly large U.S. trade deficits and the nation's declining international competitiveness—and links them with other key economic and political problems.

This book is not written for economists or theoreticians. Its intent is to provide a broad understanding of these issues for those who have an active role or interest in the formulation and execution of U.S. policies that affect the nation's international trade and competitiveness.

It is a "primer," intended to provide an overview in non-technical language. It uses contemporary data to identify and explain the linkages among trade deficits, U.S. budget deficits, international competitiveness, the future of manufacturing in the United States, the U.S. debtor position, foreign direct investment, trade policy, the difficulties of narrowing global imbalances, and several other international economic problems. Flaws in government organization that create problems in conducting U.S. international economic policy are also discussed.

A central theme of the book is that U.S. trade deficits and the nation's international competitiveness are related but different problems, requiring separate policy consideration and sometimes different policy prescriptions. The large U.S. trade deficits of the 1980s are identified as an important, dangerous, highly visible, but temporary problem. The trade deficits, however, are a problem that can be eliminated without improving the nation's international competitiveness. In fact, some policies could improve U.S. trade balances but reduce the nation's international competitiveness.

Properly defined, international competitiveness is not measured by the nation's trade balances. Rather, international competitiveness is the continuing enhancement of U.S. living standards at rates that compare favorably with those of

competitor nations while maintaining sustainable trade balances. The U.S. failure
to meet this definition of competitiveness is a more insidious, more difficult,
and even more important problem than shrinking the trade deficits. Moreover,
it is a problem that will endure and intensify in the years ahead. It is also one
that, given its low visibility, may be neglected by U.S. policymakers.

A second theme of the book is the critical role of the manufacturing sector in
determining the nation's international competitiveness. The manufacturing sector
is the U.S. economy's primary interface with the world economy and international competition. Increasingly volatile international capital flows are manifested
in wide swings in merchandise trade balances among countries. The manufacturing sectors of the economies involved bear the adjustment costs of these
fluctuations in trade balances. Large net inflows of capital to the United States
during the 1980s decimated U.S. manufacturing and inhibited the capital investment needed to achieve productivity gains and to buttress lagging U.S.
international competitiveness.

Thus, more than any other sector, manufacturing is affected by tax and fiscal
policies that alter international capital flows. The book describes the dramatic
effect of domestic tax and fiscal policies on international capital flows, investment
in the manufacturing sector, and the structure and competitiveness of U.S. goods-
producing industries. It also advances arguments for increased attention to the
manufacturing sector in policy making.

Declining U.S. international competitiveness and the devastating effect of
wide fluctuations in international capital flows on U.S. goods-producing industries are relatively new phenomena. If this book increases attention to these
problems and the factors that created them, it will have served its purpose well.

The material is presented in four parts. Part I, "U.S. International Competitiveness," defines international competitiveness, separates it from the trade
deficit problem, and identifies its major determinants.

Part II, "The U.S. Trade Deficits," deals with the decline of U.S. trade
performance in the 1980s. Growth of the deficits is traced, causes and remedial
policy actions are identified, and the implications for U.S. manufacturing are
examined. Implications of the resulting escalation in U.S. international debt for
the U.S. and world economies are also described, and causes and remedial policy
actions are identified.

Part III, "Global Adjustment Problems," examines the difficult adjustments
that both the United States and its major trading partners must make to narrow
unsustainable U.S. deficits and the complementary surpluses of some trading
partners. The role of less developed countries (LDCs) in the creation of U.S.
trade deficits and the risks they face when U.S. deficits shrink are reviewed.

The 1990s promise to be a period of risks, opportunities, turbulence, and
rapid change for the world economy. Part IV, "Coping with the Future," examines the key policy alternatives for dealing with the trade and competitiveness
issues in the 1990s and provides a broad agenda of actions to deal with both
problems. A separate chapter describes flaws in the organization of the U.S.

government that hinder the conduct of U.S. policy and U.S. international economic leadership. The book concludes with a series of policy recommendations.

The key points of each chapter are presented in a summary section at the chapter's end.

Acknowledgments

I am indebted to many people for making this book possible. I am particularly grateful to the many skilled professionals in the International Trade Administration, U.S. Department of Commerce, who tutored me in a wide range of international economic issues. Special mention must go to Jeff Lins, Gary Teske, Bill Kokarik, Martin Kohn, and Lester Davis.

A number of colleagues read drafts and made valuable comments. They include: Lisa Barry, Dan Bond, Marshall Casse, David Elliott, Robert Hill, Kempton Jenkins, Mike Johnson, Harry Kopp, Debbie Lamb, Alan Magazine, Robert Miller, Douglas McMinn, Hunter Monroe, Jim O'Connor, George Phillips, Lee Price, Tom Singley, Gillian Spooner, Norman Ture, Mike Walls, and Sidney Zabludoff.

Special thanks must go to the Council on Competitiveness, which supported early research that led to this book. I am also particularly grateful to Beth Eck, Mary McNeil, Bruce Parsell, and Cindy Stromberg, who patiently and skillfully worked with me through many iterations of the text.

PART I

U.S. INTERNATIONAL COMPETITIVENESS

Declining U.S. competitiveness is often associated with the enlarging trade deficits of the 1980s. In fact, however, the U.S. trade deficits and the nation's international competitiveness are related but different problems. A clear conceptual separation of these issues is important to effective policy making.

Chapter 1 defines international competitiveness, describes why the enlarging trade deficits of recent years are not accurate measures of U.S. competitiveness, and explains the importance of maintaining a strong U.S. competitive position. It also examines the role of foreign trade in determining U.S. living standards and international competitiveness and how the U.S. competitiveness problem evolved.

Productivity growth is the key factor in living standard gains and maintaining and improving the nation's international competitiveness. Chapter 2 identifies and reviews the key determinants of productivity growth and recent U.S. performance.

Chapter 1

Trade Deficits and International Competitiveness: Two Key Problems of the 1990s

Each year from 1983 through 1987 record trade deficits rapidly changed the United States from the world's largest creditor nation to the world's largest debtor nation. These deficits focused public attention and concern on U.S. performance in the world economy. U.S. "competitiveness" has become a major concern and a much-discussed topic. Despite much rhetoric and many programs advocated as a means to improve competitiveness, it is seldom clearly defined and has not been addressed by policymakers in a meaningful way.

Large U.S. trade deficits, expected to continue well into the 1990s, are widely believed to be caused by declining U.S. competitiveness. In fact, trade deficits and international competitiveness are interrelated but different problems. Rather than resulting from a change in competitiveness, U.S. trade deficits are a factor contributing to declines in U.S. competitiveness.

Conceptually separating these two issues is important for several reasons, not the least of which is that they may require different policy prescriptions. A key objective of this book is to clarify both the differences and the interrelationships between trade deficits and international competitiveness so that policies applicable to each can be identified.

INTERNATIONAL COMPETITIVENESS DEFINED

The large trade deficits of the 1980s are widely seen as evidence of a decline in U.S. international competitiveness. Indeed, the recent surge of U.S. attention to competitiveness stems primarily from its huge trade deficits. Trade balances alone, however, are not good measures of a nation's competitiveness. The trade balances of all nations fluctuate from year to year and have cyclical tendencies. Balances are affected not only by domestic policies and economic performance but also by the policies and economic performance of foreign countries.

Net imports of goods and services demonstrate that a nation is borrowing abroad; large deficits show that it is borrowing heavily. No country, however, can indefinitely import more goods and services than it exports because no nation has unlimited international credit. Nor can any country indefinitely export significantly more than it imports. International economic forces inherent in the world's trade and financial systems will sooner or later force changes in exchange rates, national economic growth rates, relative prices, and other factors to narrow large imbalances. This ensures that—over time—nations will achieve sustainable external balances consistent with their economic size and structure. In the long run all nations must achieve a rough cumulative balance in their goods and services trade.

Some countries, however, may grow richer as trade balances fluctuate. Others may stagnate or even become poorer. Despite these trends, over the long term even the poorest, most impoverished countries must ultimately be "competitive" in the sense of eliminating large trade deficits. Several Latin American debtor countries, for example, had trade surpluses in the later years of the 1980s. Yet few would consider those economies, with their relatively low output, productivity, and living standards, to be on an equal economic footing with the United States. Most recent Latin American trade surpluses, in fact, have been forced by debt-servicing requirements. The severe import cuts required to achieve these surpluses have reduced living standards and have constrained economic growth.

Trade balances, therefore, provide only limited information about a country's economic performance, and large trade surpluses are not necessarily a sign of well being. Neither trade surpluses nor trade deficits are reliable indicators of what a national economy is providing to its members or of the economy's longer term direction. A useful measure of competitiveness should show an economy's performance in broader terms.

A primary goal of most national economies is to achieve increasingly high standards of economic welfare for their citizens. Unfortunately, there is no single, simple statistical indicator of economic welfare. Nonetheless, various measures of change in a nation's standard of living can provide a useful gauge of longer term trends in an economy's performance. Recognizing the linkage between living standards and real incomes, the President's Commission on Industrial Competitiveness defined international competitiveness in the following way:

International Competitiveness is the degree to which a nation can, under free and fair market conditions, meet the test of international markets, while simultaneously maintaining and expanding the real incomes of its citizens.[1]

Changes in real per capita incomes—nominal incomes adjusted for the effects of inflation—are one means of measuring change in living standards and are a broad, albeit imperfect, measure of the nation's economic welfare. Thus the commission's definition implies that international competitiveness requires that long-run balances in external accounts be achieved *concurrent with maintaining or increasing the nation's standard of living*.

Such a definition, however, is incomplete. Even if a nation's living standards increase, this may not be enough. Until the recent economic reforms began, for example, living standards in the Soviet Union had continued to rise gradually since World War II. Yet the Soviet Union was forced to economic reform because its economy was performing so poorly relative to others that it was falling farther and farther behind other nations. The Soviet Union's problem was not so much that it was unable to increase its output and raise its living standards but that it was unable to do so rapidly enough both to maintain its global military power and to avoid internal dissatisfaction among its citizens, who compared the country's economic performance with that of others. Lagging performance relative to other economies forced reforms in the Soviet economic system that will be difficult to accomplish.

The implication is clear: Gradually improving economic performance and living standards may not be enough. It is not only absolute gains that matter but also relative performance. Indeed, the relation of a nation's economic performance to that of other nations is critically important, both in satisfying the expectations of its citizens and in determining its political and military power and global leadership roles.

A nation's current economic performance compared to its past performance and to its economic potential provides another useful competitiveness indicator. Increases in a country's living standards smaller than those of earlier periods not only generate dissatisfaction but also may reflect growing economic problems. On the other hand, unless financed by borrowing abroad, an escalating growth of real incomes may signal increasing competitiveness.

In large measure, a nation's current living standards are inherited from past policies, particularly those that influenced investment in the growth of production capacity. Similarly, today's policies influence the growth of productivity and production capacity that will determine living standards in future years. Nations—particularly affluent nations—that emphasize current consumption at the expense of saving and investment that would build future production are not developing fully their economic potential. They will inevitably fall behind competitors that put more emphasis on saving and investment; those who put less emphasis on current consumption and more on future consumption.

A nation's level of development is also relevant in evaluating its performance in maintaining and increasing living standards. Less developed countries with rapidly expanding populations may have difficulty generating the capital investment and other ingredients needed to increase their living standards. But if the means can be found, the LDCs may be able to achieve growth rates stronger than more advanced economies because they are starting from a low base.

Thus there is no specific rate of advance or level of living standards that alone measures a nation's "competitiveness." Rapid improvements by less developed countries signal growing competitiveness. But in one sense a nation is not truly competitive until its living standards begin to approach those of the more advanced nations. Rapid, sustained advances in living standards, while maintaining strong trade performance, may indicate competitiveness for developed economies. Competitiveness, however, is not a permanent state. Being internationally competitive implies not only that a nation achieve high living standards but also that it continue to fulfill its potential and continue to match or exceed the increases of its peers.

A competitive nation, then, is one that maintains a rough cumulative balance in its international accounts while increasing its already high standards of living at rates that compare favorably with the improvements achieved by other nations at comparable levels of development.

U.S. COMPETITIVENESS IN PERSPECTIVE: IS THERE A PROBLEM?

Measured by these criteria, is the United States internationally competitive? By most measurements, real incomes in the United States increased in the 1980s, albeit at much more modest rates than in earlier years. Nevertheless, the relative position of the United States in the global economy has changed dramatically in recent decades. The gap between U.S. living standards and those of many foreign countries has narrowed, if not disappeared. U.S. dominance of international markets is gone, and the competition facing U.S. producers has become increasingly tough. Is this disadvantageous to members of the U.S. economy? Not necessarily. Fortunately, the struggle among nations for international markets and the competition to improve living standards and increase economic power need not be a zero-sum game. In fact, they can benefit all, including those nations who advance most rapidly and those whose rates of improvement lag.

U.S. economic preeminence of the post–World War II period is over. Viewed from a global perspective, this should not be regretted. Instead, the rise of foreign economic power is evidence of successful U.S. post–World War II policies that have benefited both the United States and its trading partners. U.S. living standards today are markedly higher than those of earlier days when large gaps existed between U.S. and foreign living standards. Moreover, U.S. living standards are higher than they would be without the advance of other economies. Newly competitive foreign economies have stimulated global competition, held down U.S. prices, and contributed new goods and technologies to the U.S. and world economies. In absolute terms—the amount of goods and services available—U.S. residents are better off than they would have been if the United States had remained dominant within the world economy. Competition and contributions from other nations have generally benefited U.S. standards of living.

What is happening to the improvement of U.S. living standards when measured against other nations? How do recent growth rates compare with past performances and relate to U.S. potential? By most measurements, U.S. standards of living have continued to increase and still remain above those of other developed nations. The U.S. rate of increase has slowed, however, and is well below that of several other developed nations. As a result, the gap in living standards between the United States and many other nations has narrowed markedly. In its "Competitiveness Index," for example, the Council on Competitiveness found that during the 1972–88 period the U.S. standard of living (defined as gross national product [GNP] per capita) increased by only 31 percent, compared with 41 percent for Germany, 66 percent for Japan, and 46 percent for the other "Summit 7" countries.[2] If recent trends continue, U.S. living standards will one day lag behind those of several other nations.

In part, the faster rate of advance of foreign competitors has been due to their catch-up status, to their emulation of U.S. technology. It is easier and faster to draw on existing products and technologies than to develop new ones. Increasingly, however, competitor countries are developing their own new products and technologies. Often they are now not simply matching but are surpassing the United States.

Moreover, although U.S. living standards as measured by real incomes do show advances, this may be somewhat misleading. Much of the relatively modest increase in U.S. living standards in recent years has been supplied by large borrowing abroad manifested in the large trade deficits of the 1980s. This level of borrowing and the resulting temporary growth of current consumption and living standards cannot continue without end. Today's increased consumption that is based on borrowing abroad will be at the expense of future living standards. Sustained heavy foreign borrowing by a rich nation such as the United States and a growing external debt show an inability to constrain consumption to levels that allow it to generate its own investment capital. This may be a harbinger of significant long-term competitiveness problems for the United States.

Is there a U.S. international competitiveness problem? What is the outlook for U.S. living standards in the years ahead? Will economic growth be enough to maintain or improve U.S. competitiveness? There are signals that, without significant policy changes, improvements in U.S. living standards may at best be modest and may continue to lag behind those of other major developed countries. By most evaluations, however, the United States does not necessarily face declining real incomes and living standards in the decade ahead. Assuming reasonably intelligent U.S. policies and no major global economic mishaps, the more relevant question is, "At what rate will U.S. living standards advance compared to those of other nations?" That is, will others continue to outpace the United States, ultimately surpassing it?

Whether or not one perceives a U.S. competitiveness problem depends very much on what one sees as the nation's economic and political roles and objectives. If the United States is content simply to achieve modest gains over current living standards, defined broadly as longer life spans, more material goods, more leisure time, and improved conveniences in everyday living, most Americans will probably enjoy higher living standards in the year 2000 than today. The advance of technology alone should make such improvements possible.

But if maintaining or increasing the standard of living implies achieving a larger measure of the economy's full potential and keeping ahead or abreast of advancing standards in other countries, the United States has a problem. If being internationally competitive means retaining the economic power to provide global economic, political, and military leadership, that problem is one of growing concern. A continuation of recent trends in time will markedly alter living standard relationships among nations. In turn, this will alter global political, economic, and military power relationships and leadership roles.

It is a mathematical certainty that if recent trends continue the United States will one day no longer be the world's number one economic power. But recent trends will not necessarily continue. The United States has played a critical role in the post-war expansion of the world economy. Recent U.S. trade deficits have played particularly important roles in the successful economic development of Japan, the Asian newly industrializing countries (NICs), and other LDCs. It remains to be seen whether the rest of the world can continue to prosper and whether some high-growth countries can continue their spectacular advances when the large U.S. trade deficits that have powered their economic growth in recent years have disappeared.

The difficult task ahead is simultaneously to boost U.S. living standard rates of improvement to levels that match those of our major developed country competitors and to end U.S. trade deficits in a way that allows continued high foreign growth rates. That translates into "leveling upward," not "averaging down."

ORIGINS AND RISKS OF THE TRADE DEFICITS AND LAGGING COMPETITIVENESS

The growth, causes, and implications of the U.S. trade deficits of the 1980s are explored in Chapters 3 through 6. In brief, however, U.S. trade deficits show that the nation as a whole is consuming more than it is producing, with the shortfall filled by borrowing from abroad. This borrowing is manifested in the net inflows of goods and services that are the U.S. trade deficits.

Although some still attribute the U.S. trade deficits to foreign barriers to U.S. exports, two major macroeconomic factors have pushed the nation's consumption above its production, resulting in the trade deficits: a large increase in government dissaving—the federal government budget deficit—and a concurrent significant decline in the U.S. private-sector saving rate—an increase in private-sector consumption at the expense of saving. These phenomena have little to do with foreign trade barriers. They stem from low U.S. saving rates that are a result of many cultural and economic factors and can best be remedied by U.S. macroeconomic policies.

The international competitiveness problem manifested in lagging rates of growth in U.S. real incomes has similar origins—too much of total U.S. income has gone to consumption, too little to saving and investment. The basic determinants of international competitiveness are described in Chapter 2. In brief, however, a nation's international competitiveness—balancing its external accounts while increasing its living standards at rates that compare favorably with competitor countries—depends primarily on keeping productivity growth rates equal to or greater than those of its major competitors. Productivity growth rates, in turn, are shaped primarily by rates of investment and innovation. Low rates of investment in human and physical capital result in low productivity growth and lagging international competitiveness. High rates of investment tend to produce high productivity growth rates and improvements in international competitiveness.

Diminishing growth in U.S. productivity and living standards is not a new phenomenon of the 1980s. In fact, lagging productivity gains were in evidence well before large U.S. trade deficits began. Productivity growth slowed in the 1970s and continued to be low into the 1980s. If U.S. productivity had continued to grow throughout the post-war period at the 3.25 percent rate recorded between 1948 and 1965, U.S. output in 1987 would have been 50 percent higher than it was. The resulting median income of the American family—roughly $30,000 in 1987—would have been about $54,000.[3]

The fact is that low saving and investment rates, slowing productivity growth rates, and shrinking living standard gains presaged the large trade deficits. Then a marked increase in government deficits in the early 1980s and a concurrent decline in the private-sector saving rate triggered the large trade deficits and foreign borrowing of the 1980s.

THE ROLE OF FOREIGN TRADE IN INTERNATIONAL COMPETITIVENESS

A nation's competitiveness and living standards improve primarily through productivity growth—through growth in its output per worker. Foreign trade also plays an increasingly important and critical role in determining living standards.

In a world without foreign trade, a nation's living standards would depend only on the growth of incomes from its own resources and from its own increased productivity. But in an integrated global economy, foreign trade is more and more important to a nation's living standards. Foreign trade allows the use of foreign technologies, raw materials, and finished goods in many ways that enhance domestic production, consumption, and living standards. In addition, a nation's living standards are affected by its international trade performance in three ways: immediate effects of the trade balance on consumption, downstream effects on the trade balance and consumption, and exchange rate effects.

First, the trade balance has immediate effects on current consumption. The current account balance is the broadest measure of a nation's foreign transactions. It summarizes the difference between a nation's production and its consumption. A current account surplus indicates lending abroad that lowers current consumption and living standards below those that could be supported by current production. A current account deficit, on the other hand, indicates borrowing abroad that raises current consumption and living standards above rates that would result from current production. The large 1983–89 trade and current account deficits allowed U.S. consumption and living standards to rise significantly above the level provided by U.S. production. The 1987 current account deficit, for example, was equivalent to borrowing abroad at a rate of about $590 per person.

Second, current account deficits create debt that must be serviced by holding future consumption below future production, with depressing effects on future living standards. If U.S. external debt growth continues, debt servicing costs in the early 1990s could approximate 0.5 percent or more of U.S. GNP, lowering the nation's total consumption and living standards below the sum of production and borrowing by that amount. The net effect of the accumulated borrowing on living standards, however, will be greater than the costs of this debt servicing. It also includes the income lost from dissipating the earlier creditor position. In the early 1980s net income from foreign investments was equivalent to about 1 percent of GNP, implying a likely loss of about 1.5 percent of GNP available for consumption during the transition from large creditor nation of the early 1980s to large debtor nation of the early 1990s.

Third, currency exchange rates can change and, in doing so, can affect living standards. A declining exchange rate, for example, raises the costs of imports and puts downward pressure on living standards. Indeed, though exchange rates fluctuate as the result of changing international economic factors, the secular trend of the exchange rate is itself a good indicator of trends in a nation's international competitiveness. An exchange rate that strengthens over the long term is indicative of increasing competitiveness; a long-term downward trend is a sign of declining competitiveness.

The effects of changes in the exchange rate on living standards are difficult to quantify precisely. However, according to Lester Thurow, professor of economics and management at the Massachusetts Institute of Technology,

If American productivity grows at 1 percent per year and the productivity of our industrial competitors grows at 4 percent per year, the American dollar must fall by approximately 3 percent per year to maintain a balance in America's balance of trade. With 12 percent of GNP imported . . . [this] causes American standards of living to fall by .4 percent (.12 times .03) per year forever.[4]

As the above example shows, international trade is only one factor in determining a nation's living standards and its international competitiveness. Thurow's calculations suggest, however, that the potential impact of consistently lagging productivity gains on living standards and international competitiveness may be a significant portion of potential U.S. economic growth that typically ranges under 3 percent annually. Rates of change in productivity and living standards are primarily the result of internal production and income gains, not principally the outcome of foreign trade relationships. But during the next several years, the combined effects on living standards of productivity increases that lag behind those of competitors and of returning the United States to a balance in its external accounts are likely to be substantial.

According to Robert Lawrence, a Brookings Institution scholar, if the United States takes the actions required to end its current account deficits and foreign borrowing,

All told, U.S. living standards [in the years ahead] will be reduced through three effects: first by the need to bring spending back into line with production; second, by the permanent interest burdens that will have to be serviced; and third, by the declining purchasing power of the dollar [the fall in the dollar exchange rate] necessary to generate the trade flows required to bring spending into line with production less net foreign interest payments.[5]

Simulations performed by Lawrence show that bringing U.S. national spending into line with production (balancing the current account and ending the associated borrowing abroad) by 1995 would lower the average American's annual spending by about $700. Net interest payments on the accrued foreign debt would cost an additional $147–$178 per person, and per capita losses due to the decline in the terms of trade could range between $259 and $1,155, depending on the amount of dollar decline required to achieve balance.[6] These costs would cut into and reduce the gains achieved in per capita output from continuing productivity growth and from other sources.[7]

Assuming an annual per capita output growth rate of 1.7 percent, an amount consistent with long-term trends in productivity gains and population growth, Lawrence's estimates indicate net remaining gains in U.S. living standards for the entire 1987–95 period ranging from only about 1 percent to 10 percent, depending on the assumptions. The 10 percent gain, however, results from a combination of optimistic assumptions that is highly unlikely. Even the 10 percent improvement during the eight-year period would produce yearly gains of only slightly more than 1 percent. The net cumulative effect of recent trade deficits and the dollar exchange rate decline required to eliminate those deficits thus may be large, substantially lowering the rate of future living standard gains for several years. Not all of these reductions in living standard gains would be permanent, however. Once the effects of shrinking foreign borrowing and a declining dollar exchange rate are absorbed, living standards can return to the higher growth rates of earlier years. They can more closely parallel the potential growth in per capita output, which Lawrence believes to be about 1.7 percent annually.

The cost of servicing the foreign debt and its drain on living standards will, however, persist as long as the debt exists. Moreover, if U.S. productivity gains continue to lag those of competitors, compensating dollar depreciation will also continue to put downward pressure on living standards.

Lawrence's estimates are useful approximations of the potential effect of recent trade deficits on future U.S. living standards. In short, the effects are likely to lower living standard gains significantly below the modest levels that could otherwise be expected. National per capita living standard gain and loss calculations, however, do not tell the whole story. It will be seen (Chapter 3) that international trade is primarily in goods; relatively few services are tradeable across international borders. Swings in trade balances and fluctuations in exchange rates affect the population unevenly. They influence wage and employment levels and investment in plant and equipment and research and development (R&D) much more in the manufacturing sector than in other major sectors. The growth of trade deficits during the 1980s caused wrenching structural changes in U.S. manufacturing. It shifted investment and employment from the goods-producing to the services sector. Similarly, lowering the nation's trade deficits will require a significant—but opposite—structural adjustment within the economy. Relative shares of goods and services production will again have to alter, this time enlarging the goods-producing sector in relation to the services sector. Such swings in the size and employment of the manufacturing sector come at a price.

Finally, even though international trade performance is only one element in determining a nation's living standards, sustained poor performance is an important indicator of likely competitiveness problems in the economy as a whole. Saving, investment, and productivity growth factors determine performance in both the domestic and foreign trade sectors in much the same way. Weak performance in the foreign trade sector and a need for continued currency depreciation to balance accounts reflect weak productivity growth in the overall economy. Similarly, strong performance in productivity growth in the domestic sector will likely be accompanied by strong performance in the foreign sector and in currency appreciation.

The need for strong productivity gains clearly extends beyond goods production and foreign trade. Productivity gains in both goods and services production are critical to the growth of the domestic economy. In a more integrated world economy, access to foreign raw materials, goods, and technology will be increasingly important in the maintenance and enhancement of U.S. international competitiveness and improving the nation's living standards. The terms of international trade, reflected in the dollar exchange rate, therefore will be increasingly important in setting U.S. living standards. Matching the productivity gains and technological advances of other nations will be increasingly difficult. In a new, more competitive world it will be necessary to advance faster and faster simply to maintain one's position, let alone to improve it.

OVERVIEW OF THE TWO PROBLEMS

The trade deficits and U.S. international competitiveness are both difficult, risky problems examined in greater detail in later chapters. The trade deficits pose several large costs and risks for the U.S. and global economies. These are:

- The large U.S. trade deficits and the complementary surpluses of some trading partners are unsustainable distortions in the international flow of goods and services. Shrinking these imbalances to more sustainable levels while maintaining good economic growth rates will be difficult and will likely impose wrenching structural adjustments on some economies. The risks of adjustment include rising global protectionism and the possibility that rapid changes in capital flows and trade balances will produce a "hard landing"—a major, debilitating disruption of the global economy and international trade flows.

- Although the continued heavy international borrowing represented by trade deficits does increase current U.S. living standards, it impairs future living standards and competitiveness in two ways: First, it creates debt that must be serviced at the expense of future living standards. Second, it raises current interest rates above levels that would otherwise prevail and thereby inhibits investment and impairs future U.S. productivity and competitiveness.

- Rising concern about accumulating international debt or the perceived loss of jobs to imports could also trigger protectionist actions in the United States as well as reciprocal foreign moves.

In short, both economic and political pressures will eventually force a narrowing of the U.S. trade deficits and the complementary trade surpluses of some countries. Facilitating gradual improvement and avoiding sharp changes in economic forces and political actions that might dramatically raise U.S. and international trade barriers are difficult problems likely to continue well into the 1990s.

The risks of declining U.S. international competitiveness can also be summarized in three broad categories.

- When real income gains fall below potential, members of the economy clearly lose in the consumption of tangible goods and services; the nation's living standards are lower than they could be.

- Internationally, the relative decline in U.S. competitiveness could lead to a decline of its military, political, and international economic leadership roles and to a U.S. abandonment of some global commitments.

- Lagging economic performance compared to other societies could have far-reaching domestic political and economic consequences, including pressure to make basic economic and political systemic changes.

A decline in U.S. international competitiveness relative to those of other countries and the resulting decline in the U.S. international leadership role will occur only gradually. The elements that determine growth rates are deep-rooted in American society and in U.S. macroeconomic policies. Because the effects of slower growth cumulate gradually and subtly, and because the improvement of long-term economic growth rates may require fundamental policy changes, international competitiveness is a more enduring and important problem than the trade deficits. It is also a more difficult problem to deal with.

Separating the trade deficit problem from the competitiveness problem is important because it affects how U.S. trade and competitiveness problems are identified, the remedies that will be sought, and the policies that will be applied. These distinctions and their importance are further developed in the chapters that follow.

SUMMARY

• U.S. trade deficits and U.S. international competitiveness are essentially different problems, though in part they stem from common causes.

• "Competitiveness" is the ability of a nation to maintain a rough cumulative balance in its external accounts over the long term while making gains in its standards of living that compare favorably with other nations at comparable stages of development.

• U.S. competitiveness is an ill-defined problem and one that U.S. policy making has not focused on. A clear distinction between the trade deficits and international competitiveness is important because some actions that might narrow the trade deficit could actually impair U.S. competitiveness.

• Differentiating between the trade deficit and competitiveness problems is also important to ensure that both are adequately addressed by policymakers. It is particularly important that attention be directed to the more difficult and longer term competitiveness problem, which may be neglected because there is no visible, obvious crisis.

• A nation's trade balance is a flawed indicator of its international competitiveness because it reveals little about long-term trends in the nation's standard of living.

• The trade deficits are a relatively short-term problem that can be resolved in a few years by appropriate policy measures. Competitiveness, however, is a long-term, enduring problem that cannot be quickly resolved; it is one that will require continuing attention.

• Both problems pose serious risks to the United States. The trade deficits are accruing international debt that will impose a drain on future living standards. The costs of declining international competitiveness include lower future living standards and a reduced U.S. economic, political, and military leadership capability.

• Declining U.S. competitiveness stems from slowing productivity gains, which in turn are the result of lagging investment in human and physical capital.

• U.S. living standards are not primarily determined by the nation's performance in international trade but by productivity advances in the domestic economy, including services industries that do not face international competition. But as the world economy becomes more integrated and the United States more dependent on foreign sources for raw materials, oil, finished goods, and technology, the ability of U.S.-based production to compete in U.S. and foreign markets at favorable terms of trade will become more important.

• U.S. living standards will likely continue to increase but perhaps at more modest rates than those of some other competitor nations, resulting in a declining U.S. international competitiveness position.

NOTES

1. The President's Commission on Industrial Competitiveness, *Global Competition: The New Reality,* vol. 1, Commission Report (Washington, D.C.: U.S. Government Printing Office, 1985), 6.

2. *Competitiveness Index* (Washington, D.C.: Council on Competitiveness, June 1989), 5.

3. Robert E. Litan, Robert Z. Lawrence, and Charles L. Schultz, "Improving American Living Standards," *The Brookings Review,* Winter 1988/89, 28.

4. Lester C. Thurow, *The Zero Sum Solution: An Economic and Political Agenda for the '80s* (New York: Simon & Schuster, 1985), 93–94.

5. Robert Z. Lawrence, "The International Dimension," in Robert Litan, Robert Lawrence, and Charles Schultz, eds., *American Living Standards: Threats and Challenges* (Washington, D.C.: The Brookings Institution, 1988), 44.

6. Ibid.

7. Per capita output growth rates (the nation's total output divided by its total population) can differ from productivity growth rates as the portion of the total population that is employed changes. For example, an increase in the portion of women who enter the labor force and a decline in the unemployment rate tend to raise per capita output; an aging of the population and an increase in the ratio of retired persons to employed persons tend to lower per capita output.

Chapter 2

Determinants of International Competitiveness

PRODUCTIVITY, LIVING STANDARDS, AND INTERNATIONAL COMPETITIVENESS

A nation's standard of living is an elusive concept. In the broadest sense it may include many intangibles that determine the quality of life, ranging from health care to air quality and recreational opportunities. In the material sense, however, it can be thought of as per capita consumption. As long as unused labor is available, increases in a nation's production available for consumption can be achieved by increasing the portion of the total population that is employed. This could be done, for example, by reducing unemployment rates or enlarging the labor force through increasing the participation of working mothers. For short periods, increases in consumption may be provided by net imports that constitute external borrowing. In the longer term, however, a nation's consumption and material living standards must be derived from its productivity—the amount produced per worker. Rises in living standards must come fundamentally from productivity increases. The term *productivity,* as used in this book, not only means churning out more units of a good or service for each unit of input, but also improving quality and creating innovative new products.

In an integrated world economy, simply increasing productivity is not enough to maintain or strengthen the United States' competitive position. If a competitor's productivity grows more rapidly than that of the United States, the competitor's prices will decline relative to U.S. prices. This will increase its share of U.S. and foreign markets. Dollar depreciation and downward pressure on real wages will then be required to return U.S. external transactions to balance. In the long term, if the United States is to balance its international accounts without deteriorating terms of trade, U.S. productivity growth rates must compare favorably with those of other major trading nations.

For the most part, then, international competitiveness is a contest of productivity increases, with productivity defined to include quality gains and new products. It is a contest, however, in which all nations can gain. Strong productivity growth abroad is desirable from the U.S. viewpoint not only because it will contribute to improving global standards of living but also because some part of foreign productivity gains, embodied in imported goods and technology, will benefit U.S consumers.

How has the United States fared in the productivity growth race? Changes in output per worker-hour are a common measure of productivity growth rates. These increases in output per worker-hour result from increases in the stock of physical capital per worker and improvement in the ways in which human and physical capital work together to produce goods and services. No single statistic tells the whole story, but because the manufacturing sector interacts more directly with and is more affected by foreign competition than most other sectors, manufacturing productivity is a useful indicator of U.S. performance in international competition.

Productivity growth rates in U.S. manufacturing have improved recently (Table 2–1). Growth rates of the past few years compare favorably with those of earlier years. The productivity of major competitors, however, has consistently increased more rapidly than that of the United States. Therefore, the U.S. manufacturing sector has been losing ground relative to its competitors, a strong indicator of declining U.S. international competitiveness. During the 1973–88 period the 2.5 percent annual U.S. manufacturing productivity growth rate lagged far behind Japan's 5.7 percent rate, was significantly under the average growth rate of ten other industrial countries, and was well below even the United Kingdom's 3.3 percent growth rate.

In more recent years, U.S. productivity growth rates have increased. During the 1987–88 period, U.S. rates compared more favorably with other industrialized countries, yet still lagged behind some other major competitors. The U.S. manufacturing productivity increase of 3.2 percent for 1988 was only slightly lower than the gain of 3.4 percent in 1987. It equaled that of Canada in 1988 but fell well below manufacturing productivity growth in Japan (7.6 percent), France (5.3 percent), the Netherlands (5.0 percent), the United Kingdom (4.9 percent), and Germany (4.6 percent).

Productivity growth in U.S. manufacturing was particularly strong during the 1983–87 period, partly as a result of significant changes forced on U.S. manufacturing by foreign penetration of U.S. markets. Short-term spurts in productivity growth are often spurred by personnel cuts, making more effective use of existing resources, shutting down marginal and less efficient facilities, and cutting non-essential programs. These kinds of quick, one-time changes may be forced by foreign competition, recessions, and other factors. But strong increases in productivity sustained over the long term require consistent, continuing emphasis on those factors that underlie continuing productivity growth—improving human and physical capital stocks.

Table 2-1
Manufacturing Output per Hour, Average Annual Percentage Rates of Change, Twelve Countries

Country	1960–88	1960–73	1973–88	1973–79	1979–88	1979–86	1987	1988
United States	2.8	3.2	2.5	1.4	3.3	3.3	3.4	3.2
Canada	3.3	4.5	2.2	2.1	2.2	2.1	2.4	3.2
Japan	7.8	10.3	5.7	5.5	5.8	5.2	7.8	7.6
Belgium	6.3	6.9	5.7	6.0	5.4	5.6	3.7	NA
Denmark	4.2	6.4	2.3	4.2	1.1	1.3	.9	.0
France	4.9	6.4	3.7	4.6	3.1	3.0	1.2	5.3
Germany	4.4	5.8	3.3	4.3	2.6	2.5	1.3	4.6
Italy	5.5	6.4	4.7	5.7	4.1	4.5	2.5	2.9
Netherlands	5.7	7.4	4.3	5.5	3.5	3.7	.8	5.0
Norway	3.4	4.3	2.4	2.2	2.6	2.3	5.0	NA
Sweden	4.5	6.4	2.9	2.6	3.0	3.0	4.3	2.3
United Kingdom	3.7	4.2	3.3	1.2	4.7	4.4	6.4	4.9

Source: U.S. Department of Labor.

KEYS TO MEETING THE INTERNATIONAL COMPETITIVENESS CHALLENGE

A nation's productivity and its international competitiveness are determined fundamentally by the quality of its human capital (the quality of its work force), the amount and quality of its physical capital (the machines, buildings, equipment, and technology used in production), and how well these stocks of human and physical capital function together to produce goods and services. Consistent, long-term productivity growth and the development of new products and higher living standards depend on improving the quality of human capital, enlarging the quality and quantity of physical capital, and improving the use of the available stocks of human and physical capital.

The amounts and quality of a nation's human and physical capital normally change only gradually. Changes are influenced by many social, demographic, and economic forces. Over the long term, however, a nation's economic policies can significantly affect the size, quality, and use of its capital. Economic policies primarily affect the rates of new investment in both human and physical capital and influence the way in which these resources work together to produce goods and services.

The following are key factors in raising productivity and meeting the international competitiveness challenge:

- High national saving rates
- Strong capital formation rates
- Expanding research and development
- Continuing human resource development
- Effective trade policies

U.S. Saving Rates

Saving is the portion of an economic entity's earnings that is set aside for future consumption. *National saving* is the sum of private and public saving. High national saving rates are necessary to provide the financial capital to fund new investments at favorable interest rates. Low saving rates generate a small supply of funds available for investment, leading to high interest rates that deter investment or require borrowing capital from abroad. Saving rates should be adequate to obviate the need for large net imports of foreign financial capital for extended periods. In recent years, U.S. saving has been inadequate to finance the demand for investment goods and services. In 1988, with gross domestic saving equal to only 13.2 percent of GNP, gross private investment of 15.4 percent of GNP was financed partly by foreign investment equal to 2.4 percent of GNP (Table 2–2).

For some time, the United States has had the lowest saving rate among major

Table 2-2
Composition of U.S. Saving as a Percentage of GNP, 1980–88

	1980	1981	1982	1983	1984	1985	1986	1987	1988
Gross Saving Of Which:	16.3	17.1	14.1	13.6	15.1	13.3	12.4	12.2	13.2
Private Saving Of Which:	17.5	18.0	17.6	17.4	17.9	16.6	15.8	14.7	15.1
Personal	5.0	5.2	4.9	3.8	4.4	3.1	3.0	2.3	3.0
Business	12.5	12.8	12.7	13.6	13.5	13.4	12.9	12.4	12.2
State and Local Government Surplus (Saving)	1.0	1.1	1.1	1.4	1.7	1.6	1.5	1.1	1.0
Federal Government Deficit (Dissaving)	-2.2	-2.1	-4.6	-5.2	-4.5	-4.9	-4.9	-3.6	-3.0
Gross Investment	16.5	17.2	14.1	13.8	15.2	13.2	12.4	12.1	13.0
Net Foreign Investment	0.5	0.3	-0.0	-1.0	-2.4	-2.8	-3.2	-3.3	-2.4
Gross Private Domestic Investment	16.0	16.9	14.1	14.7	17.6	16.0	15.6	15.5	15.4
Statistical Discrepancy	0.2	0.1	-0.0	0.2	0.1	-0.1	-0.0	-0.1	-0.2

Source: U.S. Department of Commerce.

Table 2–3
Gross Saving of Selected Countries as a Percentage of GDP, 1980–86

	1980	1981	1982	1983	1984	1985	1986
United States	19.2	19.8	16.8	15.8	17.2	15.9	15.0
Japan	31.1	31.1	30.5	29.8	30.7	31.7	31.9
Germany	21.8	20.2	20.3	21.1	21.8	22.1	23.4
France	23.6	21.1	19.7	19.1	19.0	18.9	19.8
United Kingdom	18.5	18.0	18.2	18.1	18.4	19.0	18.3
Canada	22.9	22.6	19.5	18.8	19.9	18.9	18.0

Source: OECD.

competitor developed nations. The broadest and most useful comparison is in *gross* savings, the sum of personal, business, and government saving. Table 2–3 presents a comparison between six countries of gross savings as a percentage of gross domestic product (GDP).

U.S. gross saving rates are only about half those of Japan and typically below those of all major competitors. For many years gross U.S. saving was below that of other competitor countries; yet no large trade deficits were incurred. During the 1980s, however, gross U.S. saving declined relative to its earlier performance. The reduced saving rate was inadequate to fund the sum of increasing government deficits and private-sector investment. This shortfall in saving—termed the *saving-investment gap*—has raised real interest rates and has led to net inflows of capital and the accompanying trade and current account deficits. (The role of the saving-investment gap in U.S. trade deficits is discussed in more detail in Chapter 4.)

High U.S. interest rates have inhibited investment that would raise productivity in some critical sectors, thus impairing U.S. competitiveness. The effects of low saving rates on U.S. competitiveness are not limited to the 1980s. Low U.S. saving rates relative to those of foreign competitors have long played an important role in raising the cost of investment capital, lowering investment, slowing the advance of U.S. living standards, and narrowing the U.S. competitiveness edge over some other countries. The cumulative effects are now becoming evident.

U.S. saving—the portion of income not spent for current consumption—comes from both private-sector and government sources (Figure 2–1 and Table 2–2). Government saving is the excess of tax receipts of the federal, state, and local governments over government expenditures. Because the federal government has

Figure 2–1
Composition of U.S. Saving as a Percentage of GNP, 1988

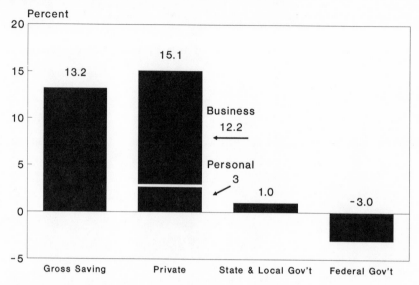

Source: U.S. Department of Commerce.

recently run very large deficits, federal government dissaving and surpluses generated by state and local governments have summed to deficits, with total government dissaving reaching 3.4 percent of GNP in 1986 and about 2.0 percent in 1988.

Private-sector saving consists of business saving and personal saving. Gross business saving (undistributed profits plus depreciation allowances) is a much larger portion of GNP than personal saving, typically running around 13 percent of GNP, compared with personal saving of about 3 percent of GNP (Table 2–2). Depreciation allowances provide the major portion of business saving, ranging around 12 percent of GNP. The undistributed profits portion of business saving is much smaller, fluctuating with business conditions and ranging from 0.6 to 2.5 percent of GNP during the 1980–88 period.

Personal saving—the difference between the disposable income and consumption of households—was close to 5 percent of GNP for most of the period since 1950 but reached new lows during the 1980s. It declined from 5 percent of GNP in 1980 to 2.3 percent of GNP in 1987, rising modestly to 3.0 percent in 1988.

U.S. personal saving rates, an important factor in total saving, have long been well below those in most competitor countries. They fell still lower during the 1980s. In 1987 the U.S. saving rate of 3.9 percent of disposable income contrasted with rates of 16.5 percent for Japan, 12.2 for West Germany, and 5.6 for the United Kingdom (Figure 2–2).

Figure 2–2
Personal Saving Rates as a Percentage of Disposable Income, Selected Years

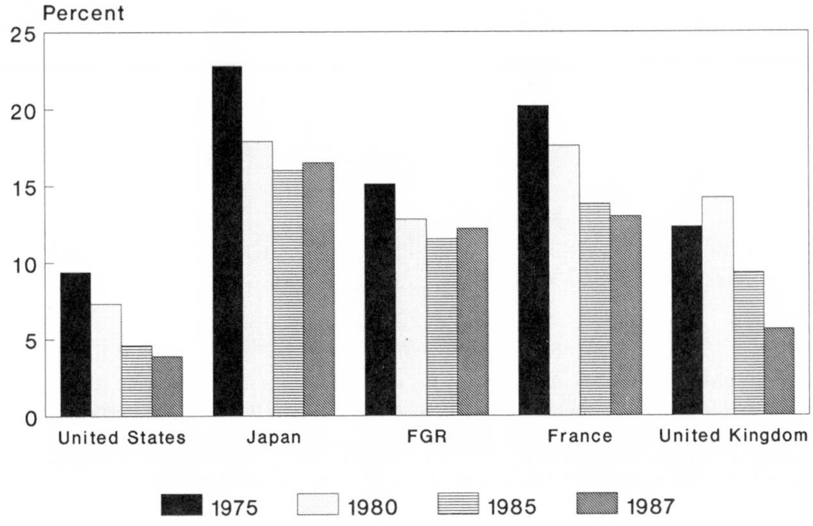

Source: U.S. Department of Commerce.

U.S. personal savings can be split into two components: the saving from employee and employer net pension fund contributions and earnings and discretionary saving. The preponderance of pension plan assets result from defined-benefit pension plans, which are fully funded by employer contributions. As the availability of employer pension funds and the balances in these funds has risen, personal saving has become more "contractual" and much less "discretionary." Decisions about most of personal saving have passed from the individual to the employer, and the discretionary portion of personal saving is declining. Indeed, since 1984 personal saving other than annual net pension fund contributions and earnings—discretionary saving—has been negative.[1] The recent decline in the U.S. discretionary saving played an important role, together with growing federal deficits, in creating the saving-investment gap and the resulting trade and current account deficits.[2]

There is uncertainty about the causes of the decline in U.S. personal saving rates during the 1980s. Some believe that rising stock market prices beginning in the early 1980s produced a "wealth effect" that mitigated the need many saw to save for retirement. A similar effect may have stemmed from continued increases in equity that many homeowners experienced during the decade's real estate boom. Some analysts also see an increasing reliance on social security to meet retirement needs as lowering the incentive to save during preretirement years. Another view is that demographic, social, and cultural changes have combined to emphasize immediate consumption, rather than provision for the future. It is noteworthy, however, that personal saving rates have also declined in competitor countries (Figure 2–2).

Raising total U.S. saving rates—the sum of government, business, and personal saving—will be difficult. Restoring personal saving rates to earlier levels, let alone raising them to levels achieved in other countries, may be particularly difficult. Personal saving rates are affected by many factors, and the effects of various policy measures are uncertain. Some argue that personal savings are primarily goal or target oriented (directed at specific targets that require given amounts of saving) and that changes in tax rates do not significantly change the "targets" or the amounts saved. Only minor changes in tax laws that might affect personal saving rates have been attempted, however, and the results have been ambiguous. Some of these changes (for example, the Individual Retirement Account [IRA]) may not have been sustained long enough to affect saving patterns fully. There can be little doubt that just as prices influence demand, significant, more fundamental changes in the methods of taxation can influence consumption and its complement saving. Taxes that add to the cost of a product (including sales taxes and value-added taxes), for example, discourage consumption and thus enhance the attractiveness of saving. On the other hand, tax-deductible interest costs lower the cost of consumption and thus encourage it. Similarly, taxes on interest and dividend income discourage saving and thus encourage the alternative—consumption.

Manipulating the tax system can probably alter personal saving rates to some degree. The exact effects of tax law changes and other factors on personal saving rates are, however, uncertain and likely to be controversial for many reasons, including those related to equity and burden sharing. Given these difficulties, one view is that the kinds of basic changes in tax laws that might produce a significant increase in the personal saving rate are unlikely; that a significant personal saving rate change may result only following a serious recession. Such a recession would increase uncertainty and concern about the future and thus motivate increased saving to prepare for it.

Another view is that the problem will take care of itself, that the decline in personal saving rates is primarily demographic in origin, and as demographics change in the 1990s, "the prospects for improving personal saving rates are very strong."[3]

Business saving—undistributed profits plus capital consumption (depreciation) allowances—is very much a function of business conditions and business profits but is also deeply affected by tax laws and regulations. These laws and regulations can strongly affect the ability and incentives of business to save. Increases in business income taxes, for example, increase the gross profits required to generate a given amount of business saving. Altering depreciation allowances also directly affects business saving. The effect of tax law changes on business saving and capital formation should not be underestimated. The 1986 tax law changes shifted about $140 billion (over five years) from individuals to corporations and, other things being equal, have lowered business saving. Since business tends to have a higher savings rate than private households, the 1986 changes thus may lower the level of *total* private savings. Moreover, the short-term effect of decreasing the federal government budget deficit by increasing business taxes is simply to decrease business saving in order to add to government saving. To a large extent, it is simply "robbing Peter to pay Paul." To the degree that costs are passed on in higher prices or lower profits, either the consumer pays or the business and personal savings available for capital formation are reduced.

In the end, all taxes are borne by all members of the economy, not by "businesses" or corporations that are inanimate legal creations. Increased business costs—including taxes—are ultimately passed on to members of the economy, whether through higher prices, lower wages, lower capital formation rates, or in other ways. Whether the *initial incidence* of a tax falls on business or individuals has important effects, however, with increased business taxes acting to discourage capital formation.

To summarize, there are three potential sources of increased saving: (1) eliminating government dissaving by balancing the budget, possibly moving into surplus to further increase total saving; (2) increasing personal saving; and (3) increasing business saving, that is, increasing retained profits and depreciation allowances. Steps aimed at increasing saving in any of these areas will likely be difficult and controversial. Moreover, it is important to recognize that the objective is to raise total national saving, that is, the sum of government, personal, and business saving. Cutting the federal budget deficit is a means to that end, not an end in itself. The objective is increased national saving and investment. Lowering the federal budget deficit by equivalent reductions in other kinds of saving (for example, by transferring programs from federal to state responsibility) does not resolve the U.S. problem. Changes in tax policies relating to one revenue source inevitably will affect the others, and cutting the federal budget deficit will not necessarily increase national investment. Indeed, some actions that might help cut the government budget deficit could actually reduce investment and harm U.S. international competitiveness. Lowered business saving, for example, will reduce the saving available for the investment needed to raise U.S. productivity. The policy alternatives and the difficulties in implementing them are reviewed more extensively in Chapter 11.

Capital Formation Rates

Strong capital formation rates will be even more critical in determining future U.S. competitiveness than in the past. Today's world is one of rapidly changing technology, a world in which foreign production capabilities often match, and sometimes surpass, those of the United States. In this environment an ever-growing flow of investment in new products, plants, and processes will be essential for a high-wage nation such as the United States to remain internationally competitive. Gross capital formation rates that may have been adequate in the past are likely to be inadequate in the future. Higher capital formation rates will be required if the United States is to maintain and enhance its international competitiveness. An increasing flow of new U.S. investments will require both financial capital at reasonable cost and the profit incentive necessary to motivate risk taking and capital formation.

Some observers justify recent U.S. trade deficits and borrowing abroad, arguing that the inflow of borrowed capital represented by the trade deficits has financed an investment boom that is increasing and modernizing U.S. productive capacity. They expect that the surge in investment will be more than ample to service the foreign debt. They assume that the borrowed capital will produce more goods and services for U.S. consumption as well as the export surpluses needed to service the accumulated debt. Has there been an investment boom? Have capital formation rates been increasing?

Investment data do not reveal any major surge in U.S. investment (Table 2–2). Indeed, gross U.S. investment has been stable as a percentage of the GNP in recent years and below earlier levels.

Moreover, there are different uses of investment capital, and not all of them are equally useful in building up the kinds of productivity gains and productive capacity needed to compete in the international marketplace. It is basically the goods-production sector—essentially U.S. manufacturing—that faces international competition. This is the sector that must be built up to meet and best foreign competition. Not all investment helps to improve the goods-production sector.

Investment in residences, for example, usually is about one-third of total fixed investment (Figure 2–3), typically between 4 and 5 percent of GNP and usually greater than plant and equipment investment (Table 2–4). Although highly desirable for other reasons, adding to the nation's stock of personal residences does little to enhance U.S. ability to compete against foreign producers of goods and services. In fact, many economists argue that the United States is "overinvesting" in housing, that housing diverts scarce capital from more productive uses, raises its cost, and reduces investment in other sectors.

Nor does all non-residential investment contribute significantly to international competitiveness. Although investments in many industries should to some degree act to increase U.S. productivity, their effect on U.S. ability to compete against foreign production varies widely, and some investments make little or no contribution. Investments in hotels, stores, shopping malls, and other aspects of the retail sector, for example, are unlikely to help U.S. producers of goods and services compete against foreign-based producers in either U.S. or foreign markets. Indeed, such investments not only compete for scarce capital and raise its cost but also may be a factor in increasing personal consumption, thereby lowering personal saving and the supply of investment capital.

Investment in manufacturing is particularly critical to meeting foreign competition, but gross investment in the manufacturing sector in 1988 was only little more than one-fifth of total U.S. fixed investment and 3.4 percent of GNP, down

Figure 2–3
Composition of U.S. Gross Investment as a Percentage of GNP, 1988

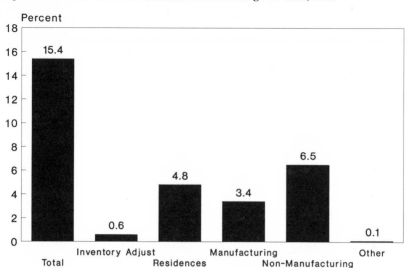

Source: U.S. Deptartment of Commerce.

from earlier levels. Seen as a portion of GNP, there is no evidence of a "manufacturing investment boom."

Indeed, the manufacturing share of U.S. investment has been declining (Figure 2–4). In 1980 manufacturing accounted for 16.9 percent of total U.S. investment. In 1988 it was only 12.5 percent of the total. In 1980 non-farm, non-manufacturing investment was 52.3 percent of total U.S. gross investment; in 1988, 57.8 percent.

Dissecting the data still further and setting aside investment in residences reveals that in 1980, capital-intensive U.S. manufacturing got 23 percent of total non-residential U.S. investment but only 17.4 percent in 1988 (Figure 2–5). During the same 1980–88 period the investment share of transportation and public utilities—another group of capital-intensive industries—also declined, from 24.4 percent to 20.3 percent of total non-residential U.S. investment.

But wholesale and retail trade, finance, insurance, real estate, and miscellaneous services all scored major gains. Construction of shopping malls and office buildings and investment in many facets of service industries appear to have increased, even though there has been no evident surge of investment in manufacturing.

The gross plant and equipment expenditures of the United States contrast markedly with those of Japan. Japan's 1988 plant and equipment spending in

Table 2–4
Composition of U.S. Gross Investment by Type as a Percentage of GNP, 1980–89

	1980	1981	1982	1983	1984	1985	1986	1987	1988	1989
Gross Domestic Investment	16.0	16.9	14.1	14.7	17.6	16.0	15.6	15.5	15.4	14.8
Of Which:										
Business Inventory Adj.	-0.3	0.8	-0.8	-0.2	1.8	0.3	0.2	0.6	0.6	0.6
Fixed Investment	16.3	16.1	14.9	15.0	15.8	15.7	15.4	14.8	14.7	14.3
Fixed Investment										
Residential	4.5	4.0	3.3	4.5	4.8	4.7	5.1	5.0	4.8	4.5
Non-Residential	11.8	12.1	11.6	10.5	11.0	11.0	10.3	9.8	10.0	9.8
Non-Residential Investment										
Manufacturing P&E	4.1	4.1	3.8	3.4	3.7	3.8	3.4	3.2	3.4	3.5
Non-Manufacturing	7.4	7.3	7.2	6.7	6.9	6.9	6.7	6.5	6.5	
Other	0.3	0.7	0.6	0.4	0.5	0.3	0.2	0.1	0.1	

Figure 2–4
Gross Real Investment by Sector as a Percentage of Total U.S. Real Private Investment

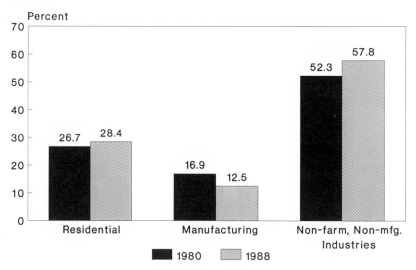

Source: U.S. Department of Commerce.

all industry sectors—including the services sectors—was about 18 percent of GNP; U.S. spending was 8 percent.

Narrowing the plant and equipment investment comparison to the critically important manufacturing sectors of the two countries is even more revealing (Figure 2–6). In 1987 U.S. manufacturing plant and equipment spending was 3.2 percent of GNP, just over half of Japan's 6 percent. Thus with an economy about half the size of the United States, Japan's manufacturing plant and equipment expenditures are nearly twice those of the United States relative to GNP and about the same amount in absolute terms. These data give advance warning that Japanese productivity gains will likely continue to outpace those of the United States. The high investment rates of other competitors make it likely that their productivity gains will also continue to outpace U.S. rates. It is, therefore, difficult to see how U.S. productivity gains can be a factor in increasing U.S. price competitiveness.

Gross annual current dollar capital expenditures in U.S. manufacturing plant and equipment have trended upward, from $112 billion in 1981 to $165 billion in 1988. But there is only a tenuous connection between capital spending and changes in the capital stock that increase productivity and capacity. Gross expenditures in current dollars include the effects of inflation and must be deflated to give an accurate representation of trends. Also, capital expenditures must both replace existing plant and equipment and add to existing capabilities. As the

Figure 2–5
Industry Shares of Gross Real Non-residential U.S. Private Investment

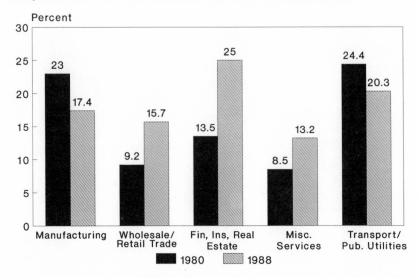

Source: U.S. Department of Commerce.

Figure 2–6
Manufacturing Plant and Equipment Investment as a Percentage of GNP

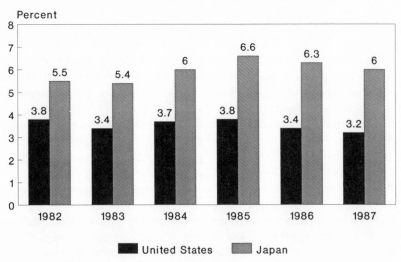

Sources: U.S. Department of Commerce and
Economic Planning Agency, Japan.

average age of capital stock increases, as has been occurring in the United States, more and more must be spent for replacement, and less and less of total spending is available to add to existing stocks. Additions to stocks are essential to increasing capacity and productivity.

Gross investment expenditures, therefore, do not tell the full story. Changes in the net real capital stock are another useful measure of investment trends and the growth of capital stock in U.S. manufacturing. These changes are estimated by calculating gross investment spending less outlays for replacement, both expressed in real terms.

Assessed in these terms, the growth of manufacturing capital stock has been slow in the 1980s. Total manufacturing net capital stock was $707 billion (1982 dollars) in 1980, rising to only $772 billion in 1988, a $65 billion, 9.2 percent, gain in eight years. Recent increases have been sharply below the levels of earlier decades. Per annum growth rates were 4.7 percent in the 1960s, 3.3 percent in the 1970s. Since 1982, growth in manufacturing capacity as measured by increases in the real net capital stock has averaged only about 1 percent yearly, accounting for only about 5 percent of the cumulative gains in the overall business capital stock during the six-year period.

Nor do the data indicate an investment surge in the years since the dollar decline began, as increases of only 0.8 percent in 1986 and 1987 and 0.9 percent in 1988 have been recorded.[4]

Moreover, detailed examination shows that the core components of "industrial capital"—the heavy machinery and industrial plants that account for more than 82 percent of total manufacturing capacity—rose only 0.3 percent in 1988 following a six-year period of virtual stagnation. Core capacity was no higher in 1988 than it had been in late 1982, following a six-year period of virtual stagnation.[5] As is evident from other investment data, this extended lack of capacity growth has unfavorable implications for productivity growth and belies impressions of an investment boom in U.S. manufacturing fed by imported capital.

There has, however, been no dearth of net investment growth in the service sector. The service sector's total net real capital stock rose nearly 5 percent in 1988 and about the same pace in the previous four years. Thus there has been a recent bias toward investment in the service industries, which generally do not face foreign competition, and away from investment in the goods producing/manufacturing sector, which is directly exposed to foreign competition.

Still another useful way to assess U.S. capital investment is to examine changes in the real per capita capital stock, that is, the amount of physical capital available per individual. Increased individual productivity implies more capital stock for each worker, providing the means for each worker to produce more. During the 1980–88 period, gross manufacturing real capital stock—the gross capital stock adjusted for the effects of inflation—grew by only 9.3 percent (Figure 2–7). Net real stock, including the effects of depreciation, grew only 1 percent in the eight years. The growth of non-farm, non-manufacturing per capita stocks, however, was much greater, 25.2 and 22.2 percent respectively.

Figure 2–7
Changes in Real Per Capita U.S. Capital Stock, 1980–88

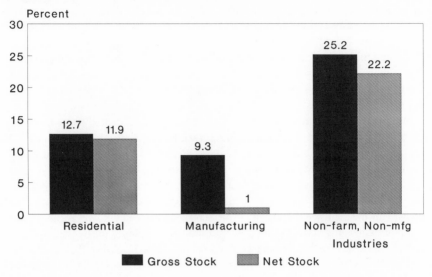

Source: U.S. Department of Commerce.

Estimating net capital stocks—taking into account the effects of depreciation and obsolescence for many thousands of different kinds of residences, buildings, plants, and equipment—is a complex process requiring aggregations, estimates, and judgments that are fraught with opportunities for error. The results are not precise. Nevertheless, unless the estimates of net capital stock are widely at variance with reality, the revealed general trends are disturbing. They indicate a bias against investment in capital-intensive manufacturing compared to other alternatives.

This lack of growth of the capital stock in U.S. manufacturing—even while manufacturing profits have increased—raises disturbing questions about whether there has actually been a genuine resurgence of U.S. manufacturing capabilities and capacities. It raises the prospect that improved profits too often may have been achieved by decreasing capacity, by retiring older, less efficient facilities without replacing them. It also implies that U.S. companies have either consciously or implicitly ceded some market share and products to foreign-based production. Although the effect of such strategies may have been to raise individual company profits in the short term, it does not bode well for an expansion of U.S.-based production. Such an expansion is essential to improving U.S. competitiveness and narrowing the trade deficits.

Even with the retirement of a lot of obsolete, inefficient production capacity, available data indicate the average age of manufacturing stock continues to increase. The average age of gross U.S. manufacturing stock, measured in 1982 dollars, increased from 10.1 years in 1980 to 11.1 years in 1988; net stock (the gross stock less deductions for depreciation) average age increased from 7.1 years to 7.8 years during the same period.

These differing kinds of measurements demonstrate what is happening to U.S. capital stock in some important areas. Taken together, they belie the theory that foreign borrowing is providing the basis for capital investment that will boost U.S. international competitiveness. The data show that investment increases have not been in the manufacturing sector. Rather, the increases have been largely in sectors that do not face international competition to the same degree as does goods production. In fact, much of the new investments will do little to enhance the international competitiveness of the U.S. manufacturing sector; some may actually inhibit gains.

The investment data collected by the U.S. government and included herein actually tell only part of the story. Several kinds of investments important to the nation's competitiveness are excluded from most assessments of investment spending. National accounts investment data, for example, do not include government spending for roads, communication and transportation systems, buildings, and many other expenditures on infrastructure that contribute to the productivity of the nation and to an improvement in its living standards. Although available data do not facilitate comparisons, there is a growing body of opinion that the nation's infrastructure is deteriorating.

Research and Development

Research and development will provide the new products and processes that spur technological advance and enhance a nation's competitiveness. They will also be more important than ever before in determining U.S. international competitiveness. Staying abreast of competitors will require a constant expansion of investment in the discovery and development of new products and processes. Because of the high degree of uncertainties involved, private-sector research and development is even more dependent on profit incentives than are plant and equipment investments.

Research and development expenditures are made primarily by the federal government and private industry, with small portions from universities, colleges, and non-profit institutions (Table 2–5). Just under half of the total is provided by the federal government and about the same portion by private industry. Despite the figures, nearly three-fourths of the actual work is done by private industry, with only some 12 percent in government labs and 15 percent in universities, colleges, and other non-profit institutions.

Measured in constant 1982 dollars, growth in U.S. research and development expenditures has been strong. Moreover, relative to GNP, U.S. expenditures for research and development compare favorably with those of major competitors (Table 2–6). A large portion of U.S. spending, however, is for defense-related research, compared to much lower portions in most other countries and a min-

Table 2-5
Research and Development Expenditures by Source of Funds and Performance Sector (Billions of 1982 Dollars)

	Total	By Source of Funds (Percent of Total)				By Performance Sector (Percent of Total)				
		Fed Govt	Industry	Univ.	Other	Fed Govt	Industry	Univ.	FFRDC*	Other
1960	43.6	64.6	33.4	1.1	.1	12.7	77.8	4.8	2.7	2.1
1970	62.4	57.1	39.8	1.8	1.3	15.7	68.9	9.0	1.9	3.5
1975	59.9	51.8	44.6	2.2	1.5	15.6	68.2	9.9	2.9	3.6
1980	73.2	47.2	49.2	2.1	1.5	12.3	70.9	9.8	3.6	3.4
1985	96.6	47.7	49.0	2.1	1.2	12.1	72.8	8.8	3.3	3.0
1987(Est)	105.4	49.4	47.3	2.2	1.2	12.1	75.9	9.0	3.1	2.9

*FFRDC = Federally Funded R&D Centers

Source: Statistical Abstract of the United States, 1988, U.S. Department of Commerce.

Table 2–6
National Research and Development Expenditures as a Percentage of GNP by Country

Year	U.S.	France	Germany	Japan	U.K.	USSR
1965	2.8	2.0	1.7	1.5	NA	2.9
1970	2.6	1.9	2.1	1.8	NA	3.3
1975	2.2	1.8	2.2	2.0	2.2	3.8
1980	2.3	1.8	2.4	2.2	N.A.	3.8
1985	2.7	2.3	2.7	2.9	2.2	3.8

Source: Statistical Abstract of the United States, 1988, U.S. Department of Commerce.

iscule portion in Japan. According to the National Science Foundation, in 1985 about 30 percent of U.S. research and development expenditures were for defense purposes; less than 1 percent of Japan's went to defense projects.

For many years, it was widely accepted that the large research and development efforts associated with developing advanced military equipment and technology had spin-off effects that significantly benefited the U.S. economy. There have, of course, been spin-off benefits. The U.S. aircraft industry has clearly gained from military research and development spending. Spin-off benefits, however, are likely to lessen as defense needs become more specialized. Moreover, there is now a growing body of opinion that large military expenditures have sapped some of the best research and development resources available, to the detriment of the development of commercial products, U.S. competitiveness in international trade, and the long-term strength of the economy.[6]

The Department of Defense spends about 75 percent of total U.S. government research and development money and about one-third of the U.S. total. The effect isn't just the preemption of money but one of diverting much of the nation's best scientific and engineering resources from developing commercial products that would enter international competition. Many of the nation's limited scientific resources are spent on research on sophisticated military equipment. Much of such research cannot be transferred to products and processes that will improve U.S. trade and international competitiveness.

Thus many see the concentration of Japan and other countries on commercially oriented projects as providing them with significant advantages in developing new products that can compete in international markets.

Declining U.S. technical dominance is reflected in U.S. patent registrations. In 1988 foreign inventors received 48 percent of the patents issued in the United

States. In 1963 the foreign share was only 19 percent. Japanese inventors received 21 percent of the 1988 U.S. patents, up from only 9 percent in 1975. These trends are likely to continue. Foreign advances in technology will increase, and the U.S. share of world advances will likely decline further. Moreover, even if defense needs decline, changing the focus of research and development would likely take many years before these diverted resources could be rechanneled into producing discoveries and applications for commercial goods markets.

Human Resource Development

Enhancement of the educational levels and skills of the nation's work force is essential to effective international competition. Indeed, studies typically impute the major portion of productivity growth to human capital factors. In today's world the pace of technological change is escalating; the workplace is becoming more dependent on specialized, new skills as well as traditional skills, such as basic mathematics and the ability to read and interpret instructions, plans, and drawings. Requirements for scientists, engineers, and mathematicians will also increase.

But U.S. performance in education is lagging at the very time that education is becoming more critical. The United States no longer has the world's premier labor force. The American functional illiteracy rate is now above that of the rest of the industrial world, and the rate of graduation from high school is below the industrial world average. American elementary and secondary students tend to fall near the bottom of many comparative international tests. U.S. universities turn out relatively fewer scientifically and technically trained people: 6 percent of American baccalaureates are in engineering versus 20 percent in Japan and 37 percent in Germany.[7]

National data do not focus strongly on investments in human capital and changes in the quality of the nation's work force. There is, nevertheless, growing awareness of a decline in the quality of the U.S. labor force relative to that of a number of competitor nations. An increasing attention to the importance of human capital—and probably increasing educational investments—will be required to raise the ability of the nation's work force to contribute to productivity gains. Making changes in education, however, will be complicated by the many layers of government involved—federal, state, and local. Significant changes will not only be controversial and slow but will also involve painfully long pay-off periods; for example, twenty or more years from initiating changes in primary education to actually achieving significant positive effects on the work force. Moreover, it will be difficult to measure the changes and even more difficult to relate these changes to particular earlier policy measures.

Effective Trade Policies

Trade policies—the laws, rules, customs, practices, regulations, and international agreements that govern U.S. and foreign participation in international trade—are a fifth important ingredient in determining international competitiveness. U.S. trade policies do not directly affect U.S. productivity but should prevent arbitrary U.S. or foreign actions from disadvantaging U.S.-based production. No matter how high U.S. productivity levels may be, for example, U.S. producers cannot be competitive in foreign markets they are barred from by non-market forces such as foreign import barriers and U.S. export restrictions. Trade policy is important, but it is far less important than other factors and is much overemphasized as a factor in U.S. competitiveness. The role of trade policy in U.S. competitiveness is discussed in more detail in Chapter 11.

Other Competitiveness Factors

The five factors noted above are the key determinants of U.S. productivity and competitiveness. How these factors function together is itself critically important. Experts on productivity and competitiveness problems rightfully draw attention to a number of other factors that affect how human and physical capital function together. Some of them are the competency of management and the attitudes of workers, the adversarial attitudes between management and labor in the United States, the business versus government adversarial processes, and the short time horizons of investors and managers. All of these things and many others are factors in determining U.S. competitiveness. Their significance varies, however, and is difficult to measure. Diagnosing the causes and prescribing remedies are even more controversial, and changes are likely to be even more difficult to accomplish than changes in the five basic factors noted above.

INTERNATIONAL COMPETITIVENESS: A NEW BUT ENDURING PROBLEM

Competitiveness is a relatively new U.S. problem, particularly for Americans of current generations. For many years following World War II the United States enjoyed overwhelming advantages in technology, manufacturing, and marketing skills. The United States emerged unscathed from World War II with the world's largest and most modern industrial complex. Rebuilding other economies provided important markets for several years. A large, wealthy domestic market provided U.S.-based production with unique economies of scale not available to foreign competitors. Large sales volumes and healthy profits facilitated investments in research and development that competitors could not afford and generated a continuous stream of new products. The U.S. labor force was better educated and more skilled than those of most foreign competitors. The quality of U.S. manufactures was high. Many U.S. products were superior to those of foreign competitors. Many were unique, with little foreign competition.

U.S. productivity was well above that of most foreign competitors and was growing rapidly. U.S. saving rates were not high, but the United States was so wealthy compared to the war-ravaged economies of the world that even relatively low savings were adequate to finance enough new investment and research and development to stay ahead of foreign competitors.

For much of the post-war period the United States had access to low-cost energy and other raw materials, much of it from domestic sources. Together, these advantages often allowed U.S. goods producers to raise wages and prices, collecting what economists call "economic rents" (the high profit margins that monopolies or unique products allow). For many years, the United States was able to balance its international accounts at favorable terms of trade that supported high and rapidly rising real U.S. wage levels in the manufacturing sector. These U.S. advantages generated high expectations and, perhaps, overconfidence, which in time led to laxity by U.S. business and labor and a disregard of trade and competitiveness factors in U.S. government policy making.

Dramatic changes, however, have occurred in the past two decades. The once favorable gap between U.S. and foreign competitors has narrowed dramatically. The pace of technological change has increased. Some key competitor economies have saved and invested in human and physical capital at high rates. War-ravaged foreign industrial plants have been rebuilt using the most modern technology. Several less developed countries have rapidly developed from agricultural to industrializing economies. The quality and productivity of foreign labor have increased rapidly in response to those investments, and foreign capital stocks and wealth have been accumulating rapidly. Economic growth, the formation of customs unions such as the European Community, and exports of goods to global markets have provided economies of scale to many producers, even in small countries. Foreign capabilities and productivity have increased more rapidly than in the United States, and U.S. advantages have disappeared. The pace of investment and productivity growth abroad has risen, increasing the stream of new investments required to maintain competitiveness, narrowing long-standing U.S. advantages, and intensifying the international competitiveness race. Also, the pace of technological change, accompanied by plant and equipment obsolescence, has required more capital investment and investment in research and development for U.S. companies to remain competitive.

The large size of the U.S. market and the open, free enterprise nature of its economy have given the United States an edge over many other economies in generating new products and new investments and in increasing productivity. Recently, however, many competitor economies have been turning away from central planning and tight government control to more market-oriented economic systems, thus increasing their efficiency and competitiveness.

At the same time, the United States is at the forefront in implementing costly new regulations to improve health, safety, and the environment. A tightening regulatory climate often imposes greater costs and uncertainties on manufacturing in the United States than exist in competitor nations. This may inhibit some investments in U.S.-based production at the expense of increased productivity and competitiveness as measured by real incomes. This is not an argument against new regulatory initiatives, only a recognition that added regulations that are more costly than those of foreign competitors disadvantage U.S.-based production. These programs should be undertaken only if they bring benefits to U.S. society that match or outweigh their costs.

In addition, U.S. dependence on imports of oil, other raw materials and goods, and foreign technology has been increasing. This increased dependency on foreign sources is largely irreversible, leaving the United States more vulnerable to external market conditions (for example, oil prices) and foreign supplies of goods and technologies. U.S. foreign trade will inevitably grow still larger as a portion of U.S. GNP. Growing dependencies increase the importance of competing successfully in world markets.

These and other changes have produced a new, very different, and permanently altered international economic environment. In short, it is a world in which the United States is no longer industrially dominant; one in which U.S. businesses and workers can no longer collect the economic rents that come from dominance and monopoly positions. But this new situation is not recognized or accepted by most in the United States. Harold L. Hodgkinson, director of the Center for Demographic Policy at the Washington-based Institute of Education Leadership, has summed it up well:

In the '50s a poorly educated man could work in a factory, have two cars in the garage, three kids and a non-working wife, and the kids could go to college. We have assumed this to be the norm, when it actually was an aberration which we have never seen before and will never see again.[8]

A general failure to recognize the new U.S. situation complicates policy making because many voters assume that slipping U.S. performance must be due either to foreign "unfairness" or to readily fixable errors made by policymakers. In fact, however, although the United States' difficulty in maintaining its international competitiveness position is a relatively new phenomenon, it is one that will continue and cannot be easily or quickly resolved. In a world of rapid technological progress and increasing global economic interdependency, competition from producers in other countries—particularly competition for manufactured goods markets—can only intensify as more and more nations strive for higher economic growth through industrialization and as production and trading capabilities in both industrialized and developing nations continue to improve.

In this new environment, the critical and enduring question is, given continuing rapid increases in foreign capabilities—often in nations with significantly lower wage levels—can the United States maintain sufficient competitive advantages for U.S.-based production to balance its trade at favorable terms of trade? That is, can it balance its trade at exchange rates and wage levels that not only improve U.S. real incomes and living standards but also provide rates of advance comparable to those of other developed nations?

The answer is unclear. It will depend on a great many factors. U.S. macroeconomic policies have not responded to this new U.S. situation but have remained aloof from consideration of international competitiveness. Indeed, several recent policy actions actually run counter to international competitiveness interests. Economic competitiveness must be given new attention if the United States is to retain its global leadership role. U.S. policymakers will have to pay new heed to the fundamental factors that affect U.S. productivity and competitiveness.

Changes in U.S. competitiveness can occur only slowly but can be influenced by government policies. Implementing policies that increase productivity gains to levels matching those of some major competitors will be difficult. It will require a public understanding of the competitiveness problem and of what is at stake.

POLICIES TO RAISE PRODUCTIVITY AND COMPETITIVENESS

Balanced U.S. trade would, sooner or later, be achieved without a strong U.S. performance in the five fundamental determinants of competitiveness described in this chapter. Trade can be balanced through dollar depreciation, by relative or absolute declines in U.S. wages, and through a U.S. recession or growth slowdown. But international competitiveness—defined as balanced trade concurrent with living standards that rise at rates comparable to those of major competitors—cannot be achieved without consistently strong performance over the long term in the basic factors that determine productivity growth.

Saving and capital formation rates, the pace of new research and development, and the enhancement of human resources are influenced by a great many social and economic forces. Cultural, demographic, and many other factors are beyond the influence of government policies, except, perhaps, over the very long term. Government, however, can influence the quality of human resources and the growth of physical capital, and hence the medium-term and longer term direction and pace of productivity and competitiveness changes.

Investment and the ways in which human and physical capital are used can be influenced by a wide variety of government laws and an enormous range of regulations. The primary government policy tools for dealing with saving, physical capital formation rates, and investment in research and development are fiscal, monetary, and tax policies. The federal government is dominant in setting these policies. Legal and regulatory environments may also be very important. Some regulatory approaches may promote new investment and productivity growth; others may inhibit them.

Education is a critical factor affecting the development of human capital, but it has traditionally been primarily under state government control. Enhancing the quality of U.S. human capital—the U.S. labor force—is a vital component in faster productivity growth and improved U.S. competitiveness. It is no less important than enlarging and improving the physical capital stock, research and development, and other factors. It is perhaps, even more important. Improving human capital is also probably an even more difficult, complex, and longer term undertaking than achieving gains in physical capital and research and development.

In short, a large number of factors influence the productivity of U.S. human and physical capital and the resulting U.S. international competitiveness. This book, however, focuses primarily on the contributions of physical capital and research and development to competitiveness and on the policy alternatives for dealing with these factors. Policies for reducing the trade deficits and improving international competitiveness are reviewed in more detail in Chapter 11.

SUMMARY

• A nation's productivity and its international competitiveness are determined fundamentally by the quality of its human capital (work force), the amount and quality of its physical capital (machines, buildings, equipment, and technology) used in production, and how effectively these assets are employed.

• The amounts and quality of a nation's human and physical capital usually change only gradually. The course and speed of changes are determined by many social and economic forces but can be influenced by economic policies.

• The key factors that determine the growth and improvement of these capital stocks and increases in productivity and competitiveness advances are national saving and capital formation rates, research and development, and continuing improvement of the labor force. Policy actions to improve these underlying factors may require many years to have an effect.

• There are no one-time quick policy fixes for international competitiveness problems. International competitiveness requires sustained attention to, and good performance in, the basic factors that determine productivity.

• Effective trade policies are important, but much less so than effective macroeconomic and other policies that improve the stocks of human and physical capital and their use.

• The international competitiveness contest is essentially one of *relative* productivity increases. Maintaining or increasing competitiveness requires not just that U.S. productivity increase but also that it grow at rates that compare favorably with those of major competitors. Rates of growth lower than those of competitors foreshadow declining competitiveness.

• Not all forms of investment will improve U.S. international competitiveness. The United States must be increasingly concerned about capital formation in the goods producing sector, which is the primary interface with international competition. Investments in residences, the retail sector, and many other sectors do little to improve the ability of U.S.-based goods production to compete against foreign production. Indeed, a surge of investment in these areas may actually preempt available capital to the detriment of investment in U.S.-based goods production.

• Total U.S. research and development spending appears to compare favorably with that of most foreign competitors. Much of U.S. spending, however, is for defense-related projects that may have only limited spin-offs to products that can compete in world markets.

• U.S. investment in human capital is not recorded in national accounts, and comparing spending with other countries is difficult. There is growing opinion, however, that U.S. education is not matching that of foreign competitors and that the quality of the U.S. labor force is declining relative to that of some other nations.

• International competitiveness is an enduring problem, one that will intensify as more and more industrialized and developing nations improve their production and marketing skills.

• The critical and enduring question is, given rapid, continued increases in foreign capabilities—often in low-wage countries—can the United States maintain its competitive advantage; can it balance its trade at exchange rates and wage levels that maintain and improve already high real incomes and living standards? The answer is uncertain but can be influenced by laws, regulations, and policies.

NOTES

1. James W. Christian, "Prospects and Policies for Higher Personal Saving Rates in the 1990s" (Paper delivered at "Saving: The Challenge for the U.S. Economy," a Public Policy Symposium sponsored by the American Council on Capital Formation, Washington, D.C., 12 October 1989), 4–7.

2. Some analysts argue that measurements of U.S. saving rates are incorrect and that, adjusted to compensate for differences in measurement techniques, U.S. personal saving rates are much closer to those of other industrialized countries. See, for example, Orawin Velz, "Concerned About Saving? Why Not Stop Taxing It!" U.S. Chamber of Commerce, Policy Working Papers, no. 21 (August 1989). Nevertheless, regardless of these arguments on measurement methodology and results, the combination of U.S. personal and corporate saving rates have clearly been inadequate to fund government deficits and U.S. investment, resulting in foreign capital inflows.

3. Ibid., 28; "Will the Baby Boomers Bail Out America?" *Business Week,* 9 October 1989, 20; John Rutledge and Deborah Allen, *Rust to Riches: The Coming of the Second Industrial Revolution* (New York: Harper and Row, 1989).

4. *Economic Perspectives* (Morgan Stanley & Co., New York), 14 July 1988; 11 May 1989.

5. Ibid.

6. For detailed assessments of the effects of defense research and development on a nation's international commercial competitiveness, see Mary Kaldor, Margaret Sharp, and William Walker, "Industrial Competitiveness and Britain's Defense," *Lloyds Bank Review,* October 1986, 31–49; Daniel S. Greenberg, "A Hidden Cost of Military Research: Less National Security," *Discover,* January 1987, 94.

7. Michael L. Dertouzos, Richard K. Lester, and Robert M. Solow, *Made in America:*

Regaining the Productivity Edge (Cambridge, Mass.: MIT Commission on Industrial Productivity, MIT Press, 1989), 21, 24.

8. Dick Kirschten, ''Going for the Breakthrough,'' *National Journal,* 18 November 1989, 2805.

PART II

THE U.S. TRADE DEFICITS

The large U.S. trade deficits that began in the early 1980s will likely continue for some years. The resulting global imbalances have already had significant effects on the U.S. and world economies and narrowing these imbalances will pose significant risks for several years. Understanding how the deficits came about is essential in forming policies to reduce them in an orderly fashion and to deal with the accompanying U.S. and foreign adjustment problems.

Chapter 3 describes the evolution of the U.S. trade deficits and the dominant role of manufactures trade, both in the deterioration of U.S. trade performance and the improvements that must ultimately occur.

Both the popularly perceived and the actual causes of the enlarging trade deficits are described in Chapter 4.

Chapter 5 looks at the costs, benefits, and implications of the deficits for the United States and the world economy. The risks of U.S. debt buildup, the possibility of a ''hard landing,'' the effects on jobs, and the future of U.S. manufacturing are also examined.

The role of foreign direct investment in growth of the U.S. debtor position and the controversial aspects of foreign ownership of U.S. firms and real estate are examined in Chapter 6.

Chapter 3

The Dominance of
Manufactures Trade

A number of factors converged in the 1980s to cause a dramatic deterioration in U.S. trade performance. This deterioration can be analyzed by reviewing trends in the major components of U.S. trade. The performance of manufactures trade, as this chapter shows, was the dominant force acting on the U.S. current account.

THE CURRENT ACCOUNT AND THE
INTERNATIONAL INVESTOR POSITION

The merchandise trade deficits reported each month are only part of total U.S. trade. A nation's international transactions include not only goods but exports and imports of a variety of services and other types of transactions. The net of all of these exports and imports for a specific period, usually a year, is the nation's international, or external, account balance, which is commonly called its current account balance. The current account provides the most comprehensive annual assessment of a nation's international economic performance.

Fluctuations in current account balances reflect changes in a nation's total production of goods and services relative to its total consumption expressed as the sum of government expenditures and private-sector consumption and investment spending. Current account surpluses indicate that a country is producing more than it is consuming, exporting the difference, and lending abroad. Current account deficits show that a country is consuming more goods and services than it is producing. Net imports and borrowing from abroad make up the difference between total production and total consumption by the government and the private sector.

Current account deficits and surpluses change a nation's international investment position (IIP). The IIP is the balance of cumulated stocks of foreign obligations to domestic holders and cumulated stocks of domestic obligations to foreign holders. If a nation's foreign holdings exceed its foreign obligations, it is said to be a creditor nation. If its foreign obligations exceed its foreign asset holdings, it is a debtor nation. Given recent rapid increases in international capital flows and the accompanying changes in trade flows, the IIPs can now change very rapidly. The U.S. IIP is reviewed in detail in Chapter 6.

During the 1980s the United States recorded very large current account deficits, reflecting large net capital inflows. Until 1983, the U.S. current account fluctuated between relatively small surpluses and deficits. Deficits then began to grow rapidly (Table 3–1). The current account deficit was $104 billion in 1984 and $133 billion in 1986. It rose to $144 billion in 1987 and then declined modestly to $127 billion in 1988 and $106 billion in 1989.

The 1987 current account deficit, equivalent to foreign borrowing of about $590 for every person in the United States, may represent a low point in U.S. trade performance. In 1989 foreign borrowing reflected in the current account deficit had declined to about $460 per person.

The current account deficits of the 1980s were also quite large relative to the size of the U.S. economy. The last current account surplus in 1981 was equivalent to only 0.3 percent of the gross national product (Table 3–1). Deficits then grew rapidly to the 3 percent range, peaking at 3.2 percent of the GNP in 1987, before shrinking to 2.6 percent in 1988 and 2.0 percent in 1989.

These current account deficits indicate that the United States consumed about 2.8 percent more goods and services than it actually produced during the 1984–89 period. Net imports—and net borrowing from abroad—supplied the difference.

As a result of continued large international borrowing, reflected in the current account deficits, the U.S. IIP has changed dramatically, from the world's largest creditor nation to the world's largest debtor nation (Table 3–1). The United States rapidly moved from a creditor position of $141 billion in 1981 to a debtor position of $532 billion at the end of 1988. Preliminary data show a further increase to $664 billion at the end of 1989.

The U.S. international debtor position is examined in more detail in Chapter 6. Briefly, however, it took seventy years for the United States to build its 1981 peak creditor position but only eight years for it to move to the 1989 debtor position, a swing of about $804 billion. Further growth in the U.S. international debtor position should be expected. In an orderly narrowing of U.S. deficits and complementary trading partner surpluses, U.S. current account deficits will shrink only gradually in the 1990s, and growth of the international debt will continue.

The U.S. debtor position at the beginning of the 1990s does not, in itself, pose large, immediate risks. The end-1989 debtor position was small relative to GNP (about 13.0 percent). This compares with, for example, a Brazilian ratio of external bank debt to GNP of about 31 percent and a Mexican ratio of about 58 percent. Some developed nations also have much higher ratios than the United States. Canada's ratio, for example, is about 40 percent. Nevertheless, the rapid

Table 3–1

U.S. Current Account by Major Component, 1981–89 (Billions of Dollars)

	1981	1982	1983	1984	1985	1986
Merchandise Trade						
Exports	237.1	211.2	201.8	219.9	215.9	223.4
Imports	265.1	247.6	268.9	332.4	338.1	368.4
Balance	-28.0	-36.4	-67.1	-112.5	-122.1	-145.1
Business Services						
Exports	44.6	44.8	45.3	54.8	56.9	70.9
Imports	32.6	33.5	36.4	49.5	53.6	59.3
Balance	12.0	11.3	8.9	5.2	3.4	11.6
Other Goods and Services						
Exports	10.6	12.6	13.0	10.5	9.5	9.1
Imports	12.9	13.9	14.3	13.4	13.9	14.8
Balance	-2.3	-1.3	-1.2	-2.9	-4.4	-5.7
International Investment Income						
Receipts	86.4	83.5	77.3	85.9	88.8	88.6
Payments	52.3	54.9	52.4	67.4	62.9	67.0
Balance	34.1	28.7	24.9	18.5	25.9	21.6
Total Goods and Services						
Exports	378.7	352.1	337.4	371.1	371.2	392.0
Imports	362.9	349.9	371.9	462.8	468.5	509.4
Balance	15.8	2.2	-34.5	-91.7	-97.3	-117.5
Net Unilateral Transfers	-7.6	-9.2	-9.8	-12.5	-15.4	-15.8
Current Account Balance	8.2	-7.0	-44.3	-104.2	-112.7	-133.2
Current Account Balance (% of GNP)	0.3	-0.2	-1.3	-2.8	-2.8	-3.1
U.S. International Investment Position	140.9	136.7	89.0	3.3	-111.4	-267.8

P - Preliminary

Table 3–1 (*continued*)

	1987	1988	1989	Change 81–87	Change 87–89
Merchandise Trade					
Exports	250.3	319.3	361.9	13.2	111.6
Imports	409.8	446.5	475.1	144.7	65.3
Balance	-159.5	-127.2	-113.2	-131.5	46.3
Business Services					
Exports	79.4	92.1	104.6	34.8	25.2
Imports	67.5	73.1	76.9	34.9	9.4
Balance	12.0	19.0	27.7	0.0	15.7
Other Goods and Services					
Exports	11.8	10.7	9.2	1.2	-2.6
Imports	16.0	16.6	16.3	3.1	0.3
Balance	-4.2	-5.9	-7.1	-1.9	-2.9
International Investment Income					
Receipts	104.7	107.8	124.7	18.3	19.7
Payments	82.4	105.5	123.7	30.1	41.3
Balance	22.3	2.2	1.0	-11.8	-21.3
Total Goods and Services					
Exports	446.1	529.8	600.4	67.4	154.3
Imports	575.6	641.7	692.0	212.7	116.4
Balance	-129.5	-111.9	-91.6	-145.3	37.9
Net Unilateral Transfers	-14.2	-14.7	-14.3	-6.6	-0.1
Current Account Balance	-143.7	-126.5	-105.9	-151.9	37.8
Current Account Balance (% of GNP)	-3.2	-2.6	-2.0	-3.5	1.2
U.S. International Investment Position	-378.3	-532.5	-663.7P	-519.2	-285.4P

P - Preliminary

Source: U.S. Department of Commerce.

change in the U.S. IIP—from a 1981 creditor position equivalent to 4.6 percent of the GNP to a 1989 debtor position of about 13.0 percent of GNP—and the long-term implications of continued large current account deficits and continued debt buildup relative to the GNP are matters for serious concern. The implications of the U.S. debtor position are examined in more detail in Chapters 5 and 6.

Future trends in capital and trade flows are uncertain. Analysts believe, however, that U.S. net foreign debt will continue to grow and that the U.S. debtor position could reach $1 trillion in the early 1990s, an amount perhaps equivalent to 15 percent of GNP.

A DISSECTION OF THE CURRENT ACCOUNT

Large U.S. current account deficits and borrowing abroad may continue for many years if foreign lenders remain willing to lend to the United States. But U.S. current account deficits must sooner or later narrow because no nation— not even the United States, borrowing in its own currency—can borrow without end in amounts that raise its foreign debt in relation to its GNP. Indeed, the process of narrowing U.S. current account deficits may have begun in 1988. A detailed look at trade performance during the 1980s can provide insights into how the dramatic decline in trade performance occurred and the outlook for the future; that is, we can determine in which kinds of goods and services the trade deficit growth occurred and in which areas performance is likely to improve.

The U.S. current account has five major components: merchandise trade, business services, international investment income, other goods and services, and unilateral transfers.

1. *Merchandise trade,* or the exchange of goods, is by far the largest and most volatile element of the current account. In 1989 merchandise trade was 60 percent of all U.S. goods and services exports and 69 percent of all goods and services imports. Recent merchandise trade deficits have overwhelmed other balances. The merchandise trade deficit in 1987 was $160 billion on a balance of payments (bop) basis (Table 3–1).[1] By 1989 it had improved to a $113 billion deficit.

2. *Business services trade* is a relatively small factor in the current account, with exports less than 8 percent of total 1989 goods and services exports. But with significantly smaller imports, it has yielded sizeable surpluses. In 1987 the surplus was $12 billion; in 1988 it rose substantially to $19 billion and in 1989 recorded a $27.7 billion surplus. Because its potential role in U.S. trade is sometimes overrated, business services are examined in more detail in the next section.

3. *International investment income* is the difference between the income paid to foreign holders of U.S. assets and the income received by U.S. holders of foreign assets. In 1979 the United States was a large international creditor and had a net income from international investments of $34.0 billion. By standard accounting methods, the United States was the world's largest international debtor in 1988. Nevertheless, in 1988 the

income from foreign assets exceeded the payments to foreign holders of U.S. assets by $2.2 billion. In 1989 the international investment income balance declined further but remained in surplus at $1.0 billion. The reasons for this seeming inconsistency—continued investment income surpluses in the face of a large debtor position—are examined in Chapter 5.

4. *Other goods and services* is a relatively small account, consisting mostly of military and U.S. government services transactions. It consistently registers small deficits. The 1987 deficit was $4.2 billion; it was $5.9 billion in 1988 and $7.1 billion in 1989.

5. *Unilateral transfers* account is primarily outlays, with very few receipts. It consists primarily of foreign aid and other external grants and payments to U.S. pensioners living abroad. It is, therefore, always a deficit account, with the deficits ranging from $14 billion to $16 billion during the 1985 to 1988 period. The 1989 deficit was $14 billion.

THE KEY ROLE OF MERCHANDISE TRADE

The deterioration of U.S. current account balances from a 1981 surplus to the record 1987 deficit was dominated by worsening *merchandise trade* performance. Of the $152 billion slippage in the current account from 1981 to 1987, $132 billion was in merchandise trade (bop basis). Moreover, analysis of the other components of the current account shows that merchandise trade must also be the dominant source of future improvements in the U.S. current account.

Because the United States is rapidly becoming a more service-oriented economy, some analysts contend that increasing surpluses in *business services trade* can offset continuing large U.S. merchandise trade deficits. Business services surpluses are important and have increased recently. Moreover, of the five components of the current account, business services is the only account, other than merchandise trade, in which significant improvements might be hoped for. Analysis reveals, however, that prospects for further major gains that would contribute significantly to reductions of annual current account deficits of more than $100 billion annually are slim.

An examination of the data reveals that business services trade is neither a large component of the current account nor one in which the United States is likely to achieve major gains. In 1987 the net surplus from business services was only $12 billion, compared with a merchandise trade deficit of $160 billion (see Table 3–2). Using new estimating procedures, the 1988 business services surplus rose to $19 billion and to $28 billion in 1989, perhaps partly reflecting the new estimating procedures. Business services exports in 1989 were $105 billion, 17 percent of total goods and services exports; business services imports were $77 billion, 11 percent of total goods and services imports.

Business services trade is made up of five components: travel, passenger fares, shipping and other transportation, royalties and license fees, and other business services. The account tends to be dominated by travel, passenger fares, and shipping. Together these items represented 61 percent of 1989 business service

Table 3–2
U.S. Business Services Trade by Component, 1981–89 (Billions of Dollars)

	1981	1982	1983	1984	1985	1986
Total Business Services						
Exports	44.6	44.8	45.3	54.8	56.9	70.9
Imports	32.6	33.5	36.4	49.5	53.6	59.3
Balance	12.0	11.3	8.9	5.2	3.4	11.6
Of Which:						
Travel						
Exports	12.9	12.4	10.9	17.8	17.9	20.5
Imports	11.5	12.4	13.1	22.7	24.5	26.0
Balance	1.4	−0.0	−2.2	−5.0	−6.6	−5.5
Shipping						
Exports	12.6	12.3	12.6	13.8	14.7	15.5
Imports	12.5	11.7	12.2	14.8	15.6	16.7
Balance	0.1	0.6	0.4	−1.0	−1.0	−1.3
Passenger Fares						
Exports	3.1	3.2	3.6	4.0	4.4	5.5
Imports	4.5	4.8	6.0	5.9	6.7	6.8
Balance	−1.4	−1.6	−2.4	−1.9	−2.3	−1.2
Royalties and License Fees						
Exports	7.3	5.2	5.3	5.6	6.0	7.3
Imports	0.7	0.6	0.7	1.0	0.9	1.1
Balance	6.6	4.6	4.6	4.7	5.1	6.2
Other Business Services						
Exports	8.8	11.8	12.9	13.6	13.9	22.2
Imports	3.6	4.0	4.3	5.1	5.8	8.7
Balance	5.2	7.8	8.6	8.4	8.1	13.4

exports and 83 percent of imports. These three travel and transportation items together typically have run deficits, registering a surplus in only one year ($0.1 billion in 1980) and deficits ranging up to $10 billion during the 1977–88 period. They did, however, produce a surplus of $0.8 billion in 1989, reflecting increasing popularity of the United States for foreign tourists and the effects of the dollar decline since 1985.

Royalties and license fees has been a significant net earner for the United

Table 3–2 (*continued*)

	1987	1988	1989	Change 81-87	Change 87-89
Total Business Services					
Exports	79.4	92.1	104.6	34.8	25.2
Imports	67.5	73.1	76.3	34.8	8.9
Balance	12.0	19.0	27.7	-0.0	15.8
Of Which:					
Travel					
Exports	23.5	29.2	33.9	10.6	10.3
Imports	29.2	32.1	34.2	17.7	5.0
Balance	-5.7	-2.9	-0.4	-7.1	5.3
Shipping					
Exports	17.0	18.9	20.4	4.4	3.4
Imports	18.1	19.6	20.7	5.6	2.7
Balance	-1.1	-0.7	-0.4	-1.2	0.7
Passenger Fares					
Exports	6.9	8.9	9.9	3.8	3.0
Imports	7.4	7.9	8.3	2.9	0.9
Balance	-0.5	1.0	1.6	0.8	2.1
Royalties and License Fees					
Exports	9.1	10.7	11.9	1.8	2.9
Imports	1.4	2.0	1.9	0.7	0.5
Balance	7.7	8.7	10.1	1.1	2.3
Other Business Services					
Exports	23.0	24.3	28.6	14.2	5.6
Imports	11.4	11.4	11.7	7.8	0.3
Balance	11.6	12.9	16.9	6.3	5.3

Source: U.S. Department of Commerce.

States. The income from U.S. sales of technology, represented by the receipts of royalties and fees by U.S. companies from foreign companies, was $10.7 billion in 1988. U.S. payments for foreign technology, however, were only $2.0 billion, yielding a 1988 surplus of $8.7 billion. In 1989 the surplus rose further, to a record $10.1 billion.

Other business services, the fifth subcategory of business services, includes a wide variety of tradeable business services such as income from communication services, construction contractors' fees, film rental income, financial and management services, and consulting services. Trade in these items netted $12.9 billion in 1988, a substantial sum. The 1989 surplus rose to $16.9 billion.

International sales of these kinds of other business services are important sources of revenue for many U.S. firms but are unlikely to become substantially larger net export earners for the United States. Other business services trade is relatively small. Exports in 1989 were only $28.6 billion, imports $11.7 billion. The contributions to international balances are relatively small because the current account receipts for many types of other business services are only the net "value added" in the home country. This may be only a small fraction of what may have been much larger transactions. Although the premium payments to U.S. insurance companies for covering foreign risks might be very large, for example, after payments of claims, foreign reinsurance, foreign administrative costs, and so forth, the U.S. "export" registered in the other business services account would be only a tiny fraction of the premium paid by the foreign insurance purchaser. Similarly, construction and other services performed abroad typically incur significant costs in the purchasing country, leaving a much smaller net "services export" to appear in U.S. accounts.

Also, although the United States is sometimes assumed to have significant advantages in those services included in other business services, whatever U.S. advantages exist may be dwindling. International competition in many services is increasing rapidly. All of the world's largest banks, for example, are now Japanese. The largest U.S. bank in terms of total assets now ranks twenty-fourth in the world.[2] Also, the Koreans and others have become very proficient and competitive in international construction.

Similarly, although royalties and license fees have been a significant source of U.S. earnings, the U.S. share of world patents that provides the base for sales of technology continues to decline. As the United States continues to buy more and more foreign technology, further major gains in this category are unlikely.

The travel and passenger fares balances have improved significantly in the past few years, by $7.4 billion in the two years since 1987. The flow of foreign tourists to the United States is increasing, both by reason of dollar depreciation and as a result of increasing wealth in foreign countries. But unless there is a very large further decline in the dollar, large U.S. travel, passenger fares, and shipping expenditures will likely persist, and increases in foreign travel to the United States will add only a few billion dollars to U.S. services exports. Further dollar depreciation could somewhat improve the balances in these three accounts, but it would take a massive fall of the dollar to turn them into major net earners.

Further dollar depreciation will, however, increase all of the five types of business service earnings in two ways. First, it will tend to increase exports and decrease imports, thereby improving the balance. Second, dollar depreciation increases the dollar value of earnings originally denominated in foreign currencies. Both effects have helped to boost business services earnings since 1985.

Some analysts have argued that data collection procedures significantly understate some elements of business services. The recent revisions to business

services data estimating procedures seem to support the view that there may have
been some modest understatements in the past. Even if current procedures continued to underestimate this item, however, the understatement would likely be
minor compared to other elements of the current account. Though business
services trade is substantial—some $181 billion in 1989 two-way trade—and is
likely to continue to grow, it is most unlikely that it will become a major factor
in improving overall U.S. trade performance and current account balances.

Like trade in business services, other non-merchandise trade components of
the current account afford little or no opportunity for significant improvement
in the current account balance. *International investment income*—the balance on
receipts from investments abroad and payments on foreign investments in the
United States—will continue its decline from the significant surpluses of past
years. The $1.0 billion 1989 surplus in this component of the current account—
the smallest in many years—is a major reversal from surpluses of $34 billion in
1981 and $26 billion in 1985. The balance will almost certainly slip into deficit
in 1990, with the deficits subsequently enlarging as the U.S. debtor position
continues to grow.

Other goods and services will likely continue to accrue small deficits. The
deficits could increase modestly, depending primarily on whether the dollar
exchange rate and other factors increase the deficit in military transactions in
this account.

Unilateral transfers deficits will also continue. A growing number of U.S.
citizens retiring abroad and increases in average pension payments to these
citizens could enlarge the deficit. A major reduction in the other main components
of this account—foreign grants and other transfers—is unlikely in the near term.

Looking to the future, neither business services trade nor other non-merchandise trade components can achieve large gains. Instead, a major improvement
in the U.S. current account deficit must be generated primarily by a turnaround
in the merchandise trade account. There is no other likely source of major
improvement.

For many years, balances in non-merchandise trade accounts summed to substantial surpluses and helped to offset merchandise trade deficits. But the balance
on non-merchandise trade items, while still in surplus, has narrowed and, as the
U.S. debtor position grows, will move into deficit. Thus a balanced current
account will require a merchandise trade surplus. No combination of "services"
transactions should be expected to offset large merchandise trade deficits. This
is an important conclusion with very significant policy implications that are
further developed in the remainder of this book.

MERCHANDISE TRADE PERFORMANCE
BY MAJOR COMPONENT

The preceding discussion has shown that international trade in "services"
will not provide major improvements in the U.S. current account. Such im-

provements can come only in the merchandise trade sector. A dissection of recent merchandise trade performance can further refine the analysis and identify the kinds of goods most affected by declining U.S. merchandise trade balances and those with the most potential for improvement.

Merchandise Trade Performance, 1981–89

U.S. merchandise trade has been in deficit since 1976. Deficits remained relatively modest through 1982, but rapid growth began in 1983 (Table 3–3). The merchandise trade deficit reached $107 billion in 1984, increased to $138 billion in 1986, and peaked at $152 billion in 1987 (imports on a customs basis). The 1988 deficit narrowed by $33 billion, to $119 billion. Performance improved more modestly in 1989, by $10 billion, to a deficit of $109 billion, with imports recorded on a customs basis.

As 1990 began, most forecasters expected little improvement in the merchandise trade balance; in fact, several predicted that the deficit would begin to grow again. Without major changes in other determinants, trade performance in the early 1990s will primarily reflect the strength of the U.S. economy, with import growth restrained if the economy weakens.

Explosive trade deficit growth in the 1983–87 period was the result of strong growth in U.S. imports, concurrent with export declines in 1982 and 1983 and subsequent slow export growth through 1987. Total merchandise imports increased rapidly through the mid-1980s and by 1987 were 56 percent above the 1981 level, with a further increase of more than 8 percent in 1988 to $441 billion. Merchandise imports growth slowed only modestly in 1989, with the total reaching $473 billion.

Export behavior was very different. After declining in 1982 and 1983, exports began a slow recovery in 1984 and in 1987 finally pushed 5.9 percent above the 1981 level. Exports in 1988 then increased almost 27 percent above 1987 levels, to reach a new high of $322 billion. Further gains were registered in 1989, with exports rising 13 percent to $364 billion.

Categorizing merchandise trade into four broad product groups shows the dominant role of manufactures trade. *Manufactured goods* accounted for four-fifths of 1989 U.S. merchandise trade—79.5 percent of exports, 80.3 percent of imports.

The other three components were much smaller. *Mineral fuels* accounted for only 3 percent of exports but 11 percent of imports. Exports were mostly coal; imports were crude petroleum and refined products.

Agricultural products were 11.1 percent of 1989 exports, 4.6 percent of imports. *"Other"* is a group of miscellaneous items, including paper pulp, wood, hides, and skins. It accounted for only 6.5 percent of 1989 exports, 4.0 percent of imports.

To illustrate the dominance of manufactures trade in determining merchandise trade and current account performance, recent performance in each of the four

Table 3–3
U.S. Merchandise Trade by Components, 1981–89 (Billions of Dollars, Imports, Customs Basis)

	1981	1982	1983	1984	1985
Total Exports	238.7	216.4	205.6	224.0	218.8
Imports	261.0	244.0	258.0	330.7	336.5
Balance	-22.3	-27.6	-52.4	-106.7	-117.7
Manufacturers Exports	171.7	155.3	148.5	163.6	167.8
Imports	149.8	151.7	171.2	231.3	257.9
Balance	21.9	3.6	-22.7	-67.7	-90.1
Agriculture Exports	43.8	37.0	36.5	38.2	29.6
Imports	17.2	15.7	16.5	19.8	20.0
Balance	26.6	21.3	20.0	18.4	9.6
Mineral fuels Exports	10.3	12.8	9.6	9.5	10.1
Imports	81.4	65.4	58.3	61.0	53.9
Balance	-71.1	-52.6	-48.7	-51.5	-43.8
Other Exports	12.8	11.4	11.1	12.7	11.2
Imports	12.5	11.2	12.4	18.6	4.7
Balance	0.3	0.2	-1.3	-5.9	6.5

Source: U.S. Department of Commerce.

components of merchandise trade is reviewed below. U.S. merchandise trade performance probably hit bottom in 1987. Examining the changes in balances of the four components during the 1981–87 period of massive deficit growth provides useful insights.

Not only does *manufactures trade* dwarf the other components, but also the

Table 3–3 (*continued*)

1986	1987	1988	1989	Change 81–87	Change 87–89
227.2	254.1	322.4	364.3	15.4	110.2
365.4	406.2	441.0	472.9	145.2	66.7
-138.2	-152.1	-118.5	-108.6	-129.8	43.5
179.9	200.0	255.6	289.7	28.3	89.7
297.0	324.9	361.4	379.6	175.1	54.7
-117.1	-124.9	-105.7	-89.9	-146.8	35.0
26.6	29.1	37.6	40.6	-14.7	11.5
21.2	20.7	21.2	22.1	3.5	1.4
5.4	8.4	16.4	18.5	-18.2	10.1
8.2	7.8	8.6	9.9	-2.5	2.1
37.3	44.2	41.0	52.6	-37.2	8.4
-29.1	-36.4	-32.4	-42.7	34.7	-6.3
12.1	15.9	18.5	23.6	3.1	7.7
9.6	15.1	17.6	19.1	2.6	4.0
2.5	0.8	3.1	4.5	0.5	3.7

massive deterioration in the manufactures balance far outweighs other changes. U.S. manufactures trade fell into deficit in 1983 (Table 3–3). The deficits then expanded rapidly, through 1987, reflecting both lagging exports and an explosion of imports. Exports peaked in 1981, declined in 1982, and declined again in 1983 before beginning a gradual recovery in 1984.

Manufactures imports, however, increased every year, with particularly dramatic gains beginning in 1984. By 1987 manufactures exports were only 16 percent above the 1981 level, but imports were 117 percent higher. In 1987 manufactures exports were $200 billion, but imports, at $325 billion, were 1.6 times as large. By 1988 manufactures exports had to grow 1.6 times as fast as imports simply to keep the manufactures deficit from expanding further.

In 1988 manufactures exports grew 28 percent to $256 billion; imports grew only 11 percent to $361 billion. But manufactures imports remained 41 percent greater than exports and the manufactures trade balance improved only $19 billion to a $106 billion deficit. In 1989 exports grew 13 percent, imports increased only 5 percent, and the balance improved another $16 billion to a $90 billion deficit.

The *mineral fuels* deficit, though it worsened in 1987, nevertheless was dramatically improved over earlier years. The deficit narrowed from $71 billion in 1981 to $36 billion in 1987, a $35 billion improvement. As a result of declining oil import prices, the 1988 mineral fuels deficit improved modestly, to $32 billion. In 1989, however, as oil prices and import volumes both increased, the deficit widened by $10 billion to almost $43 billion.

Agricultural trade provided the United States with significant surpluses in earlier years of the 1980s. Although by 1987 agricultural trade was still in surplus, the $8.4 billion surplus was $18.2 billion less than in 1981 (Table 3–3). Surpluses shrank from 1981 through 1986, declining from a peak of $26.6 billion in 1981, to only $5.4 billion in 1986, before beginning a recovery that carried the surplus to $18.5 billion in 1989.

Other goods trade, a small account, in 1987 was essentially unchanged from its 1981 balance. From 1981 to 1987 exports ranged from $11.1 billion to $15.9 billion and imports from $4.7 billion to $18.6 billion. Balances ranged from a deficit of $5.9 billion to a surplus of $6.5 billion. A surplus of $4.5 billion was registered in 1989.

The above data demonstrate that manufactures trade dominates merchandise trade and current account performance. The 1987 manufactures trade deficit of $125 billion far outweighed the $36 billion mineral fuels deficit. The modest $8.4 billion agricultural trade surplus was relatively insignificant. The manufactures trade deficit was equivalent to 82 percent of the total $152 billion deficit.

Looking Ahead

In the six years from 1981 to 1987 the *manufactures* trade balance worsened by $147 billion, significantly more than the $130 billion slippage in the whole of the merchandise trade account (Table 3–3). What can be expected in the 1990s? What components of goods trade may worsen? What are the likely areas of improvement? We must first examine the prospects for the non-manufacturing subcategories.

The balance of the mineral fuels account, dominated by oil imports, is determined primarily by the quantity and price of oil imports, both of which can change rapidly. The volume of oil imports has grown rapidly in recent years, and prices have fluctuated over a wide range. Other things being equal, each $1 per barrel change in the price of oil imports changes the United States oil import bill about $2 billion. Taking both price and import volumes into consideration, major improvements in the mineral fuels account seem highly unlikely. Although oil prices were down in 1988 from 1987 levels, import volumes were up by 10 percent. The result was a modest decrease in the oil deficit in 1988 to about $37 billion. In 1989, however, prices rose, and volume continued to climb, rising another 8 percent. This increased the oil deficit by $10 billion over the 1988 level and about $6 billion over the 1987 level. Looking into the 1990s, oil prices will likely fluctuate and could fall below levels at the beginning of the decade. However, price increases in the longer term are likely. If price increases do occur, the oil import bill could grow dramatically. Indeed, even if oil import prices remain at 1988 levels, the oil deficit will increase as U.S. oil production continues to decline, consumption continues to grow, and oil import volumes continue to increase.

The 1989 agricultural surplus was $18.5 billion, well above the lows of the decade but still short of the $26.6 billion surplus of 1981. Some further modest gains from the 1989 level may be achieved, but the prospects for significantly larger agricultural surpluses are dim. Even a return to the record surpluses of 1981 would make only a relatively small dent in the U.S. merchandise trade deficits. Most importantly, despite temporary, favorable short-term supply-demand changes, global supplies of the types of grains that dominate U.S. agricultural exports are expanding more rapidly than demand. Global food surpluses will likely continue, keeping prices low, competition for markets tough, and U.S. agricultural trade surpluses near 1989 levels.

At $4.5 billion, the 1989 other goods surplus had improved about $3.7 billion compared to 1987. "Other goods" is a small account, however, and during the next few years will likely fluctuate and not produce significant gains. It will continue to be a minor factor in U.S. trade balances.

MANUFACTURES TRADE DOMINANCE

Declining manufactures trade performance, as shown above, was the dominant factor in the growth of large merchandise trade and current account deficits. The non-manufacturing components of merchandise trade offer dim prospects for improvement during the next several years. Any major improvement in the merchandise trade balance must occur predominantly in the manufactures trade account. It follows, then, that manufactures trade will also be the primary source of improvement in the current account. There is no other likely source of major gains for either the merchandise trade or current account balances. Indeed, with escalating oil bills likely and increasing debt service costs a certainty, substantial surpluses in manufactures trade will be required to achieve a balance in the U.S. current account.

The dominance of manufactures in U.S. trade is not unique. World trade has become very much an exchange of manufactured goods, and the manufactures portion of world trade has been rising. In 1970 about 74 percent of world non-energy exports were manufactures. By 1980 the portion had risen to 79 percent, and in 1984 it was 83 percent. Trade among developed countries is even more heavily concentrated in manufactures. In 1984 more than 83 percent of industrial country non-energy exports and 79.5 percent of non-energy imports were manufactures.[3]

The manufactures portion of non-energy trade is likely to continue to expand as global demand for manufactures continues to increase more rapidly than demands for food and raw materials. The U.S. role in world manufactures trade is large. In 1986 the United States held a 12.2 percent share of world exports of manufactured goods to all world destinations. U.S. manufactures imports, however, were about one-fourth of other countries' manufactures exports to the world. The U.S. manufactures deficit alone equaled about 10 percent of manufactures exports by other countries.

Manufactures trade, it will be seen, is the "swing factor"—the key trade variable—in fluctuating international capital flows and trade balances. Manufacturing sectors are the primary beneficiaries of trade surpluses. They also bear the brunt of declining trade performance. Thus *major improvements in U.S. current account balances must come from improved manufactures trade performance.* This is a critical conclusion in understanding the effects of trade fluctuations. It has very significant implications for the U.S. economy and the nation's economic policies. To date, U.S. economic policy making has not focused on the vulnerability of the manufacturing sector to tax and other macroeconomic policies that cause large net capital inflows into the United States. The implications for U.S. policy making are explored in subsequent chapters.

The dominant role of manufactures trade in the large U.S. trade deficits of recent years and its key role in narrowing and eliminating U.S. current account deficits also has very significant implications for the world economy, particularly for certain trading partners. Because U.S. manufactures imports are so large, sudden large reductions in them could cause major disruptions in world trade patterns that would create difficult problems for countries whose economies are dependent on exports to the United States. The potential problems associated with narrowing unsustainable global trade imbalances are reviewed in Chapters 7 through 9.

MANUFACTURES TRADE BY MAJOR COMMODITY GROUPS

A more detailed look at recent manufactures trade performance can help one to understand the problems that will be encountered in narrowing the current account deficits. The deterioration of U.S. manufactures trade performance during the 1980s was rapid. Balances fluctuated through 1982 and then declined dramatically. The last manufactures trade surplus was in 1982 (Table 3–3). The

Figure 3–1

U.S. Manufactures Trade Balances by Commodity Groups, 1987 (Billions of Dollars)

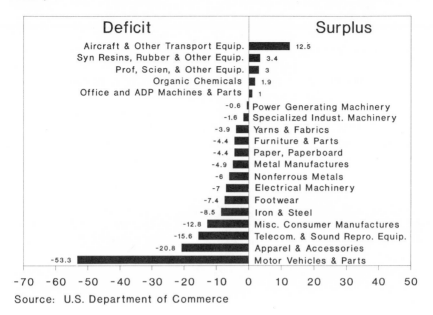

Source: U.S. Department of Commerce

$147 billion decline during the 1981–87 period was equivalent to well over 3 percent of the nation's GNP in 1987.

Sources of the 1981–87 decline can be identified by looking at performance in some product groups. Manufactures trade is recorded in forty-two two-digit product groups.[4] Twenty-four of the two-digit groups, however, accounted for 84 percent of exports and 90 percent of imports in 1987.

By 1987 the United States had surpluses in only seven of the twenty-four major manufactures groups. Only *aircraft and other transportation equipment* had a large surplus ($12.5 billion). Only two other product groups had surpluses above $2 billion (Figure 3–1).

Twelve product groups, however, had deficits exceeding $2 billion. The largest deficit was *motor vehicles and parts,* $53.3 billion, an amount equal to 1.2 percent of the 1987 U.S. GNP. Other product groups showing large deficits included *apparel and accessories* with a $20.8 billion deficit and *telecommunication and sound reproducing equipment* with a $12.8 billion deficit.[5]

From 1981 to 1987 performance worsened in twenty-one of the twenty-four groups (Figure 3–2). Particularly striking was the $40.5 billion expansion in the motor vehicles and parts deficit, though the $14 billion increase in the apparel and accessories deficit was also notable.

Significant improvements in 1988 and 1989 included motor vehicles, aircraft and transportation equipment, and non-monetary gold. Large additional im-

Figure 3–2
Changes in U.S. Manufactures Trade Balances by Commodity Groups, 1981–87
(Billions of Dollars)

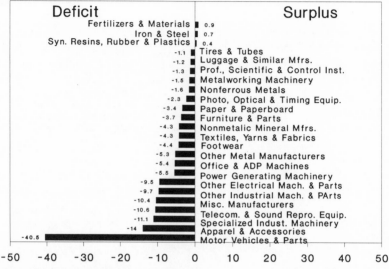

Source: U.S. Department of Commerce.

provements will be required, however, to eliminate the deficits in some key product groups and to generate the large manufactures trade surpluses needed to return to a sustainable current account balance. The prospects for the required turnaround are reviewed in more detail in Chapter 8.

Bilateral manufactures deficits with some countries grew very large during the 1980s. The 1987 manufactures deficit with Japan alone was $68 billion (imports, customs basis). Deficits with Taiwan, Germany, South Korea, and Hong Kong totaled another $47 billion. These data, reflecting a 1987 manufactures trade deficit of $115 billion—92 percent of the total—with these four trading partners give an indication of which countries will likely be most affected by the large reductions in U.S. manufactures deficits that must occur if the United States is to return to sustainable trade and current account balances.

HIGH-TECH AND NON-HIGH-TECH TRADE

Manufactures trade can also be split into high-tech and non-high-tech categories. Any split into these two categories is based on a somewhat arbitrary standard. Moreover, because technology and products are constantly changing, the definition of which specific products are high-tech must change over time. Nevertheless, it is useful to examine trade performance on the basis of technology content because some observers see concentration on the production of high-technology goods as the solution to U.S. trade problems.

U.S. trade performance in high-technology manufactures has traditionally been stronger than performance in non-high-tech manufactures. There is no single universally accepted definition of high-tech. Using perhaps the most widely accepted definition, however, high-tech manufactures trade produced a surplus of \$27.4 billion in 1981, concurrent with a non-high-tech deficit of \$5.5 billion (Table 3–4).[6] After 1981 high-tech and non-high-tech trade both deteriorated markedly. By 1987 the high-tech trade surplus had fallen to only \$2.7 billion, whereas non-high-tech trade registered a deficit of \$127.5 billion. Thus from 1981 to 1987 the high-tech balance slid \$24.7 billion; the non-high-tech balance, \$122 billion. The 1988 high-tech surplus recovered to \$8.1 billion; the non-high-tech deficit increased to \$133.8 billion.

The high-tech product group can be divided into ten subgroups. *Communication equipment,* a large deficit category, includes many consumer electronic items that intuitively may not seem to be high-tech. The deficit in this category reflects large deficits in a wide variety of consumer goods, including televisions and video cassette recorders (VCRs), as well as rapid increases in imports of non-consumer electronic goods.

Goods defined as high-tech have been increasing their share of both manufactures exports and imports. The high-tech share of exports rose from 35 percent in 1980 to 42 percent in 1987; the share in imports rose from 22 to 25 percent.

With high-tech goods making up about one-third of U.S. exports, better performance in high-tech trade will be important to improved manufactures trade and current account balances. It would be unrealistic, however, to expect that the United States can improve its manufactures trade performance primarily by emphasizing the invention, design, and production of high-tech manufactures.

Inventing and designing new products is one type of undertaking; manufacturing them in the United States at cost and quality standards that are internationally competitive is a different matter. In today's world, technology transfers occur rapidly among countries. The manufacture of many products (for example, consumer electronics) requires relatively modest supporting investment and infrastructure development. Sophisticated manufacturing capabilities now exist around the world. This widespread capability has narrowed the advantage of developed countries over LDCs as a base for manufacturing. Indeed, other countries have surpassed the United States in manufacturing skills in several product areas. Today preeminence in the development of new high-technology products no longer guarantees export surpluses in those products. Nor can it ensure that countries that develop high-tech products will not run high-tech trade deficits. Most manufactured goods—including high-tech items—can now be made efficiently around the globe. In today's more competitive world, products will not necessarily be made where they are designed and developed. Instead, they will be manufactured at whatever geographical location provides the lowest cost production and distribution site.

The United States, therefore, cannot eliminate its huge trade deficits by concentrating solely on developing new high-tech products. It will have to improve

Table 3–4
High-Tech and Non-High-Tech Trade, 1981–88 (Billions of Dollars, Imports, Customs Basis)

	1981	1982	1983	1984	1985	1986	1987	1988
Manufactures								
Exports	171.7	155.3	148.5	163.6	167.8	179.9	200.0	255.6
Imports	149.8	151.7	171.2	231.3	257.9	297.0	324.9	361.4
Balance	21.9	3.6	-22.7	-67.7	-90.1	-117.1	-124.9	-105.8
Of Which:								
Non-High Tech								
Exports	111.3	97.2	88.3	98.1	99.4	107.4	116.0	151.4
Imports	116.8	118.0	130.9	173.5	194.8	223.7	243.5	285.2
Balance	-5.5	-20.8	-42.6	-75.4	-95.4	-116.3	-127.5	-133.8
High Tech								
Exports	60.4	58.1	60.2	65.5	68.4	72.5	84.0	104.2
Imports	33.0	33.7	40.3	57.8	63.1	73.3	81.4	76.2
Balance	27.4	24.5	19.9	7.7	5.3	-0.7	2.7	8.1

Source: U.S. Department of Commerce.

its manufactures trade performance both in high-tech and non-high-tech manu-factured goods. Realistically, improvement must come primarily through better performance in non-high-tech goods. Generating U.S. manufactures trade sur-pluses will require the application of high technology not only to the invention and design of new, innovative products but to manufacturing processes as well. Developing new, advanced products and technologies must remain a top U.S. priority but this alone is not enough. The manufacturing process requires added management attention and emphasis to ensure that both high-tech and non-high-tech goods "made in the USA" are of the highest quality and are produced at competitive costs.

SUMMARY

• A nation's international trade includes a variety of goods, services, and other transactions summarized in its "current account" balance.

• The United States in recent years has experienced very large current account deficits. These deficits reflect large net capital inflows and accompanying large deficits in the exchanges of goods, services, and other transactions with the rest of the world.

• Current account surpluses indicate that a nation is producing more than it is consuming and exporting and lending the difference abroad. Current account deficits, the U.S. situation, mean a nation is consuming more than it is producing and importing and borrowing the balance from abroad.

• The large deficits of recent years have rapidly changed the United States from the world's largest creditor nation to the world's largest debtor nation.

• A deterioration of the merchandise trade component of U.S. trade was the dominant factor in the growth of huge current account deficits and the U.S. debtor position.

• Even though the United States is rapidly becoming a more services-oriented economy, increased exports of "services" do not offer an opportunity for major improvements in U.S. current account balances. Large improvements can be achieved only by improvements in merchandise trade balances.

• A balanced current account in the future will require a merchandise trade surplus. As the U.S. international debtor position continues to grow, the costs of servicing foreign debt will escalate, and larger and larger merchandise trade surpluses will be required to achieve a current account balance.

• Manufactures trade dominates the U.S. merchandise trade account: 79.5 percent of 1988 merchandise exports, 80.3 percent of merchandise imports.

• The deterioration in total merchandise trade from 1981 to 1987 was less than the decline in the manufactures component. The manufactures balance declined by $147 billion; merchandise trade as a whole fell a lesser amount, $130 billion, benefiting from a narrowing of the oil deficit by $35 billion.

• Improved merchandise trade performance must come predominantly from manufactures trade. There is no other likely source of significant improvement.

Agricultural trade could make modest gains, but oil deficits will likely widen in the years ahead and other goods trade is small, offering no prospect of major gains.

• Dramatically improved manufactures trade is, therefore, essential to major improvement in both the merchandise trade and current accounts. There is no other source of major improvement.

• High-tech goods cannot provide the major source of improvement in manufactures trade. About five-sixths of the decline in manufactures trade balances was in non-high-tech goods that must also be the principal source of improvement.

• Developing new high-technology products does not ensure trade surpluses, even in high-tech items. Sophisticated manufacturing capabilities exist worldwide. Most manufactured goods can be—and are—made around the globe. Products will not necessarily be manufactured where they are designed and developed but at whatever geographic location provides the lowest cost production site, including cost of delivery of the product to market.

• In addition to applying the latest technologies to the development of innovative new products and advanced technologies, the United States must increase its production of both high-tech and non-high-tech products. It is not enough to develop new products. To improve U.S. trade balances, the new products must be made in the United States, not abroad.

NOTES

1. This book includes U.S. merchandise trade data reported by the U.S. Department of Commerce in three ways. In both of two Bureau of Census reporting methods, U.S. exports are reported free alongside ship (fas), the value of the merchandise at the U.S. port of export. Imports are general imports, Customs import value, except where cost, insurance, and freight (cif) value is indicated. The cif valuation included the freight, insurance, and other charges incurred in bringing the merchandise from the foreign country to the first U.S. port of entry. A cif valuation therefore raises the reported cost of the import and enlarges deficits. For example, imports for 1987 on a cif basis were $424.4 billion and on a customs value basis, $406.2 billion, about 4.3 percent lower. Trade deficits expressed on a customs basis will thus be marginally smaller. Balance of payments (bop) basis foreign trade data are a Bureau of Economic Analysis translation of the original Census basis foreign trade data for use in the official U.S. international transactions accounts. In bop accounting, imports are valued excluding transportation costs, which appear in other accounts.

2. *The American Banker* (U.S. Daily Banking and Financial Services Newspaper, New York), 25 July 1989, 23.

3. International Trade Administration, U.S. Department of Commerce, *U.S. Trade Performance in 1985 and Outlook* (Washington, D.C.: U.S. Government Printing Office, October 1986), 13.

4. The data shown in this chapter's analysis of individual product groups reflect sections 5 through 9 of schedule E for exports and schedule A for imports on a cif basis.

5. For a more detailed disaggregation of recent U.S. manufactures trade performance,

see International Trade Administration, U.S. Department of Commerce, *U.S. Foreign Trade Highlights, 1988* (Washington, D.C.: U.S. Government Printing Office, June 1988).

6. The data used herein are based on the "Doc 3" definition of high-tech trade. For an explanation of that definition and a more detailed assessment of high-tech trade, see Office of Trade and Investment Analysis, U.S. Department of Commerce, *Technology Intensity of U.S. Output and Trade* (Washington, D.C.: U.S. Government Printing Office, July 1982), 12.

Chapter 4

Causes of the Trade and Current Account Deficits

The U.S. merchandise trade and current account balances declined dramatically from 1981 to 1987. The trade balance fell by $132 billion to a deficit of $160 billion (bop basis), the current account by $152 billion to a deficit of $144 billion. Commonly cited causes of the deterioration in U.S. trade and current account performances include:

- An overly strong dollar, with the exchange rate rising relentlessly from 1980 through early 1985
- More rapid economic growth in the United States than abroad after the 1981–82 global recession
- The financial troubles of some LDCs that are important U.S. markets
- Trade barriers imposed against U.S. exports by other countries
- A decline in U.S. "competitiveness"

Each of these factors is important to the U.S. trade situation, and each represents a problem that must be dealt with. But the strong dollar, the differential international growth rates, and the LDC debt problem are not themselves the root causes of the massive trade deficits. Rather, they are manifestations of U.S. and foreign national economic policies that markedly changed international capital flows.

The strong dollar, the weak growth abroad, and the LDC debt problem were the directly visible causes of the growth in the U.S. trade deficits during the 1980s. They helped to price the United States out of global competition, boosting U.S. imports and cutting into foreign demand for U.S. goods and services. But changing these three factors and their effects on U.S. trade depends fundamentally on changing U.S. and foreign macroeconomic policies, behavior, and performance.

Foreign trade barriers and a decline in U.S. competitiveness are also important issues but were not major factors in the rapid growth of U.S. trade deficits. This chapter examines the root causes of the trade and current account deficits in more detail.

UNDERLYING CAUSES OF U.S. TRADE DEFICITS

In 1981 the United States was producing slightly more goods and services than it was consuming, exporting the difference, and lending abroad. This was reflected in the modest 1981 net capital outflows and small current account surplus. The situation then changed dramatically. By 1984 huge U.S. current account deficits and capital inflows had begun. The nation was consuming more than it was producing, importing the difference, and borrowing abroad. What caused the rapid change from small current account surpluses and net capital outflows to huge deficits and net capital inflows?

A country's consumption versus its production, its net international capital flows, and its resulting current account and trade balances are determined fundamentally by its national macroeconomic policies and performance *relative to* those of other countries and by its domestic investment and saving behavior *relative to* investment and saving abroad. Changes in these international relationships can quickly and markedly alter net capital and trade flows.

The changes in U.S. macroeconomic policies and performance that triggered net capital inflows resulted from a combination of factors. Beginning in the early 1980s, the United States adopted expansionary policies—for example, deregulation, broad tax rate reductions, and investment tax credits—that encouraged U.S. economic growth and spurred both investment and consumption. At the same time, monetary policies designed to counter inflation limited U.S. money supply growth and caused U.S. real interest rates to rise relative to those in many foreign countries. The resulting combination of increased U.S. demand for funds to finance growing federal budget deficits and rising domestic private investment far exceeded U.S. domestic saving. The difference was willingly made up by foreign investors who saw the purchase of U.S. dollar-denominated assets with expected favorable rates of return as a desirable investment alternative. The result was large net U.S. imports of capital from abroad.

This net borrowing provided the funds required to finance the current account deficits that allowed U.S. consumption to rise above U.S. production. Borrowing among nations is manifested in net imports of goods and services that register as current account deficits. Changing international investment positions reflect the changing net positions of obligations (in the form of stocks, bonds, and other kinds of securities) that match the net flows of goods and services. A single year's current account deficit is the net financial capital borrowing that year and in essence the mirror image of that year's addition to the nation's international investment position.

Fundamental shifts in global economic relationships underlie the recent changes that made the United States a large net dissaver and capital importer. A dissection of the saving versus investment and government deficit relationships reveals the key factors responsible for this switch in status.

THE SAVING-INVESTMENT GAP

The Saving-Investment Relationship

The key underlying determinant in U.S. trade and current account deficits is the gap between U.S. saving and the sum of U.S. investment plus the government deficit (Table 4–1). By definition, an economy's "saving" must equal the sum of private-sector "investment" and the government deficit.[1] When domestic saving is inadequate to fund private-sector investment plus the government deficit, the shortfalls in saving are made up by net capital inflows and the associated trade and current account deficits.

The saving-investment gaps of the 1980s resulted from an enlarged budget deficit, relatively strong investment spending, and lagging U.S. saving. In 1980 the United States set aside through saving and took in through taxes $6.9 billion more than it spent through private domestic investment spending and government outlays (Table 4–1). But by 1983 an excess of private-sector investment spending and government spending created a $38.6 billion gap between the amount spent and the amount saved and taxed. By 1986 the saving-investment gap had grown to $134.0 billion, and in 1987 it was $146.2 billion.

The most critical element in producing these imbalances was the expansion of the federal budget deficit, which rose from $61.3 billion in 1980 to $206.9 billion in 1986, about 4.9 percent of GNP. It subsequently declined to $161.4 billion in 1987, about 3.6 percent of GNP, and to $145.8 billion, 3.0 percent of GNP, in 1988. Without these large government deficits, private saving probably would have been more than adequate to meet U.S. investment needs. The dollar exchange rate and U.S. interest rates would likely have been lower, and the net foreign capital inflows and accompanying large current account and trade deficits probably would not have occurred.

There is, therefore, a direct linkage between the U.S. federal budget and the large trade deficits of the 1980s. National government budget deficits, however, do not necessarily result in trade and current account deficits. During most of the 1980s the United States had large budget deficits and did experience large current account deficits. But during most of the 1980s—until 1987—Japan ran government deficits ranging from 0.8 to 4.4 percent of GNP while running large current account surpluses. The Federal Republic of Germany (FRG) also consistently ran the government budget deficits and current account surpluses during the 1980s. In 1988, for example, the FRG's budget deficit was 2.1 percent of GNP, but it had a current account surplus of 4.0 percent of GNP. That same year, the U.S. budget deficit was 2.1 percent of GNP and its current account deficit, 2.6 percent of GNP. The difference was that Japan and the FRG had

Table 4-1
U.S. Saving and Investment, 1980–88 (Billions of Dollars)

	1980	1981	1982	1983	1984	1985	1986	1987	1988
Saving									
Private Saving	478.4	550.5	557.1	592.2	673.5	665.3	669.5	663.8	738.6
Of Which:									
Personal	136.9	159.4	153.9	130.6	164.1	125.4	124.9	101.8	144.7
Business	341.5	391.1	403.2	461.6	509.5	539.9	544.6	562.0	593.8
Government Saving	-34.5	-29.7	-110.8	-128.5	-105.0	-131.8	-144.1	-110.1	-96.1
Of Which:									
State and Local	26.8	34.1	35.1	47.5	64.6	65.1	62.8	51.3	49.7
Federal	-61.3	-63.8	-145.9	-176.0	-169.6	-196.9	-206.9	-161.4	-145.8
Gross Domestic Saving	443.9	520.8	446.3	463.7	568.5	533.5	525.4	553.7	642.5
Investment									
Gross Private Domestic Investment	437.0	515.5	447.3	502.3	664.8	643.1	659.4	699.9	750.3
Saving-Investment Gap	6.9	5.3	-1.0	-38.6	-96.3	-109.6	-134.0	-146.2	-107.8

Source: U.S. Department of Commerce.

high personal and business saving rates that more than offset their government deficits, whereas the United States did not.

Thus U.S. trade and current account deficits will continue as long as saving is inadequate to cover investment plus the government deficit. The gap can be closed in several ways. Reduced private-sector investment is one alternative, but this would be undesirable since cuts in investment spending inevitably reduce future productivity gains, production capacity, and international competitiveness.

Increased private saving is a second alternative. Although U.S. saving rates are low relative to those in most other advanced economies, they are difficult to change because they are driven by deeply rooted cultural, legislative, regulatory, and other economic factors.

Given these problems, most consider progressively decreasing the federal budget deficit the best route to reducing the trade and current account deficits. Policies to deal with the deficits are discussed in more detail in Chapters 11 and 13.

Risks of a Saving Shortfall

A continuing large U.S. dependence on net capital inflows and trade deficits poses risks. Through the 1980s and into the beginning of the 1990s foreign lenders have been willing partners in transforming the United States from a net capital exporter to a net capital importer and from the world's largest creditor nation to the world's largest debtor nation. Foreign capital has continued to flow to the United States, even at unsustainably high dollar exchange rates and notwithstanding the large trade and current account deficits. Lacking policies to narrow its saving-investment gap and its excess of total consumption over total production, U.S. current account deficits and borrowing will continue as long as foreign lenders are willing.

But if foreign lenders become unwilling—or even significantly less willing— to fund continuing U.S. deficits, the resulting capital shortage could push up U.S. interest rates and cause an economic downturn. Without actions to resolve the saving-investment gap, the U.S. economy is dependent on the attitude of foreign leaders. Alternative scenarios for eliminating net U.S. capital inflows are discussed in Chapters 5 and 11.

There are mutual U.S. and foreign responsibilities and problems in trimming the U.S. trade deficits and the complementary foreign surpluses. The United States must narrow its saving-investment gap during the next few years, preferably by decreasing the federal budget deficit. But if world economic growth is to continue, several current account surplus countries must take concurrent actions to increase their consumption and investment and decrease their saving. Actions by both the United States and the surplus countries will be difficult but necessary.

The problems of narrowing unsustainable global capital flows and the resulting trade and current account imbalances are discussed in more detail in Chapters 7 through 9.

THE RELATIONSHIP BETWEEN TRADE AND CAPITAL FLOWS

In a world of integrated capital markets, a nation's macroeconomic policies can have dramatic effects on its trade balances. This is a new and not widely understood development. Previously, capital flows were considered to be primarily an offsetting adjustment to trade flows. Goods and services trade performance were thought to be the major determinants of exchange rates and other factors that affect international economic performance and a country's current account balance.

In earlier periods, there were often restrictions on international capital movements, and investors were more likely to look primarily at domestic investment alternatives and less apt to look abroad. But in recent years, international capital markets have undergone dramatic changes. Floating exchange rates, instant worldwide telecommunications, deregulation of capital markets, easing of restrictions on international capital movements, lowered transaction costs, and many other factors have led investors to look more to international investment alternatives than simply to local or national opportunities. As a result, the volume of international capital movements has become huge and volatile.

In this environment of newly integrated international capital markets, capital flows can no longer be thought of as passively financing an independently determined U.S. current account balance. Rather, the net of international capital flows now exerts an independent force on the major determinants of the U.S. trade and current account balances. The current account has been adjusting to the net of capital flows, primarily through changes in relative prices, changes in exchange rates, and income levels.

In today's environment, U.S. domestic policies and saving and investment performance *relative to* foreign policies and saving and investment performance determine the size and direction of net capital flows that, in turn, affect the primary determinants of U.S. trade and current account balances. This is a critically important conclusion. In effect, it means that major changes in the U.S. trade and current account balances will occur only to the extent that U.S. saving and investment patterns change *relative to* those abroad in ways that will cause a reduction in net capital inflows to the United States.

Thus, although lowering foreign trade barriers and opening markets abroad have important benefits, they improve the current account balances only to the extent that the reduction of foreign barriers changes U.S. or foreign saving or investment patterns and, hence, the relationship between U.S. and foreign saving or between U.S. and foreign investment.

Even more important, it indicates that there is no "right" level of saving and investment for a country. In a world of free international capital flows, as long as their credit lasts, countries that are low saving and high consuming relative to other countries will typically be net importers and borrowers from high saving and low consuming countries. Improving the balance in U.S. capital flows thus may be achieved not only by increasing U.S. saving rates but by persuading surplus countries to adopt policies that will decrease their saving rates and increase their consumption.

Although current account and trade balances are now seen as being driven primarily by international financial flows, this does not mean that capital flows are unaffected by trade performance. Net capital inflows to a nation may initially reflect foreign confidence in its economy. But continued large trade deficits and a resulting continuing enlargement of a nation's debtor position relative to its GNP will in time lower foreign investor confidence and reduce or eliminate the net inflows. This is essentially what happened to LDC debtors who for a time were willingly supplied capital by foreign lenders. Ultimately, however, continued LDC debt buildup and flawed economic performance exhausted lender confidence, and voluntary lending to many LDC debtors ended. This forced them to move from the borrowing inherent in trade deficits to the trade surpluses required to service existing debt. The evolution of LDC debt is discussed in more detail in Chapter 10.

THE CRITICAL EFFECTS OF TAX POLICIES ON TRADE FLOWS

The large and volatile international capital flows produced by newly integrated world capital markets have markedly increased the effects that domestic tax and fiscal policies can have on the nation's economy, particularly on its tradeable goods sectors. U.S. tax, fiscal, and monetary policies of the early 1980s simultaneously produced a surge in investment, strong consumer spending, and a government deficit partly funded by large net capital inflows to the United States. Net capital inflows are manifested in net inflows of goods and services. However, because many services are not tradeable across international borders, changes in net capital flows necessarily occur primarily in changes in goods flows.

The changes within goods trade caused by changes in net international capital flows are also uneven. U.S. goods trade (merchandise trade) is about four-fifths in manufactures. Moreover, world market prices of many primary commodities that are outside of the manufactures category, including oil, are set by global supply-demand relationships and denominated in dollars. Thus changes in the dollar exchange rate have limited effects on U.S. imports of these items. For these reasons, the large net inflows of capital in the 1983–87 period were manifested primarily in deteriorating U.S. manufactures trade balances. Indeed, the $147 billion deterioration in manufactures trade performance during the six years of 1981 to 1987 was equivalent to 3.2 percent of the 1987 U.S. GNP. That decline was imposed on a manufacturing sector producing roughly one-fifth of the nation's GNP. Policies that produced the capital inflows therefore primarily affected the U.S. manufacturing sector.

Future changes in net capital flows will also affect mostly the tradeable goods sector and, primarily, manufactured goods. In effect, *manufactures trade is the "swing factor" in implementing changes in net international capital flows to and from the United States.* This relatively new vulnerability of the U.S. manufacturing sector needs to be recognized in U.S. policies. David Hale provided the following description of the unanticipated effects of earlier U.S. policies:

the 1981 tax bill inadvertently hurt the competitive position of many U.S. industries it was designed to assist. The 1981 tax bill significantly lowered the after-tax cost of capital goods in the U.S. and thus increased the investment share of GNP. The tax subsidies for investment increased corporate credit demand at a time when federal borrowing was still equal to 5% of GNP (partially because of the tax revenue effects of higher depreciation allowances) and created a shortage of domestic savings which pushed U.S. real interest rates to record levels, forcing the economy to run a large trade deficit in order to generate capital inflows from overseas. The subsequent rise of import penetration led to a virtual recession in U.S. manufacturing industry, with the result that most U.S. output growth since 1984 has been concentrated in non-tradeable sectors of the economy such as commercial real estate and services. In fact . . . the U.S. tax shelter industry during 1985 and 1986 inadvertently became the Reagan administration's equivalent of the depression era Works Progress Administration. As the rising dollar depressed the U.S. manufacturing sector after 1984, the boom in commercial construction helped to prevent a full-fledged recession from developing.[2]

In other words, some policies that promote "investment" beyond amounts that can be funded by U.S. savings may cause net inflows of capital from abroad that are likely to impair, not assist, the tradeable goods sector, particularly manufacturing. Thus in a world where capital markets are integrated, differences in a nation's fiscal and tax policies compared to those of its trading partners have become extremely important. Indeed, it may be that "in a world with capital mobility, countries with pro-saving tax policies could simply end up exporting funds to countries with tax policies more favorable to investment."[3] That is, countries with pro-saving tax policies will run trade and current account surpluses; those with policies less favorable to saving will run deficits. The effects of tax policy on U.S. trade performance and international competitiveness are further examined in Chapter 11.

PERCEIVED CAUSES OF THE TRADE DEFICITS

The dramatic changes in international capital flows that began in 1983 were manifested in several ways that many perceived as the causes of the trade deficits.

The Overly Strong Dollar

Heavy net capital inflows to the United States reflected in strong demand for dollar-denominated assets pushed the dollar higher and higher through early 1985. The rise in the exchange rate held down the prices of U.S. imports and raised U.S. export prices to foreign buyers. Imports grew rapidly, exports stagnated, and the trade deficits mushroomed. Between its February 1985 peak and the beginning of the new decade, the dollar declined markedly, about 36 percent against a trade-weighted index of ten key industrial country trading partners.[4] The dollar decline, however, was asymmetrical, with not much change evidenced against some key LDC trading partners. Also, there are inevitable lags between exchange rate and trade movements. Trade performance in current dollar terms worsened through 1987, but the trade balance improved modestly in both 1988 and 1989.

The failure of the trade deficits to decrease more rapidly in the late 1980s despite significant dollar depreciation reflects the strong competitive stance of foreign suppliers. Large profit margins prior to the dollar decline, heavy cost cutting, and new investment allowed them to absorb much of the effects of the exchange rate decline. The perceived quality and service advantages of some foreign producers also allowed them to pass on price increases.

Continued capital inflows of 1987 and 1988 were sustained in part by increased foreign government holdings of dollar-denominated assets made to support the dollar exchange rate. These factors, together with consistently improving foreign production capabilities, show that a significant additional dollar decline will very likely be a precondition of a further major narrowing of the trade and current account deficits. It is unlikely that many foreign suppliers will be forced from U.S. markets by exchange rates that prevailed at the beginning of the 1990s. The role of the exchange rate in narrowing U.S. trade deficits is discussed in more detail in Chapter 8.

Stronger U.S. Economic Growth

Faster economic growth in the United States than abroad was an important factor in widening the U.S. trade deficits, especially in 1983 and 1984. Growth in U.S. exports is highly dependent on growth in foreign economies. Growth in some major trading partners lagged in 1983 and 1984, following the 1981–82 global recession. In later years of the decade, however, the growth gap narrowed. Foreign growth in a number of instances was higher than U.S. growth.

Improved foreign economic growth would help U.S. trade performance, but it is not a potential source of large gains in the U.S. trade balance. To be an important factor foreign growth rates must significantly exceed those of the United States for an extended period. The problem is that U.S. imports tend to increase more rapidly in response to U.S. economic growth than do U.S. exports in response to foreign economic growth.

Empirical data suggest that each 1 percent of U.S. GNP growth increases U.S. imports by 2 to 2.5 percent, whereas the comparable import propensities of major trading partners tend to be much lower. Some estimates indicate, for example, that for each 1 percent growth in Japan's GNP, its total imports increase by only around 1 percent. This divergence in national import propensities reflects the relative openness of the U.S. economy and the high consumption rates of U.S. consumers for foreign goods. The implication of these estimates is that, other things being equal, if the United States and its major trading partners maintained the same growth rates, U.S. trade deficits would continue to expand.

LDC Debtor Problems

Before 1982 many LDCs were incurring trade and current account deficits and borrowing internationally to fund net imports. But in 1982 a number of LDCs encountered debt servicing difficulties, and the growth of new lending slowed. These changes in capital flows forced major trade and current account alterations on a number of debtors. Necessarily, the changes occurred primarily in merchandise trade. Debtor countries expanded exports and contracted imports to produce the income required to service their external debts.

These changes in capital flows, manifested in LDCs' need to substitute trade surpluses for trade deficits, contributed significantly to the worsening of U.S. trade balances, especially in manufactures. In 1981 the United States ran a manufactures trade surplus with LDCs of $28.4 billion. By 1984 the surplus had changed to a deficit of $13.9 billion, and by 1987 the deficit was $36.4 billion, a swing nearly of $65 billion during the 1981–87 period.

The United States has been the prime target of the LDC export drives. U.S. imports of manufactures from high-debt LDCs increased from $9.0 billion in 1980 to $19.8 billion in 1986. The United States absorbed 80 percent of the increase in LDC manufactures exports to industrialized countries during that period.[5]

As long as the flow of new capital to LDC debtor countries is restricted—as long as banks will not voluntarily lend to them because they continue to be considered poor credit risks—LDC debtors must continue to restrict their imports and to press export drives. They must do so to generate the income required to service their debts and avoid default. In such an environment it will be very difficult for the United States to improve significantly its trade balance with LDCs. LDC debtor trade problems and the implications for U.S. trade performance are discussed in more detail in Chapter 10.

Foreign Trade Restrictions

Foreign barriers to imports of specific products were not a major cause of the 1981 to 1987 growth in U.S. trade deficits. Although both explicit and implicit trade restrictions clearly limit the ability of many U.S. companies to sell overseas, and although the U.S. trade deficit would probably be somewhat smaller if other countries removed all their import barriers, foreign trade barriers against specific U.S. products are not a major cause of recent U.S. trade deficits. Most foreign trade barriers existed before the 1981 deterioration in U.S. trade began. Moreover, in a number of products—sugar, autos, steel, machine tools, textiles, and apparel—the United States has imposed its own trade restrictions to limit U.S. imports, with some effects on the U.S. trade balance. Trade barriers do, however, significantly affect the composition and efficiency of trade.

The foregoing assessment of the effects of product-specific trade barriers leaves aside the effects of macroeconomic policies and customs of foreign economies that determine their general propensity to save, consume, export, and import. These factors definitely can be very important barriers to an expansion of U.S. exports but are not trade barriers in the popular sense of the term. High foreign saving rates and low consumption and import rates are important barriers to narrowing global trade imbalances but require different approaches than do specific product-oriented foreign restrictions.

Declining U.S. Competitiveness

Although some see declining U.S. competitiveness as a key cause of the dramatic decline in U.S. trade performance, trade deficits are not necessarily correlated with, and are a poor measure of, international competitiveness. Indeed, rather than being caused by declining competitiveness, the trade deficits are, as noted in Chapter 1, a factor contributing to declining U.S. competitiveness.

SUMMARY

• The strong dollar, the strong U.S. economic growth, and the LDC debt problem were proximate causes of the huge expansion of U.S. trade deficits during the 1980s but not the root causes.

• Foreign trade barriers and a presumed loss of U.S. competitiveness, though important problems, were not significant factors in the growth of U.S. trade deficits.

• The underlying cause of rapid expansion of the trade deficits was macroeconomic policies that caused the rapid change of the United States from a modest net exporter of financial capital to a large net importer of capital.

• Beginning in the early 1980s, U.S. consumption, investment, and the federal deficit expanded rapidly, causing the sum of private-sector investment and the government deficit to exceed total national saving. This saving-investment gap was willingly filled by net inflows of capital from foreign sources. Net capital inflows are necessarily manifested primarily in merchandise trade deficits, particularly in manufactures.

• The size and direction of net international capital flows are determined by the perceptions of international investors concerning risk and return on the total spectrum of international investment opportunities. Despite very large U.S. trade deficits, foreign investors perceived the acquisition of dollar-denominated assets as preferable to other international alternatives and during the 1980s willingly supplied large amounts of capital on terms acceptable to U.S. borrowers.

• The perceptions of international lenders are shaped by many factors, including interest rates, recent and prospective economic performance of the borrowing economy, and its political stability.

• The very large and volatile international capital flows produced by newly integrated world capital markets have markedly increased the effects that a nation's fiscal and tax policies can have on the nation's economy, particularly on its goods-producing sectors.

• Changes in the volume and direction of net international capital flows to and from the United States are manifested primarily in manufactures trade and affect the manufacturing sector most heavily. Some tax, fiscal, and monetary policies that induce net capital inflows may aid investment and prosperity in other sectors but at the expense of reduced performance and investment in manufacturing.

• To eliminate its trade and current account deficits, the United States must change its national macroeconomic policies and performance *relative* to those of other countries. It must eliminate its saving-investment gap and the need for net capital imports to fuel investment and economic growth. This requires increasing saving and reducing the government budget deficit.

• Very high foreign saving rates and low consumption rates are important barriers to narrowing global trade imbalances but require different U.S. policy approaches than do specific product-oriented foreign restrictions.

NOTES

1. "Saving" is the sum of private saving plus the government surplus (or minus the government deficit). Private saving is made up of saving by individuals and by business. Total individual saving is that by persons, non-profit institutions, farms, and other noncorporate business. Business saving includes undistributed corporate profits, with inventory valuation and capital consumption adjustments, corporate and noncorporate capital consumption allowances with capital consumption adjustment and private wage accruals, less disbursements.

2. David D. Hale, "Tax Reform in the U.S. and Japan: The Movement Towards International Tax Convergence" (Paper delivered to U.S.–Japan Consultative Group on International Monetary Affairs, San Diego, February 1987), 11.

3. Ibid., 3.

4. Office of Trade and Investment Analysis, U.S. Department of Commerce, *Weekly Exchange Rate Developments* (Washington, D.C., January 26, 1990).

5. William F. Kolarik, *Exports of Financially Distressed LDC Debtors to the United States and Industrial West: Trends, Outlook, Implications* (Washington, D.C.: International Trade Administration, U.S. Department of Commerce, 1988), 18.

Chapter 5

Implications of U.S. Trade and Current Account Deficits

Trade and current account deficits that cause the U.S. international debtor position to increase relative to the nation's GNP cannot continue without end. Even the United States, borrowing in its own currency, does not have unlimited credit. Although large deficits and borrowing may continue for several years, sooner or later adjustment will occur. U.S. trade and current account deficits ultimately will narrow whether or not the United States takes specific policy actions directed at its deficits.

Although the U.S. trade and current account deficits are not a permanent problem, continuing large deficits pose major risks. How and when the deficits are narrowed is of great concern, not only for the United States but also for its trading partners. Managing the transition will require careful attention and correct policies if severe global economic disruptions are to be avoided.

To lessen risks to the U.S. and world economies, a reduction of U.S. deficits and the complementary surpluses of some trading partners must be gradual. Chapter 7 describes the problems of narrowing global imbalances and the need for a gradual return to sustainable balances.

Although a gradual narrowing of U.S. trade and current account deficits is clearly the best course, slow improvement will pose difficulties, including:

- Further significant growth in the U.S. international debtor position.
- A public perception of "jobs lost" and an endangered U.S. manufacturing base.
- Concerns about the growing debt and lost jobs could increase trade-restricting actions. In turn, this could trigger foreign retaliation and an eventual trade war.

This chapter examines the implications of recent deficits and the coming adjustment process. It also describes the potential effects of the adjustment process on the U.S. debtor position, on jobs, on the U.S. manufacturing base, and on the U.S. and global economies.

ALTERNATIVE SCENARIOS FOR TRIMMING
UNSUSTAINABLE U.S. BORROWING

The large U.S. current account deficits of recent years and the external borrowing they represent cannot continue without end. Although some believe the United States could borrow far beyond current levels, no nation can borrow without end in amounts that rapidly raise its debtor position relative to its GNP. Sooner or later, U.S. current account deficits and external borrowing will narrow markedly in relation to the U.S. GNP.

Two generalized scenarios summarize different ways in which the narrowing may occur:

1. U.S. government budget deficits will decrease over the next few years, perhaps accompanied by increases in private saving. This will gradually reduce the need for capital imports and eventually return the United States to a net capital exporter position.

2. Alternatively, the excess of the combination of U.S. investment spending and the government deficit over saving will continue to generate the need for capital inflows. But in a changing international environment, international investors will begin to see U.S. investment opportunities as relatively less attractive than other foreign alternatives. This will raise the price of U.S. borrowing, shrinking the amount of such borrowing, perhaps rapidly.

The first scenario would allow a ''soft landing''—a reduction of global trade imbalances with minimal global economic disruption. Progressively shrinking U.S. trade deficits would force difficult adjustments in the manufacturing industries of trading partners, but the adjustments would be relatively gradual and more manageable. Surplus countries would have time for steps to stimulate domestic consumption, time to create domestic demand that would replace export demand as their export surpluses diminish.

Getting imbalances down to sustainable levels by this kind of process would probably require five or more years. As the trade deficit slowly declines, U.S. manufacturing would gradually increase its share of U.S. and foreign markets, and progress on reducing the trade and current account deficits would be evident. Nevertheless, even this sequence of events would not be without hazards. With deficits declining only slowly, the U.S. external debt would continue to grow, and any softening in the U.S. economy could bring renewed pressures in the United States for protectionist measures.

The second scenario risks a hard, much more dangerous and disruptive landing for the United States and the world economy. Large U.S. borrowing—and current account deficits—would continue until foreign investors change their preferences. Should those preferences change abruptly, the resulting rapid reduction of U.S. borrowing abroad could have many serious global repercussions. U.S. interest and inflation rates could rise rapidly, generating a sharp U.S. recession that would rapidly cut U.S. imports. Suddenly deprived of their key U.S. export market, some countries that had not reoriented more to domestic demand would likely experience major economic problems. In turn, this could produce domestic political unrest in some countries. Serious global recession and high interest rates could threaten the abilities of LDCs to continue servicing their debts. In turn, this could pose major problems for some industrialized country lender banks.

HOW "CREDITWORTHY" IS THE UNITED STATES?

How threatening is the prospect of a hard landing? How much time can be had for adjustment? That is, how long and how much will foreign investors willingly lend to the United States? How much more can the United States borrow without causing markedly higher U.S. interest rates and a much lower dollar exchange rate?

There is no way of knowing when the preferences of foreign lenders might turn from the United States. If saving rates abroad remain high, the United States might continue to attract large quantities of borrowed capital on acceptable terms for many years. Foreign holdings of U.S. assets are probably still well within reason. In late 1986, for example, gross claims on the United States represented only roughly 3 percent of Germany and Japan's financial assets, probably not a saturation point. It has also been estimated that U.S. net capital inflows have absorbed only about 14 percent of world savings, a rate that might be sustained for many years.[1]

International investment is a process of choosing among available alternatives. If Japan, Germany, Taiwan, Korea, and some other countries remain large net savers, producing more than they consume, where are those savings to go? To LDCs already overborrowed? To centrally planned economies that have consistently demonstrated their economic ineptitude but now are attempting difficult, politically risky economic reforms? Or will countries with surplus savings prefer to lend to the United States?

As long as foreign savings remain high, large net capital inflows to the United States can probably continue without inordinately increasing the share of dollar-denominated assets in most foreign portfolios. In deciding what portion of their portfolios should be in U.S. assets, not just the strength of the U.S. economy but the strengths and weaknesses of other economies are relevant. Many foreign economies that now seem very strong are, in fact, very much dependent on exporting to the United States. International lenders may recognize that if the United States encounters economic problems, so will those economies that have experienced high growth rates based on constantly growing exports to the United States. Couple this with the political stability of the United States and a recognition that financial capital invested there can be readily converted to land, buildings, businesses, and other physical assets at prices that appear attractive to foreigners, and one can see that willing lending in large amounts could continue for some time.

In short, it may be difficult for foreign investors to find better alternatives than the United States for large pools of saving. U.S. borrowing at acceptable interest rates and exchange rates might therefore continue for years, even in the face of relatively high and growing U.S. international debt-to-GNP ratios.

Indeed, the projections of several respected econometric models imply continued U.S. current account deficits of $100 billion or more into the mid-1990s. These models, however, are projecting U.S. capital import needs, not foreign willingness to supply capital, and capital markets are notably fickle. As an international banker said some years ago when questioned why lending to Poland was continuing, despite analyses indicating that Poland had no means to pay, "You think these decisions are made on cold, hard analysis? That's bull! It's the herd instinct."

At that time the herd instinct favored lending to Poland. At the beginning of the 1990s the herd instinct—the prevailing conventional wisdom—favored lending to the United States. Indeed, in the early months of 1990, the dollar exchange rate was strong, reflecting foreign willingness to purchase more U.S. dollar-denominated assets. But the herd instinct can be changed by many events. Growth abroad might rise well above U.S. rates, for example, or a U.S. recession or increased U.S. inflation might make investments in the United States appear relatively less attractive. Or, notwithstanding the "safe haven" image conveyed by normal U.S. political and economic stability, unforeseen political or economic events could suddenly and sharply weaken investor confidence in the U.S. economy.

Also, simply accumulating higher and higher levels of U.S. debt relative to the GNP could in time cut foreign appetites for U.S. assets. The U.S. debt-to-GNP ratio was about 10.5 percent at the end of 1988 and about 13.0 percent at the end of 1989, not yet high ratios. But in an orderly global adjustment, U.S. external debt will continue to rise well into the 1990s, both in nominal terms and in relation to the GNP.

The outer limits of the level of U.S. debt that foreign lenders feel comfortable with depend on many complex and unpredictable economic, social, and psychological factors. At some point, however, financial markets may more carefully assess the effects that growing U.S. debt-servicing burdens ultimately will have on global trading patterns and on the world economy. As U.S. debt continues to grow, the United States will need ever larger manufactures trade surpluses to balance its current account and to stop further debt growth. The massive swing in the U.S. manufactures trade balance needed to balance its accounts could severely disrupt world trading patterns. The longer that U.S. borrowing continues, the greater the potential for major disruptions of global trade and capital flows. The effect of narrowing U.S. deficits on global trading patterns is discussed in Chapters 7 through 9.

Moreover, as long as the United States continues to need large net imports of capital, it remains vulnerable to relatively modest changes in the attitudes of foreign lenders. Foreign investors need not withdraw their money from the United

States to push up U.S. interest rates and set off a "hard landing" scenario. They need not even entirely cease net new lending. Rather, they need only become sufficiently unenthusiastic about increasing their U.S. holdings to drive interest rates up to levels that will significantly impair U.S. economic growth.

The increased vulnerability of the United States stemming from its need for foreign capital, for example, was apparent in early 1990, when rises in foreign interest rates caused U.S. rates to rise, the increase being necessary to continue to attract foreign capital.

Even the Tokyo stock market now affects U.S. ability to borrow. In one hypothetical disaster scenario—unlikely, but not impossible—a plunge of Tokyo's stock prices from their lofty heights sets off a need for Japanese investors to cover their losses by selling their holdings of U.S. government bonds and other securities. In turn, this triggers a steep decline in U.S. markets and possible financial panic. A counterview, however, is that a shaky international financial situation motivates a flight of international capital to the United States, seen as an international "safe haven" in troubled times. Nevertheless, the point is that in an integrated world economy, borrower nations are particularly vulnerable to the policies and economic performance of their creditors.

Also, the dramatic developments in Eastern Europe and the Soviet Union, as well as the European move toward a full customs union (EC 1992) could stimulate increased demand for investment funds that would compete with U.S. needs and raise the cost of U.S. borrowing.

In situations in which the supply of capital from foreign private sector lenders is not adequate to meet U.S. borrowing needs, the role of foreign central banks is critically important. Such banks are "lenders of last resort" and may intervene temporarily to fill U.S. needs. There are signs that private-sector foreign investors on occasion have been hesitant to expand their U.S. holdings. A precise accounting is not possible, but it appears that a large portion of 1987 U.S. external borrowing—about $120 billion of the $144 billion total current account deficit—was supplied by foreign central bank lending.[2]

Central banks of foreign countries apparently had to step in to fill the gap when private-sector foreign lending was not available at existing market interest and exchange rates. The net buying of dollar-denominated assets by foreign central bank intervention thus supplied much of U.S. capital needs and prevented further declines of the dollar. Exchange rate expectations are, however, a critical factor in international investor decisions. It may be that private sector lenders held back from U.S. investments during much of 1987 because they anticipated a further fall in the dollar and then returned to the market when they judged further dollar decline as unlikely in the near term.

In any event, continued large U.S. borrowing abroad risks serious downstream adjustment problems, though how far downstream cannot be anticipated. The risks of growing U.S. international debt go beyond the attitudes of foreign lenders. Domestic concerns about the international debt, for example, could trigger U.S. protectionist or other actions that could cause severe disruption of international trading patterns and the world economy.

THE U.S. DEBTOR POSITION IN PERSPECTIVE

It is clear that continued large U.S. borrowing abroad cannot be sustained without end and without some risk. Such borrowing might, however, be sustained for a long period, possibly even through the 1990s. But whether borrowing can be sustained and whether continued borrowing is desirable are different questions. Just how critical a problem is the U.S. debtor position? Does it really matter?

The net negative international investment position of the United States at the end of 1989 was about $664 billion, a decline of about $804 billion from the 1981 peak creditor position of $141 billion. The 1989 debtor position was equivalent to about 13.0 percent of GNP; the 1981 creditor position, 4.6 percent of GNP. The dramatic change in the IIP occurred because U.S. borrowing abroad (foreign holdings of U.S. assets) increased faster than U.S. lending abroad (U.S. holdings of foreign assets), though both have increased rapidly since 1982.

If U.S. trade and current account deficits decline gradually during the early years of the 1990s—the preferred scenario—the U.S. debtor position will enlarge significantly. If progressive improvements in the U.S. current account returned it to balance by 1992, the U.S. debtor position at the end of 1992 would likely be $800 billion or more. This would be international debt equivalent to perhaps 12 to 13 percent of 1992 GNP, depending on the rate of growth in current dollar GNP. A slower decline in the current account deficit would further raise the debt-to-GNP relationship.

Neither the current debt level nor the prospect of an $800 billion or more 1992 debtor position is, in itself, an untenable situation. Though the United States today is termed the world's largest debtor, the U.S. position is much different from that of many other debtor nations. Brazil's end-1989 external liabilities of $113 billion, for example, were equivalent to roughly 31 percent of the Brazilian GNP; the $103 billion debt of Mexico was about 58 percent of Mexico's GNP.[3]

There are other differences. U.S. foreign debt is unique in that the United States is the only country able to borrow large amounts in its own currency. U.S. international debt is denominated almost exclusively in dollars. The United States does not have to purchase foreign exchange to service its debt. This relieves it of the major potential problem faced by those who must borrow in instruments denominated in foreign currencies—depreciation of the borrower's currency against those in which the debt is denominated.

Also, many argue that the United States is not really a debtor nation because the accounting methodology undervalues U.S. assets abroad. This argument is supported by the fact that, though the standard accounting shows a large negative IIP, U.S. holders of foreign assets in 1988 received more income from their foreign holdings ($108 billion) than U.S. borrowers paid to foreign holders of U.S. assets ($106 billion) and even in 1989 still achieved a modest surplus ($1 billion).

This anomaly stems from the fact that some kinds of assets are valued in the IIP at their book value as of the time of the investment. Such an accounting ignores the fact that, over time, inflation and growth in earnings have increased the market value of many direct investments (and some others) beyond the historical book value reflected in the IIP. Because many U.S. direct investments abroad have been in place longer than comparable foreign investments in the United States, the IIP tends to understate the market value and earning power of U.S. assets abroad compared to foreign assets in the United States.

Some also argue that the IIP overstates the U.S. debtor position in that large U.S. gold reserves are valued at $42 per ounce, much less than recent market values, which at the beginning of the 1990s ranged from $400 per ounce. On the other hand, however, book values overstate the real market value of some U.S. assets in the IIP. They include large amounts of LDC debt unlikely to be recovered at face value.

These and other methodological issues indicate that the end-1989 debtor position of about $664 billion was not a precise market value accounting of the nation's international "debtor-creditor" position. Arguments about the correct valuation of the IIP, however, miss the important point. By any accounting, there can be no doubt that a very large erosion of the United States position began in 1981. This decline reached some $804 billion by the decade's end, according to the methodology employed. The decline is also reflected in the diminishing net income on the U.S. international investment income account (Table 3–1). Net income on the international investment account peaked in 1981 at $34 billion, with the diminished 1989 surplus of $1 billion representing a swing of $33 billion, an amount equal to about 0.6 percent of 1989 GNP.

Moreover, without undesirable disruptions of the global economy that would quickly eliminate U.S. trade and current account deficits, the U.S. international investment position will continue to deteriorate for some time. The net of U.S. payments to foreign investors and foreign payments to U.S. investors depends not only on the stocks of foreign and U.S. holdings but also on economic performance in the United States relative to that abroad. Also, the earnings of U.S.-held foreign assets are usually denominated in foreign currencies. Thus U.S. earnings on its foreign assets are affected by the exchange rate at which foreign earnings are translated to dollars. Dollar decline raises the dollar value of earnings initially denominated in foreign currencies.

While neither the current U.S. debtor position nor those projected for the next few years necessarily signal a crisis, there is cause for concern. Action to narrow and stop the debt growth must be taken as soon as practical. If the capital borrowed via the current account deficits of the 1980s was used to improve the volume and efficiency of U.S. production, and if the resulting increases of national output exceed the cost of servicing the borrowed capital, living standards will be higher than had borrowing not occurred. Following this scenario the United States will benefit in the long term from its recent borrowing.

Even under this favorable view of the use of U.S. borrowings, however, the net benefits will be less than if the United States had generated enough savings to supply its own investment capital. Moreover, if the borrowed capital essentially financed increased current consumption, rather than investment in productive facilities—as most believe has been the case—debt servicing in the future will lower living standards. Consumption during the 1980s will have been increased at the expense of future consumption.

Continued expansion of the U.S. debtor position poses other problems. Debt must be serviced by net exports of goods and services. Because most services cannot readily be exported, the surpluses needed to service burgeoning debt will have to be in merchandise trade, primarily in manufactured goods. But U.S. investment gains in the 1980s have been mostly in areas other than manufacturing—mostly in the services industries (see Chapter 2). Thus large U.S. manufactures trade surpluses will be difficult to achieve. Beyond this, they will impose significant problems on a world economy that will likely be experiencing a global glut of manufactures. This problem is discussed in more detail in Chapters 7 through 10.

TRADE DEFICITS AND JOBS

International trade affects U.S. output and employment in many ways. Simplistically, exports are sometimes seen as job creating and imports as job destroying. Following this line, trade deficits are net destroyers of jobs. Indeed, concern about the large trade deficits of the 1980s was probably more related to job loss perceptions than to other factors. In fact, the effects of trade and changing trade balances on jobs and the economy are not straightforward but are very complex.

Realistic estimates of the jobs *related* to (supported by) exports can be formulated by analyzing historical data. A recent analysis of historical data, for example, indicates that, on average, in 1987 each $1 billion of U.S. exports of manufactures supported about 25,000 jobs.[4]

Unfortunately, these post-hoc estimates of jobs related to exports are sometimes erroneously translated to "jobs lost" as a result of trade deficits. Based on the assumption that trade deficits substitute foreign production for U.S. production and hence "destroy" or "export" U.S. jobs, some observers simply multiply the trade deficit times the estimate of export related jobs—25,000 jobs per $1 billion of exports—to determine the effect on U.S. employment. Following this method, the $125 billion 1987 manufactures trade deficit would imply the loss of 3,125,000 jobs (125 times 25,000), equivalent to roughly 2.6 percent of the 1987 civilian work force.

This kind of calculation is unrealistic because it implicitly assumes that U.S. trade deficits could be eliminated without related effects on other sectors of the economy. Given the complex effects of trade and capital flows on both the U.S.

and foreign economies, estimates of the effects of deficits (or surpluses) on U.S. employment require assumptions about so many interrelated variables that the end results are, in fact, determined largely by the assumptions. They are not meaningful for the purpose intended.

A reasoned estimate of the employment effects of eliminating the trade deficits, for example, would require assumptions about several factors, including:

- Is the deficit eliminated through expanded exports, reduced imports, or both? Expanded exports create new jobs. Slower import growth or a decline in imports could result from a U.S. recession, which implies lower overall employment.

- To what extent would increases in jobs associated with internationally traded goods be associated with reduced job growth in other economic sectors—for example, services?

- An improved U.S. trade balance attempted by import restrictions may trigger foreign retaliation against U.S. exports, with resulting job losses. Also, import restrictions raise the costs of inputs to other U.S. industries and may make them less competitive in foreign markets, with negative effects on the U.S. trade balance.

- Without other offsetting changes in the U.S. budget deficit and the U.S. saving rate, a reduction in the net inflow of capital to the United States would likely raise U.S. interest rates and cut domestic investment, with unfavorable effects on U.S. employment.

These are only a few illustrative examples of the problems of dealing with trade-related job loss calculations. Simplistic estimates derived by translating trade deficits to job losses are not credible.

"Jobs destroyed" and "jobs exported" analyses ignore the U.S. job creation record, which by far tops that of competitor economies that enjoyed trade surpluses. From 1980 to mid-1987, a period of rapidly expanding U.S. trade deficits, the U.S. economy created 13.1 million new jobs. Japan, despite its huge surpluses, created only 3.7 million jobs, and Germany actually lost 0.4 million jobs. Moreover, the U.S. unemployment rate declined from 9.7 percent in 1982 to 5.5 percent in 1988, whereas the unemployment rate in Germany was 7.7 percent in 1988.[5]

The net capital inflows reflected in recent U.S. trade deficits played an important role in creating the macroeconomic conditions that made it possible to create so many new jobs in the U.S. economy. "Jobs lost" analyses presume that some combination of policy actions could have produced a still better record, that by eliminating the trade deficits the performance in non-trade-related sectors would be equally as good, with still more jobs added in the trade-related sector.

Both exports and imports speed the pace of adaptation and structural change in the economy and increase its efficiency. Structural change, in turn, influences the composition and level of U.S. output and employment. Structural change, however, is also the result of the introduction of new products and technologies and the passing of old products and technologies. Most structural change is independent of trade. Much of the job displacement blamed on imports and foreign competition would occur anyway as the result of new technologies, productivity growth, and other factors. Even had foreign automobiles not taken a large share of the U.S. market, for example, the number of workers employed by the auto industry would have declined markedly, reflecting increasing automation of many facets of production.

Nevertheless, the effects of international trade on the U.S. economy are increasingly significant. A large manufactures trade deficit implies a change in the composition of employment—to the detriment of total U.S. manufacturing jobs— if not a reduction in the level of the nation's total employment. Similarly, eliminating the large U.S. current account deficits through large manufactures trade surpluses implies some medium-term increases in manufacturing employment in absolute numbers and, probably, relative to other sectors. Over the longer term, however, the more rapid increase of productivity in manufacturing than in most other sectors indicates manufacturing employment will probably decline, both in absolute and relative terms.

Should the economy turn downward and unemployment increase while the trade deficit remains high, a resurgence of concern about "jobs lost" could occur, which might lead to new protectionist measures. In a world of intensifying competition for global markets new U.S. restrictions could provoke foreign retaliation and begin a series of tit-for-tat protectionist actions and reactions.

THE FUTURE OF U.S. MANUFACTURING

The large U.S. manufacturing deficits have raised concerns about the survival of U.S. manufacturing. The U.S. manufacturing base has been seen by some as withering away. Calls have been made for an "industrial policy" that would preserve U.S. manufacturing. A 1985 *Business Week* cover story raised the possibility that the United States might become "a nation of hollow corporations"—one essentially devoid of manufacturing operations, with corporations performing design, marketing, and research functions but with most manufacturing performed abroad.[6] In addition to creating many other problems, such a demise of manufacturing would raise serious national security concerns.

Will U.S. Manufacturing Survive?

What has happened? Has U.S. manufacturing withered away? Is the United States deindustrializing? What is the future of U.S. manufacturing? As measured by U.S. statistics, the U.S. manufacturing base has not declined in an absolute sense. The manufacturing component of the index of industrial production had climbed to all-time highs and at the end of 1989 was 36 percent above the 1981 level. In constant dollar terms, manufacturing has remained a constant portion of the GNP, about 20 percent throughout the post-war period.[7]

Manufacturing employment did decline from 20.2 million in 1981 to 18.4

million in 1983 as a result of the recession but had recovered to 19.1 million in 1987 and 19.5 million in 1989. Employment gains have lagged behind industrial production, primarily as a result of productivity gains. In addition, there is reason to believe that the manufacturing jobs statistic has been altered downward by changes in operating methods. Company cafeteria, guard, and janitorial services, for example, are now often subcontracted to service organizations whose employees are included in national job tabulations of service industries. Earlier, when company employees performed these services, they were included in the count of manufacturing jobs. Also, many firms today are relying more and more on temporary help ("temps") to stabilize employment. These temps are often employees of a contract service provider and are excluded from the manufacturing total.

The United States thus appears to have experienced simultaneously a rapidly increasing manufactures trade deficit, rising to about 3.0 percent of GNP in 1987; industrial output rising to new highs; and a recovery in manufacturing employment. How is the seeming inconsistency explained? Is U.S. manufacturing declining or holding its own?

One explanation is that the performance of manufacturing was substantially improved during much of the 1980s by the U.S. defense buildup.[8] Also, some have argued that industrial production data overstates U.S. production.[9] Regardless of other statistics, however, the continuing large manufactures trade deficits of the 1980s are proof of a degree of "hollowing" of U.S. manufacturing output compared to U.S. consumption of manufactures. Given that U.S. manufacturing represents only about one-fifth of total U.S. output, a manufactures trade deficit equivalent to 3.0 percent of the 1987 GNP reveals a much larger shortfall in manufacturing output relative to consumption of manufactures.

Precise data are lacking, but one estimate is that in 1987 U.S. output of manufactured goods was about 14 percent less than the total U.S. consumption of manufactures; that is, net manufactures imports were about 14 percent of the total manufactures consumption. The manufactures trade deficit was the key element in a 1987 current account deficit of $144 billion (Figure 5–1).

Thus a degree of "hollowing" does seem to have occurred. How far might it go? If the hollowing of U.S. manufacturing were to continue until net imports were equivalent to, say, 25 percent of total consumption, the result would be an annual current account deficit equivalent to more than 6 percent of GNP— about $275 billion in terms of 1987 GNP. Deficits of such large size would initially raise the U.S. international debtor position about $275 billion each year. The annual current account deficit and additions to the debtor position, however, would increase as debt servicing costs expanded to match the escalating debt.

As noted several times, the international economic system ensures that large imbalances do not persist indefinitely. U.S. deficits much larger than the peak levels of the 1980s would surely concern foreign lenders and exceed their appetite for dollar-denominated assets. In turn, this would trigger exchange rate changes, relative price and income movements, and other changes that would adjust

Figure 5–1

U.S. Manufacturing Output, Percentage of U.S. Consumption of Manufactures

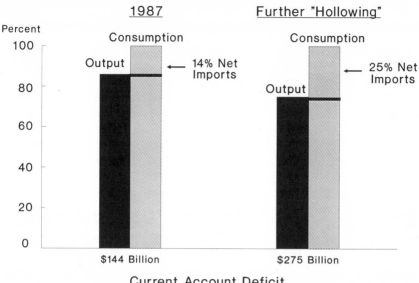

Current Account Deficit

international capital flows and shrink the U.S. current account and trade deficits to sustainable levels.

Thus because of the dominant role of manufactures in U.S. trade, the United States cannot for long run large manufactures trade deficits. There is no source of large export surpluses in other accounts to offset large manufactures deficits. The hard fact is that the United States cannot consistently run large manufactures deficits and pay its way in the world economy. Indeed, over the longer term, the United States must run substantial manufactures trade surpluses to balance its external accounts.

In effect, then, the workings of the international economic system ensure that the United States will not become "a nation of hollow corporations" and that it will retain a large manufacturing base. In time, the United States will return to a situation in which U.S. manufacturing output is roughly equal to or greater than total U.S. consumption of manufactures.

Most other industrial nations are in a generally similar position to the United States. That is, over the longer term most will have to maintain a rough balance in their manufactured goods trade. Few will be able to maintain either large continuing deficits or surpluses far beyond those needed to pay for imports of primary products and other goods and services.

It can be unequivocally stated that *the United States will not deindustrialize* and that *it will not become a nation of hollow corporations*. The survival of U.S. manufacturing, however, is not the real issue. The real question is, *"On what terms will U.S. manufacturing survive?''* That is, how much of the improved U.S. price competitiveness necessary to restore balance in U.S. external accounts will stem from dollar exchange rate decline, how much from stagnant or falling real wage levels, and how much from productivity improvements (including quality improvements and new products)?

The linkage between the competitiveness of U.S. manufacturing and U.S. international competitiveness is critical and unequivocal. Manufacturing is the key sector through which the United States interacts with the world economy. Manufacturing represents only about one-fifth of the U.S. economy on a "value-added" basis, but it must provide the major portion of the exports of U.S. goods and services required to pay for imports of oil, other essential raw materials, and foreign goods and to service foreign debt. Moreover, dramatically improved U.S. manufactures trade performance must dominate in the trade gains required to narrow and eliminate U.S. current account deficits. There is no other source of large gains. Thus how the manufacturing sector achieves these gains will provide a clear indicator of the direction of the nation's international competitiveness.

Productivity gains in U.S. manufacturing are typically higher than in the rest of the U.S. economy. Nevertheless, manufacturing productivity growth in recent years has been lower than those of several major U.S. competitors. If a consistently declining dollar in real terms is necessary to sell U.S. manufactures abroad in sufficient quantities to balance U.S. accounts, it will be virtually impossible for U.S. living standards to rise at rates comparable to those of major competitors.

In essence, whatever happens to the international competitiveness of U.S. manufacturing will happen, albeit more slowly, to the competitiveness of the U.S. economy. To the extent that U.S. manufacturing survives through further dollar exchange rate declines and lower real wages, there will be downward pressure on U.S. living standards and competitiveness. To the extent that it survives through increased productivity, quality, new products, and improved efficiency, U.S. living standards will be enhanced.

The Terms of Survival for U.S. Manufacturing

Though one can be confident that the discipline imposed by the international economic system will ensure that the United States will maintain a large manufacturing base, there is no assurance that U.S. manufacturing will remain sufficiently competitive to pay high, consistently increasing real wages. Nor is it assured that U.S. manufacturing will be sufficiently competitive to generate the exports needed to pay for a constantly growing volume of imports. In short, there is no assurance that the surviving manufacturing base will contribute in full to rising national living standards. The outcome is uncertain but will be shaped by how well U.S. manufacturing can compete in the international marketplace in the years ahead. In turn, the competitiveness of U.S. manufacturing will be determined by a number of factors, including U.S. government policies, laws, and regulations that affect capital formation and productivity.

U.S. manufacturing has become aware that it is, indeed, the "swing sector" in U.S. interaction with the world economy. It is the sector primarily affected by the net balance of international capital flows and by changes in U.S. and foreign macroeconomic policies that determine the size and direction of those flows. This awareness is bound to inhibit new investment in U.S.-based manufacturing. Tax and other policies, that cause net capital inflows, increase the cost of investment, raise direct and indirect taxes on business, transfer costs from individuals to business (child care, retirement pensions, health care), or lay social costs on business (environmental protection) will affect the manufacturing sector much more strongly than other sectors (such as retail and wholesale trade) that do not have to meet foreign competition.

U.S. and foreign firms today are able to serve both U.S. and foreign markets by locating their production abroad. In this new environment, the new investments in U.S.-based manufacturing required to match foreign investment levels and productivity gains will be increasingly a function of the dollar exchange rate and the mix of U.S. and foreign government policies, laws, and regulations that affect capital formation and productivity in manufacturing. The more unfavorable that U.S. government policies are, the greater the dollar depreciation will be required to motivate investment in U.S. manufacturing. Moreover, the greater the fall in the dollar exchange rate, the larger the portion of that investment will be in foreign acquisitions and foreign investments in other forms.

The new, more competitive global environment and methods of production have wrought other important changes, including the kinds of labor needed and the wages that can be commanded by some kinds of labor. Based on the post–World War II advantages of U.S. firms over foreign competitors and the bargaining power of unions, wages in some manufacturing industries (such as steel and automobiles) had increased to levels well above the U.S. average. This created an impression that manufacturing jobs are inherently "high value-added," high-wage jobs. But although the wages paid and the value added in these industries were partly a function of high productivity, they also stemmed partly from competitive advantages of U.S. products and U.S.-based production that allowed selling prices that supported high wages. Workers in these industries were, in effect, collecting a portion of the "economic rents" that can accrue to monopolies or unique products and capabilities. Yet the unique competitive advantages of U.S. products and U.S.-based production of earlier periods have now largely disappeared. With increased international competition and reduced opportunities to collect economic rents, it cannot be assumed that U.S. manufacturing jobs will necessarily be high value-added and high-wage jobs. Moreover, with the increasing move from heavy industry to light industry and automation, the educational requirements for many manufacturing jobs have increased. One result of all these changes is that less educated workers will have fewer opportunities to command high wages in manufacturing jobs.

Several factors operate to inhibit the new investment in U.S. manufacturing needed to raise productivity levels and make it more competitive, particularly investment to serve export markets. As industries "globalize," major markets will more and more be served by production located in those markets. Moreover, the high cost of capital in the United States and uncertainty about U.S. tax and environmental laws and regulations will also be increasingly important.

U.S. policies will critically affect investment in U.S.-based manufacturing and R&D and hence the terms of the survival of U.S. manufacturing and the sector's contributions to U.S. international competitiveness. U.S. policies can either aggravate or mitigate investor concerns about U.S.-based production. The volatile nature of international capital flows and the decimating effects of large net capital inflows are not lost on U.S. manufacturing. As the sector most affected by U.S. fiscal, tax, and other policies that alter international capital flows, manufacturing decision makers will watch these policies closely and nervously. Existing environmental and other policies and regulations that are seen as disadvantaging U.S.-based production and uncertainty about future policies and regulations will further inhibit investment in U.S.-based manufacturing plant and equipment and research and development. To the extent that a resurgence of investment in U.S. manufacturing is discouraged by U.S. policies that are less favorable than those of competitor countries, improved manufactures trade performance will become more dependent on a persistently declining dollar exchange rate.

Alternative U.S. tax and regulatory policies and their effects on U.S. manufacturing are discussed in more detail in Chapter 11.

IMPLICATIONS OF U.S. DEFICITS FOR THE U.S. AND WORLD ECONOMIES

The extended period of net capital inflows and U.S. trade and current account deficits during the 1980s has greatly affected the U.S. and world economies. Many more changes are yet to come.

Huge net capital inflows into the United States and the resulting strong dollar were manifested in a surge of imports of foreign goods into the U.S. market. In the short term, imports widened consumer choices and brought lower prices. Imports also forced restructuring and modernization of U.S. industry. Some industries, such as automobiles, machine tools, and steel, had not been challenged by foreign competition before. They had let wages and other costs rise above competitive levels, even as quality deteriorated, passing the increases on to U.S. and foreign consumers. The ability of these and other U.S. industries to pass on increasing costs has now been tempered by foreign competition. This has benefited consumers and has led to greater efficiency in the U.S. economy. U.S. industry emerged from the 1980s with higher productivity and improved quality. To recognize the benefits of foreign competition one need only consider what the price and quality of U.S. automobiles—and a variety of other products—would be today without the presence of foreign competition that challenged U.S. manufacturing during the 1980s and continues to challenge it today. The benefits of foreign competition will continue if the economy remains open.

The large net inflow of lower-priced foreign goods was an important factor in holding down U.S. inflation rates during the 1980s. The huge U.S. deficits also provided an outlet for foreign production in a difficult period when the LDC debt problem threatened severe economic disruptions for debtors and creditors alike.

These benefits did not come without a price. U.S. manufacturing would almost certainly have come under steadily increasing pressures from foreign competitors, even without the macroeconomic policies that produced the continuing influxes of foreign capital and goods. Although it was highly desirable for U.S. manufacturing to trim costs and to modernize, the speed and depth of the changes imposed by the overly strong dollar may have been more than optimal. Now this hollowing of U.S. manufacturing must be reversed; there must be a substantial restoration of U.S. manufacturing. Domestic manufacturing output must increase in relation to U.S. consumption. On the other hand, the huge influx of U.S. imports has created distortions in some foreign economies that may have overstretched themselves because they have been relying on U.S. trade deficits that cannot be sustained. As U.S. deficits decline, several surplus countries probably will have to make significant cutbacks in manufactures production. Applying hindsight, somewhat less restructuring and cutbacks in the United States and the growth of somewhat less capacity abroad would probably have been better for all concerned in the long run.

During the 1980s U.S. inflation was lowered by foreign imports, and the benefits of foreign competition will continue to restrain inflationary pressures. The adjustments ahead, however, will add to U.S. inflation. Switching U.S. spending from foreign-made to U.S.-made goods will in most cases require higher prices on foreign imports. This will likely come about mostly through dollar depreciation. This will raise the dollar price of imports and also allow U.S. producers to raise their prices. A significant addition to inflationary pressures is implicit in reducing the U.S. trade and current account deficits.

While the large U.S. trade deficits helped absorb imports from LDCs and indirectly aided in keeping foreign markets open to LDC debtors, the primary beneficiaries of U.S. deficits were the four surplus countries: Japan, the Federal Republic of Germany, Taiwan, and Korea. Moreover, although U.S. deficits helped purchase valuable time to deal with the LDC debtor problem, that problem has been postponed, not resolved.

The large U.S. net capital inflows and trade and current account deficits have also wrought an enormous global transfer of wealth from the United States to the surplus countries. Whether this reallocation has been optimal for the United States and for the world economy is a very important question. There are doubts. David Hale has written:

On a global basis, one can also question the optimality of resource allocation resulting from the interaction of highly divergent tax systems within a framework of uncontrolled capital mobility. Should the United States, for example, be exporting manufacturing jobs to an overcrowded chain of Asian islands, where per capita incomes now exceed $16,000 per annum but 60 percent of the homes are not yet connected to sewers, so that its workaholic citizens can generate a savings surplus which is then recycled back across the Pacific via the Treasury debt market to subsidize the construction of more vacant office buildings in Houston and Los Angeles?[10]

The debt accumulating as a result of this wealth transfer must sooner or later be serviced by net outflows of goods and services from the United States. The United States will then have to consume less than it produces, and the foregone consumption will be at the expense of its standard of living.

There are additional, more subtle potential effects on U.S. living standards. To the extent that the strong dollar invited foreign competitors to the United States and allowed them to get a toehold in this market, the dollar may now have to decline farther to achieve balance in external accounts than would have been necessary, absent the foreign invasion.

Probably more important is that servicing the U.S. foreign debt will require large manufactures trade surpluses in future years. The principal weapon in wresting markets from foreign competitors to allow this debt servicing is likely to be significant additional dollar depreciation.

The huge deficits of recent years are likely to change U.S. "terms of trade" significantly over the longer term. Dollar decline—which worsens the terms of trade—in itself has significant wealth transfer effects. This occurs because as the dollar depreciates the United States must export an increased quantity of goods and services to pay for the import of a given quantity of foreign goods and services.

The large net inflow of foreign capital has also been accompanied by an influx of foreign direct investment—the purchase of U.S. businesses and real estate by foreigners. This has raised concerns about a "selling of America" that could lead to disruptive restrictions on direct foreign investments. These concerns are examined in Chapter 6.

It is difficult to draw a balance sheet on the costs and benefits of the large U.S. net financial capital and goods and services imports. In large part it depends on how well the difficult and risky process of returning to sustainable global balances is managed. From the U.S. viewpoint, judging the balance of costs and benefits also is very much dependent on whether one thinks the net capital inflows were used to modernize and enlarge U.S. tradeable goods-production capabilities or simply temporarily lifted current consumption at the expense of future consumption and living standards.

The requirements and difficulties of the adjustment process are discussed in more detail in Chapters 7 through 10.

SUMMARY

• Two alternative outcomes summarize how U.S. trade deficits could be narrowed. A "soft landing" would see U.S. budget and trade deficits gradually narrowing, with continued good U.S. and global economic growth rates. But in another outcome, continued need for large net foreign capital inflows could lead ultimately to a loss of confidence by foreign lenders and a shrinking supply of foreign capital. The result could be rapidly rising U.S. interest rates, a U.S. recession, and a precipitous decline in U.S. imports that could trigger a global recession.

• During the several years that may be required to reduce U.S. deficits under a soft landing scenario, the U.S. debtor position would continue to grow. This could lead to resurgent concerns about a decline of the U.S. manufacturing base and ''jobs lost'' due to trade deficits.

• The U.S. international investment debtor position, about $664 billion at the end of 1989, is not an immediate danger. The external debt, which may actually be overstated by accounting practices, was equivalent to only about 13.0 percent of GNP compared with Brazil's 31 percent and Mexico's 58 percent.

• The rapid transition from creditor to debtor nation, a swing of about $804 billion during the 1981–89 period, and the prospects for continued debt growth do, however, merit immediate attention. Actions to ensure that reductions in borrowing are accomplished in an orderly fashion must be undertaken as rapidly as is practical.

• Meaningful calculations of jobs presumed ''lost'' because of foreign trade deficits cannot be made. The job creation record of the United States during the 1980s is far better than that of U.S. trading partners whose trade surpluses were expanding.

• The $125 billion 1987 manufactures trade deficit, equivalent to 3.0 percent of GNP, is convincing evidence that, to some degree, the U.S. manufacturing base during the 1980s ''hollowed'' relative to total U.S. consumption of manufactures.

• The United States cannot pay its way in the world economy and consistently run large manufactures trade deficits. Instead, balancing international accounts will require U.S. manufactures trade surpluses; manufacturing production in the United States will again have to be greater than manufactures consumption.

• Over the longer term, dollar exchange rates, economic growth rates, and other factors will adjust to reduce manufactures trade deficits and to increase U.S. manufacturing output to levels that match and exceed consumption.

• There was never any realistic possibility that the United States would ''deindustrialize''—that it would not retain a large manufacturing base. The discipline of the international economic system ensures that the United States will retain a large manufacturing base.

• The real question is about the terms of trade on which U.S. manufacturing will survive; that is, how much of improved manufactures trade performance will stem from dollar depreciation and downward pressure on real wage rates and how much from improved productivity and quality? In part, this will be determined by U.S. laws, regulations, and economic policies, particularly those that influence capital formation and productivity gains.

• The surge of low-cost imports and the strong dollar held down U.S. inflation rates during much of the 1980s. Narrowing the trade deficit, however, will necessarily add to U.S. inflationary pressures.

• Competition from foreign imports during the 1980s pressed U.S. industry to modernize and restructure. But U.S. deficits and manufacturing cutbacks and foreign additions to production exceeded sustainable levels and must now be reversed, a difficult process.

• The continuing large U.S. current account deficits have accomplished a huge international transfer of wealth. Growing debt servicing requirements have also probably wrought a long-lasting impairment of U.S. terms of trade that will affect future U.S. living standards.

• Large U.S. deficits bought time to deal with the LDC debt problem, but the problem has only been deferred, not resolved.

• In large measure the outcome of a costs versus benefits assessment of the huge trade deficits and accumulated international debt depends on whether one believes the net capital inflows financed modernizing and enlarging U.S. tradeable goods-production capabilities or simply temporarily lifted current living standards at the expense of future living standards.

NOTES

1. Jane Sneddon Little, "Foreign Investment in the United States: A Cause for Concern?" *New England Economic Review*, July–August 1988, 57.

2. Bank for International Settlements, *58th Annual Report* (Basle, Switz., 13 June 1988), 188–189.

3. *World Debt Tables, 1989–90*, vol. 1 (Washington, D.C.: World Bank, 1989), 30.

4. For an assessment of the relationship between exports and jobs, see International Trade Administration, U.S. Department of Commerce, "U.S. Trade Facts," *Business America*, 28 March 1984, 40.

5. These "jobs created" and unemployment data were drawn from the official statistics of the indicated countries. Jobs created are considered to be the difference between employment at the beginning and ending points of the period cited.

6. "The Hollow Corporation," *Business Week*, 3 March 1986, 57.

7. Rudiger Dornbusch, James Poterba, and Lawrence Summers, *The Case for Manufacturing in America's Future* (Rochester: Eastman Kodak Co., 1988), 9.

8. Ibid.

9. Robert Kuttner, "U.S. Industry Is Wasting Away—But Official Figures Don't Show It," *Business Week*, 16 May 1988, 26.

10. David D. Hale, "The World's Largest Debtor: The Risks of America's New Role as a Capital Importer," *Policy Review*, Fall 1986, 28.

Chapter 6

The U.S. Debtor Position and Foreign Direct Investment

In only four years, from 1982 to 1986, large trade and current account deficits changed the international investment position of the United States from the world's largest creditor nation to the world's largest debtor nation. U.S. foreign borrowing has continued, and by the end of 1989, the debtor position had reached $664 billion. In an orderly adjustment of global imbalances it will continue to grow.

The U.S. international or external debt consists of many different kinds of obligations. Most controversial to Americans, however, is the expansion of foreign direct investment in the United States (FDIUS), the foreign ownership or control of businesses and real estate in the United States.[1]

CHANGING INTERNATIONAL INVESTOR POSITIONS

The large, continuing current account and capital flow imbalances of the 1980s have markedly changed the international investment positions of several countries. In the eight years from 1981 to 1989, the U.S. IIP moved from a 1981 creditor position of $141 billion to a 1989 debtor position of about $664 billion, a decline of over three-quarters of a trillion dollars (Table 6–1).

Japan at the end of 1988 was the world's largest creditor nation, reflecting an improvement of $281 billion over its 1981 position. The Federal Republic of Germany and Taiwan also had markedly improved positions over 1982. The FRG's position improved some $173 billion, and Taiwan's position reached $73 billion in 1988, a huge improvement relative to its GNP. Although Korea remained a debtor at the end of 1989, reflecting heavy borrowing to develop its industries during the 1960s and 1970s, its position has dramatically improved since 1981. Its foreign debt was down from $40 billion in 1985 to only $11 billion in 1988. Korea's earlier vulnerability is rapidly receding as its debt continues to decline, but it remains very dependent on international trade.

International investment positions expressed as a percentage of a nation's GNP offer additional insights about the need and ability of countries to adjust to changing situations (Table 6–1). The 1988 U.S. foreign debt, though the largest in dollar terms, at 11 percent of GNP was relatively much smaller than that of Canada (39 percent in 1986). Because of recurring current account deficits and resulting external borrowing, Canada is a very large debtor relative to its GNP.

Japan is the world's largest creditor and at the end of 1988 had a dollar value position 70 percent greater than that of the United Kingdom, though the United Kingdom's position was much larger relative to its GNP—21 percent of GNP for the United Kingdom, 10 percent for Japan. The FRG also held a large creditor position, 17 percent of GNP.

Taiwan, however, is by far the largest creditor in relative terms. Taiwan's net foreign holdings, mostly in the form of huge dollar reserves held by its central bank, were equivalent to 60 percent of its GNP at the end of 1988. Moreover, continued strong growth in Taiwan's creditor position is likely for several years. Further significant growth in the U.S. debtor position and offsetting improvements in the IIPs of the other three major current account surplus countries is also likely for several years into the 1990s.

CAPITAL FLOWS AND THE DETERIORATION OF THE U.S. IIP

A direct linkage exists between the U.S. current account balance, international capital flows, and the U.S. IIP. Net capital flows are the mirror image of the current account balance. Net capital inflows are current account deficits; current account surpluses are net outflows. U.S. capital inflows accumulate in the form of an increasing stock of foreign-owned investment in the United States (U.S. liabilities). U.S. capital outflows accumulate as an increasing stock of U.S.-owned investments abroad (U.S. assets). In effect, net capital inflows and accompanying current account deficits change a country's IIP, which is the balance sheet of its international assets and liabilities. Net inflows of capital, which appear as net imports of goods and services, decrease creditor positions or increase debtor positions. These net inflows of foreign goods and services allow a borrowing nation's total consumption (government spending and private-sector spending for personal consumption and investment) to exceed its total production. Total national consumption can exceed production as long as net borrowing continues. This was the U.S. situation during most of the 1980s.

In exchange for net inflows of goods and services, net debt accumulates in the form of promises of future payment to creditors. These promises to pay are in various forms, primarily in government securities, the stocks and bonds of private-sector firms, and bank deposits. In whatever form, however, these promises to pay are claims on future production. When net borrowing ceases, the accumulated debt must be serviced by net outflows of goods and services. These

Table 6-1
International Investment Positions, Selected Countries, 1981-88

	1981	1982	1983	1984	1985	1986	1987	1988	Change 81-88
In Billions of Dollars									
United States	141	137	89	3	-111	-268	-378	-533	-674
Japan	11	25	37	74	130	180	241	292	281
FRG	33	37	40	52	58	93	159	206	173
United Kingdom	61	69	80	94	120	166	169	170	109
Canada	-110	-106	-112	-110	-119	-141	n/a	n/a	110
Taiwan	n/a	n/a	n/a	n/a	29	45	63	73	73
Korea	n/a	n/a	n/a	n/a	-40	-35	-25	-11	-11
Percentage of GNP									
United States	4.7	4.4	2.7	0.1	-2.8	-6.4	-8.5	-11.1	-15.8
Japan	0.9	2.3	3.1	5.9	9.8	9.2	10.2	10.3	9.3
FRG	4.8	5.6	6.1	8.4	9.3	10.5	14.2	17.1	12.3
United Kingdom	12.0	14.2	17.4	21.9	26.4	29.9	24.8	20.7	8.7
Canada	-37.3	-35.2	-34.3	-32.3	-34.3	-39.1	n/a	n/a	n/a
Taiwan	n/a	n/a	n/a	n/a	46.7	59.6	62.3	59.7	n/a
Korea	n/a	n/a	n/a	n/a	-43.1	-33.1	-19.0	-6.4	n/a

Sources: Official statistics of countires concerned; Taiwan and Korea IIPs, U.S. Department of Commerce estimates.

outflows reduce the borrowing nation's total national consumption below its total national production. This will be the U.S. situation sometime in the future.

Even while the U.S. debtor position has been growing rapidly, total U.S. investments abroad have continued to increase without interruption. The U.S. IIP changed from a $141 billion 1981 net creditor to a 1989 net debtor of about $664 billion because foreign investments in the United States increased more rapidly than U.S. investments abroad. In the six years from 1982 to 1988, total U.S. investments abroad increased from $825 billion to $1,254 billion (Table 6–2). But during the same period, foreign investments of all kinds in the United States more than doubled, increasing from $688 billion to more than $1,786 billion. Preliminary reports indicated that in 1989 U.S. assets abroad increased another $147 billion, but foreign assets in the United States grew by $280 billion.

COMPOSITION OF THE GROWING DEBTOR POSITION AND ITS EFFECTS ON THE CURRENT ACCOUNT

The large changes in the IIP have had important feedback effects on the U.S. current account. Even though the United States became a debtor nation in 1986, it continued through 1989 to earn positive balances on payments and receipts resulting from its international investment position. Total net receipts from international investments, however, peaked in 1981 at $34.1 billion and then trended downward, even though they were still substantial in 1987 at $22.2 billion (Table 3–1). As the U.S. debtor position continued to grow, the net U.S. income balance on international investments continued to shrink, declining to $2.2 billion in 1988 and to $1.0 billion in 1989. The United States has continued to receive net income on international investments despite a large net debtor position principally because the earnings on U.S. direct investment abroad (USDIA) have continued to be strong enough to offset growing net U.S. government payments on foreign debt.

The U.S. international investment position consists of many different kinds of assets and obligations. The U.S. government holds only about 11 percent of total U.S. assets abroad; the remainder is held by private citizens. U.S. bank claims—deposits and lending abroad—is the largest asset category, about 50 percent of the total (Table 6–2). Portfolio investment (stocks, bonds) was 12.5 percent of the total at the end of 1988, and U.S. direct investments abroad were 26.1 percent, more than one-fourth of the total.

The composition of foreign investments in the United States is somewhat different. About 5.4 percent of the total at the end of 1988 was in foreign holdings of U.S. treasury securities. U.S. bank liabilities to foreign banks were 34.1 percent of the total, and 22.0 percent was in portfolio investments. Foreign direct investment in the United States, however, was only just over one-sixth (18.4 percent) of the total, compared with the more than one-fourth of U.S. assets abroad held in the form of direct investments.

Table 6–2
U.S. International Investment Position, Selected Years, 1980–88
(Billions of Dollars)

	1980	1982	1984
Net U.S. Investment Position	106.3	136.7	3.3
Total Assets			
(U.S. Investment Abroad)	607.1	824.9	896.1
U.S. Government	90.5	108.5	119.8
Private	516.6	716.4	776.3
Direct Investment	215.4	207.8	211.5
Portfolio	62.7	75.5	89.1
U.S. Claims on Unaffiliated Foreigners Reported by U.S. Non-Banks	34.7	28.6	30.1
U.S. Claims Reported by U.S. Banks	203.9	404.6	445.6
Total Liabilities			
(Foreign Investment in U.S.)	500.8	688.0	892.5
Foreign Official Assets in U.S.	176.1	189.1	199.2
Private	324.8	498.9	693.3
Direct Investment	83.0	124.7	164.6
U.S. Treasury Securities	16.1	25.8	58.2
Portfolio	74.1	93.0	127.3
U.S. Liabilities to Unafilliated Foreigners Reported by U.S. Non-Banks	30.4	27.5	31.0
U.S. Liabilities Reported by U.S. Banks	121.1	228.0	312.2

Table 6–2 (*continued*)

	1986	1988	1988 % of Total
Net U.S. Investment Position	-267.8	-532.5	
Total Assets (U.S. Investment Abroad)	1071.4	1253.7	100.0
U.S. Government	138.0	133.3	10.6
Private	933.4	1120.4	89.4
Direct Investment	259.6	326.9	26.1
Portfolio	133.2	156.8	12.5
U.S. Claims on Unaffiliated Foreigners Reported by U.S. Non-Banks	33.3	32.9	2.6
U.S. Claims Reported by U.S. Banks	507.3	603.8	48.2
Total Liabilities (Foreign Investment in U.S.)	1340.7	1786.2	100.0
Foreign Official Assets in U.S.	241.7	322.1	18.0
Private	1098.9	1464.1	82.0
Direct Investment	220.4	328.9	18.4
U.S. Treasury Securities	91.5	96.6	5.4
Portfolio	308.8	393.6	22.0
U.S. Liabilities to Unafilliated Foreigners Reported by U.S. Non-Banks	26.6	35.5	2.0
U.S. Liabilities Reported by U.S. Banks	451.6	609.5	34.1

Source: U.S. Department of Commerce.

Despite the increasing U.S. attention to foreign purchases of U.S. businesses and real estate, the FDIUS portion of total foreign investment in the United States has not changed markedly in recent years, and indeed for a time it declined modestly. A surge in direct investment in 1988, however, returned the FDIUS portion of total foreign investment to the 18.4 percent level of 1984. A continuing enlargement is likely.

U.S. direct investments abroad at the end of 1987 still totaled more than foreign direct investments in the United States, but in 1988 FDIUS exceeded USDIA for the first time in many years. The book value of USDIA at the end of 1988 was $326.9 billion; FDIUS was $328.9 billion (Table 6–2). Preliminary data, however, indicated continued strong growth in FDIUS in 1989, raising it to $400.8 billion compared with $373.4 billion for USDIA. The actual market value of USDIA, however, is probably much greater than its book value.[2] This is reflected in the continuing large net income from U.S. international direct investment. U.S. receipts from USDIA in 1988 were $48.3 billion, and payments for FDIUS were $16.7 billion, leaving a net positive balance of almost $31.5 billion. Income from USDIA continued in 1989 to outpace payments for FDIUS, $51.1 billion to $14.9 billion, raising net income on direct investment to $36.2 billion.

At the end of 1988, the United Kingdom at $102 billion (31 percent of the total) was the single largest direct investor in the United States (Table 6–3), well ahead of Japan (16.2 percent), the Netherlands (14.9 percent), and Canada (8.3 percent).

Manufacturing continues to hold the largest portion of FDIUS, 36.9 percent of the total (Table 6–3). About one-fifth of the total FDIUS is now in wholesale and retail trade, reflecting in large measure the relatively new manufacturing operations of Japanese auto makers. Some Japanese auto manufacturing operations are classified under wholesale trade because they are subsidiaries of U.S. affiliates whose principal activity is in wholesale trade. Real estate at the end of 1988 was 9.7 percent of all FDIUS, up from 9 percent in 1987.

HOW DIRECT INVESTMENTS OCCUR

Additions to FDIUS as reported in U.S. national accounts can occur in the following ways:

• Start-up of new establishments

• Acquisitions of existing U.S. firms or real property

• Equity increases in existing U.S. affiliates

• Increases in the net worth of existing affiliates through reinvested earnings

Table 6–3
Geography and Industry of U.S. International Direct Investment, 1988

	U.S. Direct Investment Abroad		Foreign Direct Investment in U.S.	
	Billion Dollars	% of Total	Billion Dollars	% of Total
By Host Country				
All Countries	326.9	100.0	328.9	100.0
Canada	61.2	18.7	27.4	8.3
Europe	126.5	38.7	216.4	65.8
Of Which:				
Germany	21.7	6.6	23.8	7.2
Netherlands	15.4	4.7	49.0	14.9
United Kingdom	48.0	14.7	101.9	31.0
Switzerland	18.7	5.7	15.9	4.8
Japan	16.9	5.2	53.4	16.2
Developing	76.8	23.5	17.0	5.2
Other	48.5	14.8	14.7	4.5
By Industry				
All Industries	326.9	100.0	328.9	100.0
Petroleum	59.7	18.3	34.7	10.6
Manufacturing	133.8	40.9	121.4	36.9
Wholesale Trade	34.4	10.5	50.2	15.3
Banking	16.1	4.9	17.5	5.3
Financial Insurance	60.6	18.5	22.4	6.8
Real Estate	n/a		31.9	9.7
Other	22.3	6.8	50.8	15.4

Source: U.S. Department of Commerce.

• Increases in the intercompany debt of existing U.S. affiliates through lending by the foreign parent

Most FDIUS transactions are not start-ups of new establishments. Of the more than 1,300 transactions recorded from public sources by the Department of Commerce in 1987, only 263 were new establishments (164 new plants and 99 joint ventures), whereas 547 were the result of mergers and acquisitions.[3] The form of investment, however, is not important to the overall U.S. investment picture since investment capital is fungible. The mergers and acquisitions produced net inflows of foreign capital that added to the total pool available for investment elsewhere in the United States, providing the same additions to total U.S. investment as would new plant start-ups and other forms of direct and portfolio investments.

FDIUS IN PERSPECTIVE

Despite recent increases, FDIUS is small in relation to the size of the U.S. economy. Direct foreign investment in Canada, France, the FRG, and the United Kingdom, countries that host large amounts of U.S. direct investment, is relatively much larger.[4] Measurements are tenuous but indicate that the portion of total U.S. assets held by foreign-owned or controlled U.S. affiliates in manufacturing in 1986 was only 12 percent, up from 10 percent in 1981. The portion of total U.S. employment by foreign-owned or controlled U.S. affiliates in manufacturing was 8.8 percent in 1986, up from 6.9 percent in 1981.[5]

SOME CONTROVERSIAL ASPECTS OF FDIUS

The policy of the United States is that, with a few internationally recognized exceptions, market-determined forces should allocate the flow of international direct investment among nations. This policy is based on the belief that the private marketplace is the most efficient allocator of the limited international resources available for the production of goods and services. The United States has advanced this policy globally, and these general policy guidelines are widely followed among Western countries, though national policies do vary.

U.S. policy is among the least restrictive, allowing with few exceptions a free flow of inward and outward direct investment. The U.S. policy is essentially one of "national treatment"; that is, investments in the United States by foreign firms are treated the same as investments in the United States by U.S.-owned firms. The United States opposes government intervention in investment decisions, both by incentives and by restrictions. The U.S. government, however, does limit FDIUS in areas related to the national security, such as broadcasting and nuclear and hydroelectric power.[6]

Much of the concern about FDIUS reflects a fear that foreigners may operate against U.S. national interests. There are, however, the previously noted U.S. regulations on FDIUS in some particularly sensitive areas. Moreover, foreign firms are taxed and regulated in the same fashion as U.S.-owned firms, and the government can impose export controls, seize assets, and direct all firms in the United States to give priority to defense contracts. These powers, plus the fact that foreign-owned firms invariably are largely manned by U.S. citizens, make concerns about FDIUS largely groundless. Indeed, once made, foreign investments become hostage to, and have little choice but to cooperate with, the host country government.

In addition to foreign capital, FDIUS often brings foreign technology and management techniques that are increasingly important to the productivity and efficiency of the U.S. economy. Continued significant increases in FDIUS will almost certainly be a major positive factor in narrowing U.S. current account deficits.

As previously noted, in book value terms, by the end of 1989 FDIUS was about $31 billion greater than USDIA. In real value terms, however, USDIA no doubt still significantly exceeds FDIUS. Nevertheless, FDIUS is an emotional issue to many people and has generated concern and controversy. For whatever reasons, the one-sixth of total U.S. obligations to foreigners that is FDIUS generates much more concern than the five-sixths in stocks, bonds, treasury securities, and other claims on future U.S. production. A number of issues lie behind the concerns and controversy.

"Jobs" Impact of Direct Investment

When USDIA was increasing rapidly, American labor unions complained that U.S. jobs were being "exported" by U.S. firms locating production abroad. The response was that USDIA actually increased U.S. exports by enlarging foreign markets and supplying components and other inputs to foreign assembly plants.

Now FDIUS is creating the same concerns about lost jobs as did the earlier rapid increase in USDIA. Many states solicit foreign direct investment for their job-creating benefits. Unions, however, sometimes complain that FDIUS simply displaces other U.S. jobs, or that the jobs created are low-paying assembly operations ("screwdriver plants"), whereas the high paying, high value-added jobs remain abroad. Recently, some accounts have claimed that FDIUS actually costs U.S. jobs.

Which is correct? Do both USDIA and FDIUS create U.S. jobs or do both cost U.S. jobs? The answer depends on the assumptions used in making the comparison. The U.S. jobs involved in supplying a given amount of a particular product would certainly be greater if the product were made in the United States and exported than if some or all of the production were done abroad. Thus when production moves abroad, it may seem to involve job losses. But in a competitive world, prohibiting U.S. direct investment abroad and insisting on supplying foreign markets by exports from the United States could result in losing most of those markets and *all* the jobs associated with them. Similarly, although FDIUS may begin with U.S. assembly operations largely fed by production abroad, the impact on U.S. jobs in the affected industry is more positive than importing the finished product from abroad. Moreover, the U.S. content—the U.S.-made materials and U.S. jobs—used in the output of foreign-owned U.S. plants will likely increase over time.

The idea that jobs are lost by FDIUS reflects the fact that some new foreign direct investments may displace existing U.S.-owned firms. The addition of Japanese-owned auto manufacturing in some states, for example, may result in the shutdown of some capacity by U.S.-owned firms in other states. If employees at U.S.-owned plants in the United States are displaced by foreign direct investments, that is unquestionably bad for the displaced employees. But at the same time, jobs will have been created for other U.S. workers, and U.S. workers and the economy as a whole will benefit from increased competition and efficiency. The important point is that a free flow of international capital allows the best allocation of international resources and the best opportunity for an economy to remain competitive. At the same time it should provide the most efficient production and the best-paying jobs. Restricting either the outflow or inflow of direct investment in major ways is an attempt to isolate an economy from foreign technology and competition. In the end, such restrictions can only be detrimental. Estimates of jobs lost or gained from direct investments in the United States and abroad are simplistic and misleading because they implicitly assume that, absent direct investment, U.S.-based production could continue to hang on to foreign and domestic markets and remain globally competitive. These are fallacious assumptions. Estimates of jobs lost and gained can be made for local economies on specific investments, but estimates of the nationwide job creation caused by direct investment have little validity or usefulness.

Competition Among States for Foreign Direct Investment

There is frequently intense competition among states for new foreign direct investments, and various forms of "sweeteners" are often offered to make some potential sites more attractive than other competing sites. Some see the states as "engaged in economic fratricide. They vie with each other to see who can offer the most tax abatements, grants, real estate, and loans, while the foreign multinationals sit back and wait for the best bargain."[7] To counter this foreign bargaining power it has been suggested that the United States should develop "a mechanism for coordinating state efforts to avoid giving away more resources than are necessary to attract foreign investment."[8]

State incentive programs are not directed solely at foreign investors but to all investors, U.S. and foreign. As a practical matter, however, foreigners often may be the principal source of new investments, particularly in states that do not presently have much manufacturing. Foreign investors have often been prominent in the construction of new manufacturing facilities and in investments that have revitalized acquired companies. Although the incentive programs may have been overly generous in some instances, it is difficult to imagine how the federal government could police the incentive programs of sovereign states and local governments. Moreover, if the federal government did take on the job, would it police only "foreign" investments or would it also make judgments on incentives offered to domestic investors? Federal shortcomings in doing the job would include, but not necessarily be limited to, lack of legal authority, lack of competence, and a shortfall in political will.

OUTLOOK FOR FDIUS

Large U.S. trade and current account deficits will likely continue for some years. This will bring further significant growth of FDIUS. But even without U.S. deficits, continued growth of direct investment in the United States and abroad will occur. Increasingly, firms see participation in the world market as essential to the large sales volumes that are needed to absorb large spending for research and development. Increasingly, a manufacturing presence in the market to be served—not just a sales and service presence—is considered essential to meet competition. A manufacturing presence in major markets is also increasingly often considered important in providing a hedge against the rise of protectionist barriers and fluctuations in currency exchange rates.

Much of FDIUS during the next several years will likely be in real estate and in manufacturing. For example, heavy Japanese investment in automobile manufacturing in the United States is occurring. Still more will be required to replace exports from Japan when yen appreciation makes large-scale automobile exports from Japan uneconomic. These investments will likely initially be primarily in auto assembly plants. Then direct investments in the United States by Japanese suppliers to the automobile industry will follow. Thus the U.S. value added in Japanese nameplate automobiles assembled in the United States will initially be low, limited to that added by assembly operations, but will gradually increase. Because the U.S. automobile industry already has excess capacity, additional foreign investments may result in a shakeout in the industry that will eliminate some production capacity of U.S. firms. This may make additional Japanese investment in this sector particularly controversial.

Increasing FDIUS is, however, unlikely to be limited to the automobile industry. A major reduction in U.S. current account deficits will require the movement to the United States of much manufacturing for the U.S. market now done outside the United States. Indeed, U.S. trade deficits may be narrowed more by recapture of the U.S. market than by export expansion. (See Chapter 8 for an examination of the role of import substitution in improved U.S. trade performance.) When market conditions begin to make U.S.-based production more price competitive than foreign production, foreign companies in a wide variety of products will relocate their production to the United States, rather than lose their U.S. markets. Major increases in FDIUS will result.

There is every reason to be concerned about the growing U.S. international debtor position, and steps to slow and halt the debt growth should be taken. But there is no important reason to restrict direct investments beyond the national security-oriented rules already in place. There are, however, important reasons not to restrict FDIUS. In addition to the improved technology that often comes with such investment, the ability to continue U.S. borrowing is becoming more sensitive to inflows of FDIUS. In 1988 FDIUS increased by $58 billion, almost half the net borrowing evidenced by the $127 billion current account deficit that year. In 1989 it increased by $61 billion, equivalent to well over half the $106 billion current account deficit. This was in marked contrast to earlier years, when foreign debt accumulation was primarily in U.S. government securities and other forms of portfolio investments. This turn toward FDIUS will continue and probably enlarge as foreign investors seek to hedge against inflation and anticipate the need for U.S.-based production to stay competitive. Restricting direct foreign investments in the United States would invite increased foreign restrictions on U.S. direct investments abroad. Even more important, it would risk the loss of confidence of foreign lenders and discourage all forms of capital inflows. With the United States still dependent on foreign capital, shrinking those inflows would raise the interest rates on all foreign borrowing and lower U.S. investment. Thus the United States has not only become dependent on net inflows of foreign capital, but it cannot safely mandate the forms of capital inflows it will accept.

Slowing and eliminating further growth of the U.S. international debtor position should be a primary U.S. objective. This may slow the growth of FDIUS, but it will not likely stop it. Rather, FDIUS and USDIA will likely both continue to grow as a natural result of the continuing integration of the world economy and the "globalization" of individual industries. It is likely that the "foreign controlled" portion of U.S. industry will continue to enlarge, even if growth of the U.S. foreign debt ends.

SUMMARY

• The large global current account imbalances have markedly changed international investment positions, moving the United States from the world's largest creditor nation in 1982 to the world's largest debtor in 1989 and making Japan the world's largest creditor nation.

• The U.S. IIP changed because, although U.S. investments abroad continued to increase, foreign investments in the United States increased much more rapidly. U.S. investments abroad reached more than $1.41 trillion in 1989 while foreign investments in the United States grew to $2.08 trillion.

• About one-fourth of the U.S. investment abroad is in the form of direct investment; in other words, the ownership or control by U.S. firms of foreign companies or real estate in other countries. Only about one-sixth of foreign holdings in the United States is in the form of direct investment, the foreign ownership or control of U.S. firms and real estate. In recent years, however, the FDIUS portion of new net inflows has increased. The 1988 increase in FDIUS was equivalent to almost one-half the net capital inflow that year. The FDIUS portion of total foreign investment in the United States will likely continue to increase.

• At the end of 1988 the United Kingdom held the largest share of FDIUS, about 31 percent of the total. Japan held 16.2 percent, the Netherlands 14.9 percent, and Canada 8.3 percent.

• The book value of U.S. direct investments abroad at the end of 1989 was less than that of foreign direct investments in the United States, a total of $373 billion versus $401 billion. The gap will likely continue to widen during the next several years.

• Measurements are tenuous, but data covering 1986 show that about 12 percent of U.S. manufacturing assets were foreign owned or controlled. The degree of foreign ownership in Canada, the United Kingdom, and a number of other industrialized countries is higher.

• Direct investment not only provides additions to financial capital but also access to foreign technology and management techniques that help in keeping the economy efficient and competitive.

• Although foreign direct investment is only one-sixth of total foreign investment in the United States, it generates more controversy than the other five-sixths of the total.

• Estimates of "jobs lost" and "jobs gained" as the result of direct investments in the United States and abroad cannot accurately capture the effects on the national economy and are not useful additions to the debate.

• Nevertheless, increased foreign direct investment will likely play a key role in narrowing U.S. current account deficits because foreign producers will move their production to the United States to retain sales in the U.S. market.

• Large additional Japanese direct investments in auto production in the United States are likely. These investments will further increase excess global and U.S. auto production capacity and may generate controversy.

• Eliminating current account deficits and stopping growth of the U.S. international debtor position may slow somewhat the growth of FDIUS but will likely not halt it. Even without net inflows of capital to the United States, FDIUS will continue to grow as a natural result of continuing integration of the world economy.

NOTES

1. FDIUS is defined in the collection of U.S. statistics as the ownership or control, directly or indirectly, by one foreign corporation or person of 10 percent or more of the voting securities of an incorporated U.S. business enterprise or an equivalent interest in an unincorporated U.S. business enterprise.

2. Direct investments are valued in official data at the book value of the original investment. Many U.S. direct investments abroad have been in place many years and have a current market value much greater than the original book value.

3. International Trade Administration, U.S. Department of Commerce, *Foreign Direct Investment in the United States Transactions, 1987* (Washington, D.C.: U.S. Government Printing Office, 1988), 30.

4. International Trade Administration, U.S. Department of Commerce, *International Direct Investment: Global Trends and the U.S. Role* (Washington, D.C.: U.S. Government Printing Office, 1988), 47.

5. Ibid., 48.

6. An excellent review of U.S. policy and other aspects of international direct investment can be found in ibid.

7. Martin Tolchin and Susan Tolchin, *Buying into America* (New York: Times Books, 1988), 265.

8. Ibid., 271.

PART III

GLOBAL ADJUSTMENT PROBLEMS

The huge U.S. trade deficits of the 1980s produced complementary large surpluses for some trading partners and temporarily distorted global trading patterns. The difficulty of narrowing these unsustainable imbalances while maintaining good rates of economic growth in the world economy is not widely understood. It will likely be a central problem of the world economy for several years, a difficult, risky process stretching well into the 1990s.

Chapter 7 reviews why the unsustainable imbalances require action by both the United States and the surplus countries and provides an overview of the problems facing the United States and the surplus countries.

A detailed assessment of the size and composition of the U.S. manufactures trade performance improvement required to eliminate the U.S. current account deficit and likely improvement scenarios are set out in Chapter 8.

The critically important roles of Japan, the FRG, Korea, and Taiwan in the adjustment process and the difficulties they face are reviewed in Chapter 9.

The implications of the resulting intense struggle for world markets on LDC debtors who must service debts by maintaining export surpluses are reviewed in Chapter 10.

Chapter 7

Narrowing Global Imbalances: Central Problem of the 1990s

In the global trading system, one country's exports are the imports of its trading partners. Trade surpluses and deficits are complementary, or offsetting, among countries. In an error-free accounting, the surpluses and deficits of all countries of the world would sum to zero. Within the trading system, however, deficits by some nations require surpluses by others. Therefore, the large U.S. trade and current account deficits of the 1980s resulted in large, complementary surpluses for some other nations. These wide imbalances are temporary distortions of global capital flows and trading patterns that, for both economic and political reasons, cannot be sustained permanently. Narrowing these large global imbalances is a problem for both the United States and its trading partners. The narrowing will entail difficult adjustments not just for the United States but also for those countries that have been experiencing large surpluses. The narrowing of these large external imbalances is a problem that will likely stretch well into the 1990s. The process poses high risks for the world economy.

This chapter provides an overview of the difficult adjustments that must be made by the United States and the surplus countries. Chapters 8 and 9 explore these adjustments in greater detail.

SUPPLYING CAPITAL TO THE UNITED STATES

The large global trade imbalances of the 1980s were the manifestation of large net capital inflows to the United States. The U.S. need for net capital inflows and the concurrent foreign ability and willingness to provide capital at acceptable exchange and interest rates resulted from the confluence of several events. A U.S. saving-investment gap developed in the early 1980s as the personal saving rate declined and consumer spending increased. At the same time, the U.S. federal budget deficit and private-sector investment spending grew rapidly. These events pushed total national consumption (consumer spending, government

Figure 7–1

U.S. and Surplus Country National Output and Consumption

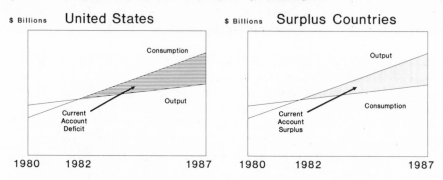

spending, and investment spending) above national output (conceptually illustrated in Figure 7–1).

Meanwhile, conditions in some foreign countries allowed their outputs to rise above their total national consumptions. Typically, these countries were concentrating on developing their manufacturing and other industries and had saving rates that had long been high in relation to total national output. These savings, supplemented by external borrowing, were used to finance high rates of investment. Capital goods and technology were imported as part of the investment buildup. Investment was particularly strong in export-oriented manufacturing industries and essential supporting infrastructures. As these investments paid off in increased output, exports began to replace borrowing as the means of financing imports required for further growth of their expanding industrial bases. Living standards also rose, but frugality and high saving rates were maintained. As growth continued, saving rates and investment in manufacturing remained high, though the need for foreign borrowing to finance investments had disappeared. In time, exports became large enough both to finance imports and to service debt. As production grew still larger, saving rates continued at high levels and became more than needed for debt servicing and export-oriented investment. A strategy of high saving and investment rates and export-led growth had paid off.

At this stage of economic development, it would be logical for a developing economy to use its gains to improve its living standards more rapidly and to increase spending for infrastructure and other forms of investment not directly related to export-oriented industries. That is, it could make policy changes designed to guide the economy to consume more or to reinvest domestically the fruits of its export success. Policies could have moved toward maintaining a rough balance in external accounts rather than running large export surpluses. Instead, several countries continued their export-led orientation and their concentration on export expansion. They achieved large trade surpluses as U.S. trade deficits grew in the mid-1980s.

Under normal circumstances, it would not have been possible for several countries simultaneously to run large surpluses because such surpluses require complementary, offsetting deficits and borrowing by other countries. In normal circumstances, creditworthy borrowers willing and able to absorb the large surpluses simultaneously experienced by some countries would not have been available. But U.S. macroeconomic policies that began in the early 1980s created the need for large net capital inflows and the opportunity for further significant export expansion and surpluses by its trading partners.

Several trading partners obliged by increasing exports to the United States. But they did not use all of the proceeds to increase their imports. They did not use the export-generated income to increase domestic personal consumption more rapidly or to increase spending on non-export-oriented infrastructures of their economies. Instead, U.S. current account deficits grew large, and some U.S. trading partners generated large current account surpluses. That is, their savings rates remained high, domestic investment did not expand enough to absorb all those savings, and they had growing current account surpluses and were lending abroad.

This is a very simplified description of an increase in the ability and willingness to lend of three of the four major surplus countries: Japan, Taiwan, and South Korea. The FRG's surpluses also stem from an emphasis on export growth and policies that have restrained national consumption and increased production. The FRG economy is, however, a more mature economy and does not have the high gross saving rates of Japan, Taiwan, and Korea.

In any event, high foreign saving rates in countries with manufacturing capacities directed at export markets made possible U.S. borrowing on acceptable terms. Had excess foreign saving and manufacturing capacity not existed, U.S. borrowing would probably not have been so large. Thus both U.S. and foreign actions contributed to unsustainably large imbalances. The problem of the 1990s is to return to sustainable levels of net international capital flows without severely disrupting the global economy. This will require adjustments both by the United States and all its trading partners but principally by the current account surplus countries.

NARROWING GLOBAL TRADE IMBALANCES: A MUTUAL PROBLEM

Narrowing the large global current account imbalances of recent years while maintaining good world economic growth rates and doing so in ways that will not aggravate the problems of LDC debtors promises to be difficult. Indeed, it will likely be a central problem of the world economy well into the 1990s. Narrowing the global imbalances is not just a U.S. problem. The fact that trimming U.S. trade deficits will force difficult changes on some foreign economies is not widely appreciated. These changes will be difficult for those trading partners that have generated large offsetting current account surpluses. Indeed, because of their greater dependence on international trade, some surplus countries probably have even more at stake in an orderly return to sustainable balances than does the United States. The adjustment problems facing U.S. trading partners have often been ignored in the United States and are not highlighted by the surplus countries for domestic political reasons. As a result, the difficulties and risks of the transition are probably underrated.

World trade has become largely an exchange of manufactured goods (see Chapter 3). The imbalances that exist today were generated primarily in manufactures trade, and the coming adjustments will also be primarily in manufactures trade. As a result, many of the effects of narrowing global imbalances will be concentrated on manufacturing industries in the United States and on the manufacturing industries of its four trading partners with large surpluses.

During much of the 1980s, widening U.S. trade deficits evidenced competitive problems that forced many U.S. industries to cut back. Many plants closed or scaled down as foreign competition pushed U.S.-based production from its domestic and export markets. In the period ahead, however, absent a difficult and unlikely coordination of U.S. and foreign economic policies, it will often be manufacturing industries in other countries that will have to bear the brunt of unpleasant adjustments. This provides a motivation for surplus countries to delay the inevitable and to characterize the global imbalances as a U.S. problem— one the United States must solve by changing its behavior. Foreign interests argue, for example, that the United States must trim its budget deficits, improve the quality of its output, and become more cost competitive.

The United States does need to make these changes. But unsustainable global imbalances do not stem just from U.S. behavior, and U.S. actions cannot spare trading partners the difficult adjustments that will be forced on them in shrinking their surpluses. Rather, the behavior of surplus countries contributed to the imbalances and is a complementary problem. Surplus country saving rates have been too high relative to domestic needs; consumption and investment in sectors not oriented to exporting have lagged. U.S. saving rates have been too low; consumption has been too high. An orderly narrowing of global imbalances will require that surplus countries reduce their saving and expand consumption, the opposite of the prescription the United States must follow. Growing trade surpluses powered much of the economic growth of the surplus countries during the 1980s. But in the 1990s, shrinking surpluses will tend to depress their employment and economic growth and force the restructuring of some industries—a painful, unwelcome process.

Surplus countries may rightly criticize the United States for its failure to move promptly to reduce its budget and trade deficits. The criticism is, however, sanctimonious. For the most part, they are moving no more rapidly to make their own adjustments, and they must surely privately welcome the slow U.S. progress because it defers the difficult adjustments they will be forced to make.

The surplus countries are aware of the significant effect the required narrowing of U.S. trade deficits will have on their economies. The same procrastination influences both the United States and the surplus countries. The U.S. delays the difficult budget decisions required to lower total U.S. consumption in relation to total U.S. production. Similarly, the surplus countries naturally want to delay necessary, but painful, adjustments they will have to make.

Although there is motivation for all parties to delay difficult steps, the long-term interests of the United States and its trading partners lie in shrinking the imbalances in an orderly, gradual, but promptly begun process that would stretch over several years. The United States must reduce its dependence on imported capital, and the surplus countries must shrink their capital exports.

COMPLEMENTARITY OF U.S. DEFICITS AND TRADING PARTNER SURPLUSES

When U.S. current account performance deteriorated over the 1981–87 period, offsetting improvements necessarily occurred in the accounts of other countries. Similarly, when U.S. current account balances improve, there must be complementary, offsetting declines in the balances of others.

There are five major current account imbalance countries in recent international trade performance: one very large deficit country, the United States, and four large surplus countries, Japan, Germany, Taiwan, and Korea. The huge swings in capital and trade flows since 1981 have affected all of the global economy. These four surplus countries, however, were probably the most directly affected by the growth of U.S. deficits during the 1980s and will likely be the most affected by the trimming of U.S. deficits during the 1990s.

During much of the 1980s, the United States was a "locomotive" for economic growth abroad. From 1981 to 1987 the U.S. current account balance declined by $152 billion dollars (Table 7–1). During the same period the current accounts of the four surplus countries improved by $163 billion. By 1987 global imbalances had grown very large. The $144 billion 1987 U.S. current account deficit was complemented by surpluses of Japan, Germany, Taiwan, and Korea totaling $160 billion (Table 7–1). The $127 billion 1988 U.S. deficit was offset by surpluses of about $153 billion in these four countries.

Current account imbalances relative to GNP had also become large. The 1987 U.S. deficit was 3.2 percent of GNP (Table 7–1); Japan's surplus was 3.6 percent of GNP; Germany's surplus was 4.0 percent. Taiwan's surplus was equivalent to a whopping 17.7 percent of GNP, indicating that that country's total consumption was only slightly more than four-fifths of its production, with the balance of output going to net exports. The effect was net lending abroad equivalent to almost one-fifth of Taiwan's GNP. Korea's current account surplus was also very large in relation to its GNP (7.5 percent), reflecting very high export growth. The 1987 surplus, however, was only Korea's second significant current account surplus. Deficits over a number of prior years had caused a very large Korean external debt that has been reduced by the recent surpluses. Imbalances relative to GNP changed significantly in 1988, registering declines in several countries. In part this reflects the effects of dollar depreciation, which enlarged

Table 7-1

Current Account Balances, Selected Countries, 1981–89 (Billions of Dollars)

	1981	1982	1983	1984	1985	1986	1987	1988	estimate 1989*	Sum 81–89	Change 81–87	Change 87–89
United States	8.2	−7.0	−44.3	−104.2	−112.7	−133.2	−143.7	−126.6	−105.9	−769.3	−151.9	37.8
Japan	4.8	6.9	20.8	35.0	49.2	85.9	87.0	79.6	57.0	426.1	82.3	−30.0
Germany	−3.6	5.1	5.3	9.8	16.4	39.2	45.2	48.5	52.7	218.7	48.7	7.5
Taiwan	0.5	2.2	4.4	7.0	9.2	16.2	17.9	10.2	10.5	78.1	17.4	−7.4
Korea	−4.6	−2.7	−1.6	−1.4	−0.9	4.6	9.9	14.2	5.0	22.5	14.5	−4.9
United Kingdom	13.9	8.2	5.9	2.8	4.3	0.2	−4.8	−25.9	−33.4	−28.7	−18.7	−28.7
Canada	−5.1	2.3	2.5	2.1	−1.5	−7.6	−7.1	−8.4	−16.3	−39.1	−1.9	−9.3

(As a Percentage of GNP)

	1981	1982	1983	1984	1985	1986	1987	1988	estimate 1989*	Avg 81–89	Change 81–87	Change 87–89
United States	0.3	−0.2	−1.3	−2.8	−2.8	−3.1	−3.2	−2.6	−2.0	−1.7	−3.5	1.2
Japan	0.4	0.6	1.8	2.8	3.7	4.4	3.6	2.8	2.0	2.2	3.2	−1.6
Germany	−0.5	0.8	0.8	1.6	2.6	4.4	4.0	4.0	4.5	2.0	4.5	0.5
Taiwan			8.4	11.8	14.8	21.5	17.7	8.3	7.0	11.8	n/a	n/a
Korea			−1.9	−1.6	−1.0	4.3	7.5	8.3	2.5	2.2	n/a	n/a
United Kingdom	2.7	1.7	1.3	0.6	0.9	0.0	−0.7	−3.1	−4.0	0.4	−3.4	−3.3
Canada	−1.7	0.8	0.8	0.6	−0.4	−2.1	−1.7	−1.7	−3.1	−0.6	0.0	−1.4

* 1989 data are from early end of year reports by the reporting countries. The translation of foreign currencies to U.S. dollars is significantly affected by the dollar exchange rate, and may differ marginally from final OECD report.

Source: OECD, International Monetary Fund, and official statistics of reporting countries.

the dollar valuation of the GNPs of those countries whose currencies had appreciated against the dollar. The ratios also reflect narrowing imbalances in some instances. Nevertheless, imbalances remain dangerously large from both economic and political standpoints.

The current account balances cited above are "global" balances; that is, the balances of each country with the world. Reducing U.S. imbalances must be viewed in a global perspective, one in which U.S. bilateral trade and current account balances are only one part of the picture. Reducing the U.S. global deficit will inevitably involve a narrowing of its deficits with Japan, the FRG, Taiwan, and Korea. However, a country's global imbalances—not its bilateral imbalances—are the measure of its need to adjust in an integrated world economy. The thrust of U.S. deficit reduction should not be solely on its bilateral imbalances but rather on adjustments that will narrow the global imbalances of the United States and the surplus countries. Although the United States typically runs large merchandise trade deficits with Canada, for example, Canada in turn had large current account deficits in 1987 and 1988 on its trade with the world. Thus U.S. and global imbalance problems would not likely be resolved by U.S. efforts to eliminate its trade deficits with Canada.

Although large U.S. trade deficits were the "locomotive" for economic growth abroad during much of the 1980s, shrinking U.S. trade deficits in years ahead will substitute a "drag" on the economies of trading partners with large surpluses. The coming adjustment process will alter world trading patterns in many ways.

Many countries will be affected. Nevertheless, it will likely affect the five major imbalance countries more than others. Indeed, if the U.S. deficit is to shrink, there is no apparent alternative to a major reduction of their surpluses. The surpluses and foreign lending of Japan, Germany, Taiwan, and Korea must shrink substantially. This must happen as U.S. deficits narrow because there is no other country or group of countries sufficiently creditworthy to borrow enough to allow them to continue their large export surpluses and lending as U.S. deficits and borrowing shrink. That is, there are no alternative creditworthy borrowers to absorb the surpluses made possible by U.S. deficits and borrowing.

To summarize, then, throughout much of the 1980s, growth of the U.S. trade deficits evidenced significant substitution of foreign-produced manufactures for U.S.-produced manufactures and fostered an expansion of foreign manufactures output. The result was widespread restructuring of U.S. industry, a painful process. Now, however, the adjustment process of the 1990s promises an expansion of U.S. manufacturing that may force painful cutbacks on the manufacturing industries of some trading partners. To avoid or postpone the pain of restructuring, each surplus country will struggle to keep its surpluses. But the major portion of their surpluses must disappear if U.S. trade deficits are to narrow significantly. Must the adjustment process be painful? Not necessarily. But it probably will be.

CHANGING THE UNDERLYING FUNDAMENTALS

"Better coordination of economic policies" is a frequently cited cure for narrowing the existing global imbalances. Most often this is interpreted as a call for faster growth abroad. Faster growth abroad is desirable but is unlikely to be the major factor in narrowing imbalances. More difficult and more wrenching changes in fundamentals—changes in saving and consumption rates relative to total production—are required in the imbalance countries. Put in simple macroeconomic terms, the United States must consume less and save more relative to its total production. The surplus countries must do the opposite—consume more and save less relative to their total production.[1] Increased domestic investment would provide a means of soaking up excess savings of surplus countries that are now loaned abroad. Such investment, however, should be directed toward domestic needs, not export demand. These changes, gradually accomplished concurrent with good global economic growth rates, could provide the optimum adjustment scenario.

Translated into effects on trade, the United States must either export more, import less, or combine in some way these two changes. Conversely, the surplus countries must import more, export less, or combine the two. The best outcome for all concerned would be one in which the imbalances are narrowed predominantly by increased U.S. exports and increased imports by the surplus countries. This would be least disruptive to world trade and would minimize the restructuring required within the imbalance countries.

How a Smooth Transition Could Occur

In theory, the required transition could occur while global economic growth continues and without traumatic adjustment-related disruptions to existing industries. That is, the imbalances could be narrowed and eliminated without cuts in U.S. imports that would hit exporting industries in partner countries. Ideally, growth in U.S. output would allow for a decline in total consumption relative to output without the need for an absolute decline in total consumption. Meanwhile, saving would rise, both in absolute and relative terms. Imports could stabilize in volume terms or even continue to grow modestly, albeit slower than the U.S. economy. In this scenario, exports would grow much more rapidly than the rest of the economy, providing a major stimulus to U.S. production.

The major surplus countries would make complementary changes. Their exports would need to stabilize or might continue to grow modestly but at slower rates than the rest of their economies. Concurrently, increased domestic demand in the surplus economies would maintain domestic production and power a rapid growth of their imports (Figure 7–2).

In essence this "ideal" outcome would require the United States, the deficit country, to reduce its reliance on infusions of foreign capital by reigning in domestic consumption, thus freeing production for export markets. The surplus

Figure 7–2
Desired Convergence of U.S. and Surplus Country National Output and Consumption Relationships

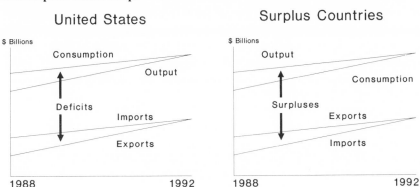

countries would need to switch from export-led growth to domestic-demand-led growth. The increase in domestic demand would reduce their reliance on exports as an outlet for production and as a source of economic growth.

The transition would be a delicate process, but in time wide imbalances would disappear. Large current account imbalances would narrow, as would the wide differences in saving and consumption patterns between the United States and the surplus countries. There would be minimal disruption to global production and trade patterns. U.S. export-oriented industries (presumably the country's most efficient industries) would increase their output and capacity. There would not be undue disruption to the export-oriented industries of surplus countries, presumably their most efficient industries, since they would not have to cut their exports. Strong import increases by Japan, for example, could narrow its current account surpluses without a major further strengthening of the yen and without a major decline in exports of automobile and other manufactures to the United States that would disrupt Japan's economy.

There are, however, at least two fundamental difficulties that make such a smooth and relatively painless transition unlikely. First, individual countries will have great difficulty in quickly and smoothly changing their saving and consumption ratios; second, it will be difficult for the world economy, particularly the surplus countries, to absorb the additional large amounts of manufacturing output implied in narrowing U.S. deficits primarily by expanded U.S. exports.

U.S. and Surplus Country Adjustment Problems

Significant changes in the saving and consumption ratios and export and import propensities of the five imbalance countries would negatively affect many different interest groups within each nation and would raise difficult issues. Some of these issues are discussed in this section, first for the United States and then for the surplus countries.

Difficult and far-reaching tax policy and other changes will probably be required to increase U.S. saving and eliminate the U.S. saving-investment gap. There is no assurance that the United States can "grow" its way out of its current situation in which total national consumption exceeds total national production. Rather, there is an ever-present tendency for perceived social and other needs to keep government spending ahead of government revenues. Continued government dissaving is likely, and there is little reason to expect that business saving will increase markedly. Indeed, recent tax law changes seem likely to decrease business saving relative to GNP.

U.S. personal consumption habits and expectations will also be difficult to change because they reflect deeply ingrained expectations and cultural mores. A London banker once characterized the United States as "the most efficient consumption society the world has ever known." She allowed that she used her business trips to New York as occasions to shop because "they make everything so easy for you."

It's true. Nowhere else in the world is there the intense pressure to consume and nowhere else is it made so easy. Television, radio, newspaper, and magazine advertising incessantly bombard potential consumers. Most Americans can receive several TV channels twenty-four hours a day—dozens if they are cable subscribers. Almost all U.S. TV broadcasts are heavily laden with advertising. In the United Kingdom there are four channels. The two BBC channels carry no advertisements and transmit only eighteen hours per day. The two commercial channels normally transmit less than twenty-four hours per day. A Sunday *Washington Post*—mostly advertisements exhorting every conceivable form of consumption—typically weighs in at around five pounds, several times the bulk of a week of the *London Times*.

Americans are deluged by dozens of junk mail solicitations that press credit cards and offers of loans on them for any purpose, from home remodeling to vacations and exercise spas. Easily obtained credit and credit cards facilitate shopping, and the stores are ever ready to help deliver customers of their money. Shopping malls in the United States are open seven days a week, often twelve hours a day, Monday through Saturday, and six or more hours on Sunday. In the FRG and much of Europe, stores close at noon on Saturday and don't reopen until Monday. Japan remains on a five-and-a-half-day work week, with an average of only six paid holidays per year versus eleven in the United States. This helps to hold down Japan's leisure expenditures.

In the United States bumper stickers boast "born to shop," and the average American spends 5.7 hours a week shopping versus 2.8 hours on housecleaning. In the past twenty years shopping malls have become "efficient temples of consumption." Twenty years ago "few envisioned how television's siren song would unleash cravings to be satisfied with the flick of a magnetically coded plastic card, or how malls would proliferate in response."[2]

The U.S. social security system is also an important factor in lifetime consumption patterns. Though it was originally intended to supplement personal saving rather than replace it, many have come to think of social security as the principal income required for retirement and old age, reducing the perceived need for preretirement saving.

In short, the U.S. economy is keyed to developing demand and consumption like no other. As long as the economy remains strong and incentive systems unchanged, current patterns of consumption and saving will probably not change dramatically without some new causal factor. Even marginal changes in personal saving and consumption habits will likely require significant changes in policies and attitudes to move the nation toward saving and away from the ever-present urge to spend.

Thus changes are likely to be difficult and to come slowly. Without major pressures for change, total U.S. consumption (expenditures by government, consumers, and investors) could well continue to grow rapidly enough to stay ahead of total production.

One might think the task of surplus countries—raising consumption relative to production and thus raising living standards—would be much easier. Perhaps. It is more likely, however, that changes to increase consumption and raise living standards in these countries will be resisted because change invariably is difficult and not in the interests of some groups. An important step in changing Japan to a more consumption-oriented society, for example, would require reducing the Japanese work week from the current 5.5 days per week to create more time in which to spend. Perhaps more important is the time to enjoy leisure goods purchased. But employer industries will resist this change, fearing the effect on their international competitiveness. Increasing Japanese consumption to higher levels will also require changing an archaic distribution system and displacing many merchants who operate small, inefficient stores and do not want to give up their livelihoods. More spending on housing—a logical expansion of Japan's consumption and living standards—will require freeing up land from agricultural uses and displacing small, inefficient farmers who cling tenaciously to a traditional way of life.

Other factors, however, may over the longer term change national saving rates and the adjustment process. In a prizewinning essay, William Emmott noted that Japan's ratio of personal saving to disposable income has fallen steadily from 23 percent in 1975 to a low of 16 percent in 1985 as Japan's pensions and social security schemes have become more generous. Emmott also saw the new post-war generation as less prone to save, implying a further continuing fall in the saving rate. He posited that the aging of Japan's population may, in time, significantly further reduce the saving rate. Old people typically spend more than they save, and, other things being equal, the older a population, the lower will be its saving ratio. This demographic factor, however, would not begin to have significant effect until 1995.[3]

Thus events may be moving in the right direction but probably not rapidly enough to satisfy U.S. and international investor concerns. A gradual change in saving and consumption patterns in Japan and elsewhere may result from rising affluence and aging populations. Results, however, are uncertain and will likely be slow. Speeding the convergence of U.S. and foreign life-styles and saving and consumption patterns will require major changes in tax and fiscal and other laws and policies in the United States and abroad. Such changes will be controversial and will take time to implement. But U.S. policies and international investor attitudes will probably not sustain continuing large U.S. borrowing for many years while awaiting such changes. Instead, more certain and faster policy solutions will likely be sought. The risk to the world economy is that, unable or unwilling to tackle the difficult and controversial measures required to narrow imbalances in an optimal manner, governments may turn to protectionist measures with the United States attempting to reduce its deficits and trading partners trying to maintain the status quo.

A Global Glut of Manufactures?

A second and potentially even more important obstacle to a trouble-free adjustment is that, in supplying U.S. deficits, the manufacturing sectors of the surplus countries may have grown too large. If U.S. trade and current account deficits are to narrow significantly, U.S. manufacturing will have to expand output to satisfy a larger portion of U.S. and foreign demand for manufactures. This expansion will have important effects on world trade and on some individual economies. An improvement of $200 billion or more in the U.S. manufactures trade balance from 1987 would be required to balance the U.S. current account by 1992 (discussed in Chapter 8). This would represent a substantial part of total world manufactures trade and would cause major alterations in world trade flows. Increased U.S. manufacturing output and declining U.S. trade deficits may force a significant downsizing of the manufacturing sectors in some surplus countries.

There has been a significant "hollowing" of U.S. manufacturing—a decline of total U.S. manufactures production relative to U.S. consumption (Chapter 5). In 1987 U.S. manufacturing output was equivalent to, perhaps, only 86 percent of U.S. manufactures consumption, with net imports making up the difference. Now, with large oil deficits and growing debt servicing requirements, a balanced U.S. current account will require manufactures trade surpluses. To bring U.S. accounts back into balance, U.S. manufacturing output will have to rise to more than 100 percent of U.S. consumption of manufactures, perhaps to 103 percent in 1992, if the deficit is to be eliminated by that year. Such an expansion of U.S. manufacturing output would be a significant addition to world manufacturing capacity and global supplies.

Which countries will absorb the U.S. manufactures exports required to balance U.S. accounts? Which countries will take the net exports of Japan, the FRG, Taiwan, and Korea still being absorbed by the United States at the beginning of the 1990s? Without the growth of complementary deficits by other borrowers, their large surpluses must disappear.

Can the surplus countries themselves adjust in a way that will allow them to maintain manufacturing output at current levels? To do so, they must either import more to narrow the surplus, or they must divert to domestic uses manufacturing output that is currently being exported. Eliminating their surpluses by increasing their imports would allow their consumers both wider choices and increased consumption of goods and services. Diverting production of their own manufactured goods to domestic consumption would allow increased consumption but restrain their consumers' choices to domestically produced manufactures.

Either alternative would require significant increases in domestic demand in relation to total production. Taiwan, whose manufacturing sector is grossly oversized in relation to domestic needs, would likely have little chance of sustaining domestic manufacturing output at existing levels by diverting export surpluses to domestic uses.

Some important conclusions flow from this assessment of the adjustment process to come: a growing global oversupply of manufactures and a resulting intensifying global competition for manufacturing markets is likely. A downsizing of the manufacturing sector will probably be necessary in some surplus countries. This will force them to switch more employment and production to service-oriented industries. The more rapid the necessary restructuring, the more difficult it will be.

THE OUTLOOK FOR CHANGE

Given the problems of accomplishing difficult, controversial, and far-reaching changes in a timely fashion, a relatively painless, smooth narrowing of global imbalances is unlikely. It will be difficult to keep total output growing in surplus countries while switching demand growth from manufactures exports to domestic demand, much of which is oriented to services rather than manufactures. In the United States a complementary early, smooth decline of total national consumption relative to production that continues to increase will be similarly difficult and unlikely.

Regrettably, a significant current account narrowing will more likely be driven eventually by market forces than by intelligent policy choices. Such market forces may produce more abrupt and painful changes. The U.S. adjustment will likely occur partly through strong export growth, but will probably occur mostly through significant import cuts, at least in volume terms, if not in nominal terms. (Further support for this conclusion is in Chapter 8.) Conversely, the surplus countries will narrow their surpluses partly through significant import growth but will probably also experience substantial export declines, at least in volume terms. These changes will likely be forced or accompanied by significant further dollar depreciation.

If so, the result may be a disruptive global industrial restructuring. In the United States, manufacturing output will grow, partly to satisfy expanding exports but mostly to substitute U.S.-based production for imports.

In surplus countries, exports may decline, putting a drag on their domestic economies. This could reduce total output unless the exporting industries successfully increase domestic demand for their products and reorient their output toward products used to satisfy increased domestic consumption. For example, at the beginning of the 1990s a large portion of Japan's automobile production was exported to the United States. Without large increases in Japanese imports that would narrow Japan's surplus and obviate further large yen appreciation, a major portion of the large segment of the Japanese automobile industry devoted to supplying the U.S. market will probably have to relocate to the United States. This will leave idle capacity in Japan and add additional excess capacity in the United States. With little room for expansion of auto sales in Japan, a successful transition would require switching excess Japanese domestic auto production capacity to new products that would satisfy increased Japanese consumption. (The key role of Japanese motor vehicle exports in narrowing the U.S. deficits is reviewed in more detail in Chapter 8.)

For surplus countries whose manufacturing sectors are significantly oversized in relation to their potential domestic consumption, the disappearance of large export surpluses may mandate downsizing the manufacturing sector, even if domestic demand for manufactures can be successfully stimulated.

The surplus countries recognize that declines in their exports to the United States will cause them major adjustment problems and that significant structural changes will be required, particularly in their manufacturing sectors. This is why they fear and resist major declines in the dollar. On more than one occasion following the beginning of dollar decline in 1985, FRG and Japanese officials complained that the dollar had fallen far enough because it was "beginning to hurt exports." But without expansion of their imports, their exports must be constricted if the trade imbalances are to narrow. For the most part, actions by the surplus countries to increase domestic demand and consumption relative to production and to increase their imports have not been adequate.

Unfortunately, the surplus countries have procrastinated in taking difficult adjustment actions in the same way the United States has avoided taking difficult budget-cutting measures. If the situation does not change, trimming U.S. current account deficits will, sooner or later, require significant further depreciation of the dollar. The dollar will need to fall to levels that surplus country exporters cannot adjust to—exchange rates they "cannot live with." The result could be sharp, disruptive changes for the global economy.

Continued structural change must occur in every economy to implement technological and other changes. The wide swings in international trade and capital flows that occurred in the 1980s, however, have imposed difficult and perhaps wasteful changes on affected industries. Barring a major global recession, the worst of the structural changes forced by loss of its own U.S. market may be over for U.S.-based manufacturing. Earlier, much of U.S. manufacturing downscaled in adjusting to tough foreign competition and an overly strong dollar. The employment cuts and plant closings often involved were painful and disrupted the economies of many communities. But now, in an orderly move back toward balanced accounts, U.S. manufacturing employment and output will be stimulated, both by export expansion and by the substitution of U.S. production for foreign production in satisfying domestic demand. U.S. manufacturing output, investment, and employment will increase—a pleasant prospect. U.S. consumers, however, will have to accept slower growth in their consumption relative to the GNP.

In an "export less" narrowing of imbalances scenario, surplus country trading partners with declining surpluses will be forced to stimulate domestic demand to take the place of declining export demand. They will probably also have to downsize some export-oriented industries, changing their output to other product lines better suited to expanding domestic needs. In some industries the effects could be wrenching, perhaps leading to increased protectionist pressures in the affected countries.

The more slowly imbalances narrow, the less painful and disruptive it is likely to be for both the United States and the surplus countries. Unfortunately, the slower the narrowing of the imbalances, the larger the U.S. debt accumulation, the greater the potential for U.S. protectionist actions, and the larger U.S. manufactures trade surpluses must ultimately be to balance U.S. accounts. Without immediate pressure, such as would be provided by further dollar depreciation, the natural tendency may be for both the United States and the surplus countries to continue deferring painful changes.

SUMMARY

• Narrowing global trade imbalances is not just a U.S. problem but one that will require difficult actions and adjustments, both by the United States and by major surplus countries.

• There are five major imbalance countries: The large U.S. current account deficits of the 1980s were offset principally by the surpluses of Japan, Germany, Taiwan, and Korea.

• Narrowing global imbalances requires that the United States consume less and save more relative to its total production. The surplus countries must do the opposite, save less and consume more, relative to their production.

• Translated to trade effects, the United States must export more, import less, or some combination of the two. The deficit countries must import more, export less, or some combination of the two.

• Narrowing the imbalances without serious repercussions for the world economy requires gradually changing the consumption and saving patterns of the United States and the major surplus countries while maintaining good world economic growth rates.

• Gradually changing these consumption and saving patterns and export-import relationships will be difficult, both for the United States and the surplus countries, and will probably require major changes in fiscal, tax, monetary, and other policies. Such changes will be difficult and controversial and are unlikely to be accomplished quickly.

• A slower narrowing of imbalances allows more time for adjustment, but there is no assurance that the time will be used effectively. At the beginning of the 1990s, there was little evidence of adequate progress in making these changes, either in the United States or in the surplus countries.

• Wrenching adjustments abroad could trigger foreign protectionist actions. On the other hand, a very slow narrowing of the U.S. trade deficits and resulting continued growth of the U.S. debtor position could increase protectionist pressures in the United States.

NOTES

1. A nation's consumption as referred to here is its total expenditures for goods and services by consumers, for investment purposes, and by the government.

2. Ellen Graham, "The Pleasure Dome," *Wall Street Journal*, 13 May 1988.

3. William Emmot, "The Limits to Japanese Power," *International Economics and Financial Markets* (AMEX Bank Review Prize Essays, New York: Oxford University Press, 1989), 15.

Chapter 8

Trimming the U.S. Trade and Current Account Deficits: How It Will—and Won't—Occur

Chapter 7 provided a macroeconomic overview of the global adjustment process, that is, how saving rates and consumption patterns must alter in narrowing global imbalances. These macroeconomic changes will have wide and varying effects on international trade patterns and on production in individual industries. This chapter reviews some of the likely effects of trimming the deficit in the United States. Chapter 9 looks at potential adjustment problems in the surplus countries.

NARROWING THE GLOBAL IMBALANCES

A narrowing of unsustainably large global trade and current account imbalances—U.S. deficits and the complementary surpluses of some trading partners—began in real terms in 1987. In 1988 improvement in current dollar terms began to be evident, with the merchandise trade deficit narrowing from $152 billion in 1987 to $119 billion in 1988 (imports, customs basis), a more than one-fifth reduction. Total 1988 U.S. merchandise exports in current dollars were up 27 percent over 1987; imports increased only 9 percent. The current account balance improved a lesser amount, from a deficit of $144 billion in 1987 to a $127 billion deficit in 1988 and $106 billion in 1989. The manufactures trade balance improved by $19 billion in 1988 and an additional $16 billion in 1989, leaving a 1989 deficit of $90 billion.

These were clearly favorable changes. Improvement in U.S. trade performance, however, had slowed markedly as the 1980s ended. As the 1990s began, most analysts foresaw little further trade balance improvement in 1990 if the U.S. economy remained strong; some forecast that the current account deficit would begin to grow again in 1990 or 1991.

Nevertheless, during 1988 and 1989 improvements were cited by the incumbent administrations as the beginning of a new trend, and they projected continued improvements in 1990 and beyond. Moreover, other authoritative voices offered continuing assurances, in a variety of languages: English, German, Japanese, and others. They argued that the dollar exchange rate prevailing at the beginning of the decade would allow global imbalances to narrow at an appropriate pace and that further declines in the dollar would be "counterproductive."

From these facts and assertions one could reasonably conclude that U.S. trade and current account deficits could disappear over the next few years and that shrinking the large global trade imbalances of the 1980s may not be too disruptive to the world economy.

Will it be that easy? Can recent U.S. current account deficits and the complementary large surpluses of some trading partners be significantly narrowed to more sustainable levels without major difficulties and risks to the global trading system?

Opinions differ on what lies ahead. One approach in assessing the outlook is to analyze saving and investment balances in the United States and other countries (Chapters 4 and 7). Reducing the U.S. budget deficit in the next few years could set up forces that would trim the U.S. trade deficit. Another approach is to examine recent changes in global trade patterns and the effects on some U.S. trading partners that will likely follow from narrowing global trade imbalances. Given the pivotal role of U.S. trade in the world economy, there has been remarkably little assessment of this kind. Drawing on much more detailed and extensive unpublished work, this chapter seeks to give a more specific sense of the size, duration, and difficulty of the adjustments ahead.[1] To provide perspective, world manufactures trade is quantified for a recent period, changes in trade flows required to restore U.S. current account balance by 1992 are projected, and potential changes in some key individual manufactures product groups are examined. Conclusions are then drawn about how quickly imbalances will narrow and how global trade and direct investment patterns will be affected.

SIZING UP THE REQUIRED TURNAROUND

Earlier chapters showed that manufactures trade was the key element in the decline of U.S. merchandise trade during the 1980s. A detailed examination of U.S. goods and services trade showed there can be no significant improvement in the U.S. current account without a major turnaround in U.S. manufactures trade performance (Chapter 3).

Indeed, to restore current account balance, manufactures trade must improve by even more than its $153 billion 1981–87 decline (imports, cif basis).[2] The additional improvement will be necessary to offset deteriorating performance elsewhere, including increasing debt servicing costs. In fact, a balanced U.S. current account will require large manufactures trade surpluses, even if oil deficits do not increase from 1987 levels.

To illustrate, in 1987 the manufactures trade deficit of $137.7 billion (imports, cif basis) was accompanied by a large oil import deficit and imbalances in other accounts—some surpluses, some deficits—that resulted in a current account deficit of $143.7 billion. That 1987 current account deficit could have been eliminated by an equivalent manufactures trade balance improvement of $143.7 billion.

It will take time to narrow U.S. deficits and complementary trading partner surpluses, however, as noted in earlier chapters. A fast turnaround in one or two years would have wrenching and potentially disastrous effects on the U.S. and global economies. A more gradual but consistent movement toward a balanced U.S. current account—perhaps during the five-year period from 1987 to 1992— is a more desirable scenario because it would allow time for structural changes in affected economies.

But a gradual correction requires even more improvement in the manufactures trade balance. Until a current account balance is achieved, each year's current account deficit will further increase the U.S. international investment debtor position. The resulting increase in debt servicing payments will widen the gap that must be closed by improvements in the manufactures trade balance. For example, assuming that five years is needed to eliminate the current account deficit, the U.S. debtor position would further enlarge by about $400 billion, to an end-1992 total approaching $800 billion.

Compared to the end-1987 debt level of $378 billion, an additional $400 billion would likely generate new annual debt servicing costs of $40 billion or more. Thus assuming (optimistically) no increase in the net U.S. oil import bill from 1987 levels and no major negative changes in other accounts, a balanced current account in 1992 would require a manufactures trade balance improvement of about $200 billion. This is the amount of improvement required to offset the 1987 current account deficit of $144 billion *plus* a projected growth of about $40 to $50 billion dollars in debt servicing payments (Figure 8–1). To the extent that U.S. oil import deficits increase, a further manufactures trade improvement will be required (in fact, the 1989 oil deficit was $6 billion larger than in 1987). On the other hand, if the cost of U.S. oil imports declines—an unlikely event— the manufactures improvement required to balance accounts will lessen.

A MASSIVE U.S. MANUFACTURES TRADE IMPROVEMENT: HOW?

An improvement in the manufactures trade balance can be achieved in any of the following ways:

• Export growth that exceeds import growth
• Import reductions
• A combination of export growth and import reductions

An infinite number of export and import growth rate combinations would result in the $200 billion manufactures trade improvement required to restore

Figure 8–1
U.S. Manufactures Trade Improvement Required to Balance the Current Account by 1992

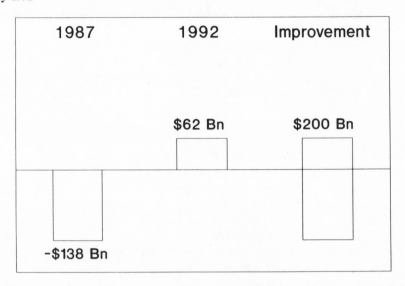

current account balance by 1992. Table 8–1 provides seven possible combinations.

Roughly, to restore the current account to balance by 1992 would require manufactures export growth rates expressed in current dollar terms about 15 percentage points higher than import growth rates each year of the five-year 1988–92 period. For example, a consistent modest annual export growth of 6 percent and a 10 percent annual decline in imports—one combination providing the required differential—would provide a $200 billion improvement by 1992.

THE GLOBAL ENVIRONMENT FOR A
U.S. TRADE TURNAROUND

Beginning from an export base that had seen little growth since 1981, in 1988 U.S. manufactures exports increased dramatically, about 27.8 percent over the same period of 1987. Import growth, however, was only 11.2 percent, a difference of 16.6 percentage points. Thus U.S. performance in 1988 was excellent, slightly better than the 15 percentage point difference needed to achieve a $200 billion improvement by 1992. In 1989 manufactures trade performance continued to improve, but with exports up 13.3 percent and imports 5.0 percent, the 8.3 percentage points difference was well below the needed 15 percentage points. Can the U.S. reach and maintain the large margin of export growth over import growth needed for several consecutive years to achieve a balanced current account by 1992 or shortly thereafter? Many factors will determine the answer.

Table 8-1
Manufactures Export Growth Required from 1988 through 1992 to Balance the
U.S. Current Account by 1992* (Under Various Manufactures Import Growth
Rate Assumptions)

Assumed Annual (Compounded) Manufactures Import Growth Rate	Required Manufactures Export $ Value Increase by 1992**	Required Manufactures Compounded Growth Rate
+5%	$291 Bn	20.0%
+2%	$234 Bn	17.2%
0%	$200 Bn	15.3%
-2%	$168 Bn	13.3%
-5%	$125 Bn	10.5%
-10%	$ 65 Bn	6.0%
-15%	$ 16 Bn	1.6%

* Actual manufactures trade annual growth rates were:

	Exports	Imports
1981-86	0.1%	14.4%
1986-87	11.2%	9.3%
1987-88	27.8%	11.2%
1988-89	13.3%	5.0%

1987 U.S. manufactures exports = $200 billion.

** $Bn=Billions of dollars

Effects of Trading Partner Economic Growth

Faster economic growth abroad is a frequently cited means of narrowing U.S. trade deficits. Strong foreign economic growth can increase U.S. exports and narrow global trade imbalances, but its potential role is widely overrated. Econometric models, for example, typically indicate that each additional 1 percent of industrialized country economic growth raises U.S. exports by only about $5 billion to $9 billion annually. Each additional 1 percent of U.S. economic growth, however, increases the demand for U.S. imports even more, by $6 billion to $12 billion annually. Thus it is the difference between U.S. and trading partner growth rates that is critical. Other things being equal, trading partner growth rates well above those of the United States for several years—an unlikely prospect—would be required to make a major contribution to reducing global imbalances.

But even if differences between U.S. and foreign growth are not wide, U.S. and global adjustment problems will be eased if world trade levels and manufactures imports by other countries do somehow grow rapidly. In a rapid trade growth scenario, U.S. balances could be improved by taking only a moderately

Table 8–2
World Exports of Manufactures (SITC 5–9) to World and to the World Less
United States, 1981 and 1986

	Billions of U.S. Dollars			Percent		
			Change	Growth	Share Total Mfrs.*	
	1981	1986	1981–86	1981–86	1981	1986
World Exports						
To World	1019.2	1354.3	335.1	5.85	100.0	100.0
To Non–U.S.	869.0	1064.4	195.4	4.14	100.0	100.0
U.S. Exports						
To World	164.2	164.8	.6	.06	16.1	12.2
To Non–U.S.	164.2	164.8	.6	.06	18.9	15.5
Japan Exports						
To World	148.1	205.4	57.3	6.76	14.5	15.2
To Non–U.S.	109.5	124.5	15.0	2.60	12.6	11.7
EC Exports						
To World	469.5	625.2	155.7	5.90	46.1	46.2
To Non–U.S.	436.0	563.5	127.5	5.30	50.2	50.9
German Exports						
To World	152.4	213.8	61.4	7.0	15.0	15.8
To Non–U.S.	141.6	190.5	48.9	6.11	16.3	17.9
LDC Exports						
To World	81.3	137.9	56.6	11.2	8.0	10.2
To Non–U.S.	42.4	56.6	14.2	6.7	4.9	5.5
Asian NICs						
To World	42.0	78.5	36.5	13.3	4.1	5.8
To Non–U.S.	20.7	30.7	10.0	8.2	2.4	2.9

*Explanation of Terms:
  Percentage share of Total Mfrs.
  To World: The % share of the indicated country in total manufacturers
  exports to the world, including the U.S.
  To Non–U.S.: The % share of the indicated country in total manufac-
  tures exports to non–U.S. destinations.

larger slice of a more rapidly expanding "world exports pie," leaving U.S. competitors with export volumes and domestic production levels not so badly hit, even as the U.S. achieves significant export gains. But if import growth in non-U.S. markets is slow or stagnant, balancing U.S. accounts over a five-year period will require taking a much larger slice of a slowly growing world export pie. In that kind of environment, improved U.S. trade performance would require significant export declines of trading partners, with depressing effects on their output and employment that could lead to protectionist actions.

The Growth of World Manufactures Trade, 1981–86

How large is world manufactures trade and how rapidly does it grow? From 1981 to 1986 world manufactures exports to all destinations, including the United States, grew at an annual rate of 5.85 percent (Table 8–2).[3] In current dollar terms, growth was $335 billion, bringing the 1986 manufactures export total to $1,354 billion. Sharp increases in U.S. imports, however, absorbed $140 billion,

Figure 8–2
**U.S. Competitor Shares of World Exports of Manufactures to Non-U.S.
Destinations, 1981–86**

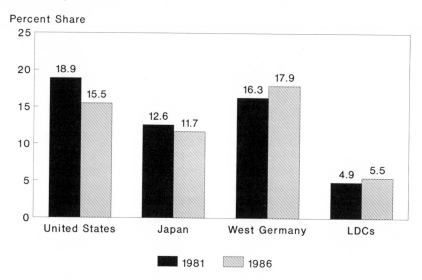

Percent Share

Source: U.S. Department of Commerce.

or 41.7 percent of the growth, raising the U.S. share of world manufactures trade imports from 15.3 percent in 1981 to 22.8 percent in 1986. In assessing U.S. export opportunities, however, one must look at world exports *less* those to the United States, that is, the market available to U.S. exporters. In 1986 world manufactures exports to destinations other than the United States were about $1,064 billion, up by only $195 billion from the 1981 level, an annual growth rate of 4.1 percent, which is well below the 5.9 percent rate achieved in world exports to all world destinations including the United States.

During the 1981–86 period, U.S. manufactures exports first declined and then recovered by 1986 to levels slightly above those of 1981, resulting in a compound annual growth rate of only 0.06 percent. At $164.8 billion, the U.S. share of 1986 world exports to non-U.S. destinations was 15.5 percent, down from 18.9 percent in 1981, when the United States had a $15.4 billion manufactures trade surplus. Table 8–2 provides additional insights.

The data show that U.S. manufactures trade deficits grew partly because U.S. exports stagnated and the U.S. market share declined. This was not the main problem, however. Had the United States maintained its 1981 share (18.9 percent) of world manufactures exports to non-U.S. destinations, U.S. exports would have been only about $37 billion larger in 1986 (Figure 8–2). Retaining the 1981 export market share thus would have only modestly narrowed the 1981–86 manufactures trade balance deterioration, from $144 billion to $107 billion.

Clearly, the growth in U.S. trade deficits primarily manifested a marked increase in foreign penetration of U.S. markets rather than a decline in U.S. export market share. This is an important point because it implies that closing U.S. trade deficits primarily through export expansion would require very large increases in the U.S. share of world export markets. In fact, it would require increases to levels well beyond those achieved in 1981 before the decline in U.S. market share began.

If one assumes 1988–92 growth of world manufactures exports to non-U.S. destinations at the 1981–86 rate (4.1 percent per annum compounded), the 1992 market available to U.S. exporters would be $1,357 billion, $250 billion larger than 1987. If U.S. imports stabilized at 1987 levels—no growth in current dollar terms—the U.S. current account could be balanced in 1992 by an increase in U.S. manufactures exports of about $200 billion over 1987 levels. Thus even if U.S. manufactures imports did not grow through 1992, the United States would have to capture four-fifths of the projected $250 billion growth in manufactures exports to non-U.S. markets. If U.S. imports grow above the 1987 level (in fact, they did grow by $36 billion in 1988 and another $18 billion in 1989), a still larger market share will be required to achieve the needed improvement in performance.

Moreover, in doubling its manufactures exports from $200 billion in 1987 to $400 billion in 1992 the United States would increase its 1992 export market share to almost 29 percent, nearly twice the 1986 level of 15.5 percent and much larger than the Japanese 11.7 percent and German 17.9 percent shares the same year. Such an increase would be extremely difficult to accomplish in a world in which manufacturing competition is intensifying as production capabilities expand rapidly around the globe. In fact, even recovery of the considerably smaller 18.9 percent 1981 export market share would likely be a difficult task. Regaining the 1981 share by 1992 would, however, result in a U.S. manufactures exports increase of only about $70 billion over 1987 levels, just over one-third of the $200 billion increase required if U.S. imports hold through 1992 at 1987 levels. To the extent that U.S. manufactures imports increase through 1992, the required manufactures export gains to achieve a balanced current account will also grow.

Export Expansion or Import Substitution?

These data support some important conclusions. First, completely eliminating the U.S. current account deficit by 1992 while meeting other economic objectives will be extremely difficult and is unlikely. U.S. trade performance improved in 1988 and 1989 but in 1989 fell well behind the pace needed for a balanced current account by 1992. Because of the size and likely growth rates of world exports to non-U.S. markets and the importance of U.S. markets to trading partners, it would be very difficult to sustain U.S. export growth rates 15 percentage points above imports for five consecutive years while maintaining good U.S. and trading partner economic growth rates.

Second, faced with intense global competition and absent strong foreign economic growth that would greatly enlarge world export markets, it is most unlikely that the United States can achieve the huge increases in exports required to close its trade deficit solely by export expansion. The very large U.S. shares of non-U.S. export markets that would be required do not seem attainable, even in years beyond 1992.

The United States, however, need not shrink its trade deficit only by export expansion. Reducing imports and substituting domestic production are equally as good for U.S. production and employment in the short term as an equivalent amount of export gains. The implied shrinkage in trading partner exports that would result from U.S. import substitution, however, may cause economic disruptions for trading partners that, in turn, may have both political and economic implications for the United States.

Nevertheless, U.S. deficits grew primarily through foreign penetration of the U.S. domestic market, and absent major changes in consumption versus saving patterns of key surplus countries, the world market has limited potential for absorbing additional U.S. exports. These facts make it apparent that the largest share of a major narrowing of the U.S. current account will likely come not from export expansion but from import substitution—by U.S.-based production capturing a larger share of the U.S. market.

Enlarging the "Made in the USA" Share: The Role of the Dollar Exchange Rate

Reducing the federal government budget deficit and bringing total U.S. consumption into line with total U.S. production are essential steps to avoiding an abrupt, disruptive global adjustment that could have serious global economic implications. These U.S. macroeconomic changes, however, will not in themselves change the trade balance. Rather, they must affect individual transactions in markets in ways that will increase U.S. exports and decrease U.S. imports.

At the microeconomic, individual transaction level, the trade balance must be narrowed by a combination of expenditure reduction (cutting total U.S. demand relative to total U.S. production) and expenditure switching (switching demand from imports to U.S.-based production). The gradual braking of U.S. demand growth caused by a progressive elimination of U.S. budget deficits will reduce total U.S. demand below levels that would otherwise obtain. Without a recession, however, this demand reduction alone is unlikely to cut U.S. demand for imports by large amounts. That is, each billion dollars of budget deficit reduction will not translate directly to a billion dollar reduction in demand for imports. In fact, reducing government spending alone would have little direct effect on imports because the government purchases few imports compared to the private sector. Within the private sector, other things being equal (for example, with exchange rates remaining the same), only a fraction of reduced total U.S. demand would be at the expense of imports.

Thus dampened U.S. aggregate demand and increased foreign aggregate demand alone are unlikely to result in the $200 billion improvement in manufactures trade required to balance the current account. Instead, a $200 billion improvement will require significant gains in the shares of U.S. and foreign markets supplied by U.S.-based production. It will require that both U.S. and foreign buyers switch a portion of their expenditures from foreign suppliers to U.S. suppliers. Individual buyers do not switch to new suppliers because of macroeconomic policy changes or because of changes in aggregate demand. The market mechanism that will motivate switching to U.S.-based production must be some combination of improved price, quality, and uniqueness of U.S.-made products.

Wresting large market share gains from foreign competitors in both U.S. and foreign markets will be difficult. Some years ago many U.S.-made products were unique in technology and quality and often did not face tough foreign competition. Today, U.S.-made products are seldom unique in design, capabilities, or quality. Now, enlarging the "Made in the USA" share of both U.S. and foreign markets usually means winning head-to-head competition with foreign products primarily on the basis of quality and price. Customer perceptions of U.S. quality can be enhanced over time by design and production improvements. At best, however, switching demand as a result of perceived improvements in quality will occur only slowly. Price-based competition will thus dominate in most products. U.S. products can become more price competitive in three basic ways:

• Holding wage rate growth below that of competitors
• Improved productivity relative to competitors
• Dollar depreciation

Analysis of the outlook in these three factors makes it clear that dollar depreciation will play the lead role. U.S. wage growth has been more restrained recently than in previous years but even so often exceeds productivity growth. Wages in many competitor countries rise less rapidly relative to productivity gains than do U.S. wages.

Productivity increases contribute to more competitive prices, but to achieve competitiveness gains U.S. productivity must increase at more rapid rates than those of foreign competitors. Recent U.S. manufacturing productivity increases have been strong but not often significantly above those of major competitors. Even these recent increases may not be sustained. Productivity increases are extremely important factors in long-term economic performance and in determining living standards. But their effects cumulate only slowly by consistently outperforming the competition, something the United States has not done in recent years. Rather, when threatened with loss of their export markets by U.S. dollar depreciation, foreign export industries have shown remarkable ability to cut their costs and prices through productivity improvements and wage restraint.

Rates of investment in manufacturing in many competitor countries are well above U.S. rates, offering little hope that U.S. productivity gains will soon top those of major competitors. Thus during the next several years, neither productivity gains nor wage restraint are likely to be major factors in improved U.S. price competitiveness and trade performance.

The dollar exchange rate will likely be the dominant factor in achieving dramatic growth in the U.S. share of the U.S. and world manufactures markets. Competitor economies may for some time be able to hold down or cut wages, and they may maintain productivity growth rates equal to, or exceeding, U.S. rates. For a time, in efforts to retain their export surpluses, they may be able to hold down the market price of their currencies by purchasing U.S. dollars. They may also be able to subsidize exports in other ways. In the end, however, the market will set exchange rates that will shrink unsustainable global imbalances.

Eliminating or sharply reducing U.S. current account deficits during the next several years will, therefore, likely depend primarily on switching demand to U.S. products. This will result from improved price competitiveness of U.S.-based production. Improved price competitiveness will come primarily from a lowered dollar exchange rate. The rate will have to be one that significantly increases the U.S. share of world manufactures exports (export expansion) but even more markedly reduces the share of the U.S. manufactures market supplied by foreign production (import substitution). Will exchange rates of the early 1990s facilitate these changes? The disaggregated product analysis that follows provides some insights.

U.S. MANUFACTURES TRADE DISAGGREGATED

The dollar devaluation that had occurred by the end of 1989 markedly aided U.S. products in both U.S. and foreign markets. There are wide differences, however, in the price and quality competitiveness of U.S. firms and industries. Some industries were already competitive in home and foreign markets, even at earlier, higher dollar exchange rates. Each subsequent further downward movement of the dollar improved the competitive stance of U.S. manufacturers. But individual firms and industries make major gains in their competitiveness at different exchange rates. Thus a look at trade patterns and factors affecting performance in individual product groups can provide insights about changes in the exchange rate that are needed to induce a major narrowing of global imbalances.

Limited Export Expansion Prospects

Table 8–3 summarizes the roles of twenty-three key manufactures trade product groups in the worsening of the manufactures trade balance from 1981 to 1987, the low point of U.S. trade performance in current dollar terms. These products

Table 8–3

The 1987 Role of Key Product Groups in U.S. Manufactures Trade

Sch. E/A#	Description	Billions of U.S. Dollars				Percent of Total	
		Exports	Imports	Balance	1981-87	Exports	Imports
51	Org Chem & Rel Prod	7.6	5.7	1.9	-1.0	3.8	1.7
54	Med & Pharm	3.2	1.5	1.7	0.2	1.6	0.4
56	Fert & Fert Mat'ls	2.3	0.9	-0.1	0.9	1.2	0.3
58	Syn Res, Rub, & Plas	5.5	2.1	3.4	0.4	2.8	0.6
59	Chem Mat & Prod NSPF	3.2	1.4	1.7	-0.2	1.6	0.4
65	Yarns, Fab & Articles	3.0	6.9	-3.9	-4.3	1.5	2.0
66	Nonmetal Min Mfrs	2.7	9.5	-6.8	-4.3	1.4	2.8
67	Iron & Steel	1.3	9.8	-8.5	0.7	0.7	2.9
68	Nonferrous Metals	2.2	8.2	-6.0	-1.6	1.1	2.4
69	Mfrs of Metal Nes	3.6	8.5	-4.9	-5.3	1.8	2.5
71	Power Gener Machines	10.5	11.1	-0.6	-5.5	5.3	3.3
72	Spec Indust Machines	9.6	11.2	-1.6	-11.1	4.8	3.3
74	Indust Mach & Parts	8.4	11.5	-3.1	-9.7	4.2	3.4
75	Office & ADP Mach	20.0	19.0	1.0	-5.4	10.0	5.6
76	Telecom & Sound Rep	5.7	21.3	-15.6	-10.6	2.9	6.3
77	Elec Mach NSPF & Pts	18.0	25.1	-7.0	-9.5	9.0	7.4
78	Road Vehicles	21.5	74.8	-53.3	-40.5	10.8	22.1
79	Trans Equip NSPF	18.2	5.8	12.5	-0.9	9.1	1.7
84	Wearing App & Acces	1.2	22.0	-20.8	-14.0	0.6	6.5
85	Footwear	0.2	7.7	-7.4	-4.4	0.1	2.3
87	Prof Sci & Cont Inst	7.7	4.6	3.0	-1.3	3.9	1.4
89	Misc Mfrs NSPF	8.3	21.1	-12.8	-10.4	4.2	6.2
95	Mil Arms, Ammo & Veh	2.3	0.3	1.9	-0.1	1.2	---
	Total-Above Groups	166.2	290.0	125.3	137.9	83.6	85.5
	Other Groups	33.8	47.8	12.4	15.2	16.3	14.5
	Total all Manufactures	$200.0	$337.8	$137.7	153.1	100.0	100.0

Source: U.S. Department of Commerce

make up about 85 percent of U.S. manufactures trade. A detailed assessment of each leads to several conclusions.

Exports should increase across a wide spectrum of products. There is, however, no single U.S. export product group that appears capable of producing quantum dollar value export gains over the next several years. There is no product group that can be expected to produce export gains similar to the $45 billion increase in U.S. motor vehicle imports during the 1981–87 period. Export gains in most product groups will be relatively small compared to the minimum $200 billion improvement required to balance the current account by 1992. In fact, some products that have been key export earners have only limited expansion potential.

Aircraft exports (Table 8–4), for example, have consistently produced the single largest U.S. manufactures surplus, $10.8 billion in 1986 (imports, cif basis), $12.5 billion in 1987, $15.3 billion in 1988, and over $18 billion in 1989. U.S. aircraft exports may further marginally expand, but surplus increases of more than an additional few billion dollars in the next two to three years are

Table 8-4
Aircraft World Exports and U.S. Trade, 1981-86*

| | Billions of U.S. Dollars | | | Percent | | |
	1981	1986	Change 1981-86	Annual Growth 1981-86	Share of Total Mfrs.** 1981	1986
World Exports:						
To World	47.8	47.9	.1	.06	4.7	3.5
To Non-U.S.	44.1	43.3	-.8	-.36	5.1	4.1
U.S. Trade:						
U.S. Exports	16.5	16.4	-.1	-.1	37.4	37.9
Imports	3.3	5.6	2.2	10.8	7.0	11.6
Balance	13.2	10.8	-2.3	n.a.	n.a.	n.a.

* Corresponds to SITC 79, Transportation Equipment, NSPF.
**Explanation of Terms:
   Percentage Share of Total Mfrs. Exports
      To World: The % share of this component in total manufactures
      exports to the world including the U.S.
      To Non-U.S.: the % share of this component in total world
      manufactures exports to non-U.S. destinations.
   U.S. Trade:
      U.S. Exports: The U.S. share of total world exports of this
      product group to non-U.S. destinations.
      U.S. Imports: U.S. imports as a % share of total world exports in
      this product group to all world destinations, including the U.S.

unlikely. Production lines are at full capacity. Also, U.S. import increases may hold the surplus near recent levels. Large current account gains from aircraft exports are even more difficult in that the net U.S. value added in some new aircraft has declined to about 60 percent of the export price. This reflects the continuing internationalization of the industry, with aircraft manufacturers now drawing from a variety of different country sources for major components. Thus even a major increase in world aircraft exports (world exports totaled only $43.4 billion in 1986 and did not increase during the 1981-86 period) or a difficult to achieve increase in the U.S. share of world exports to non-U.S. destinations (38 percent in 1986) would not necessarily produce large trade surplus gains.

Chemicals has traditionally been one of the largest surplus sources in U.S. manufactures trade. Its 1986 surplus was $7.8 billion (imports, cif basis), and it rose to $9.6 billion in 1987, $11.5 billion in 1988, and improved an additional $3 billion in 1989 (estimated cif basis). Exports will likely grow during the next few years, but continued import increases are also expected. Modest further increases in the industry's trade surplus may occur in the early 1990s. Large gains, however, are unlikely for several reasons.

During the late 1980s, chemicals exports were constrained in some key export products by lack of capacity. There is, however, some hesitancy to investing in new U.S. capacity, in part because of uncertainty that the dollar will remain at levels where U.S.-based production is competitive. In addition, large investments by many energy-rich countries pose the threat of coming global overcapacity in some petrochemical products, long a major source of U.S. export earnings. Uncertainties about tax, investment credits, and regulatory and environmental restrictions are also significant impediments to major new U.S. investments and to expanded export surpluses.

Similarly, the U.S. remains competitive in office machines and electronic data processing equipment, registering a $1.0 billion surplus in 1987. But intense foreign competition in this "high-tech" area and subcontracting of parts and components to foreign suppliers will make it difficult to recoup the $5.4 billion 1981–87 slippage in the trade balance (Table 8–3). Indeed, although the trade balance in this category increased modestly in 1988, a small deficit was incurred in 1989.

Stubborn Imports

At current exchange rates continued growth is likely in clothing and apparel imports, products in which it will be difficult for U.S.-based production to become competitive. Import growth may also continue in several other manu-factured goods that have been big contributors to U.S. deficits but now have little or no U.S.-based production. Telecommunications and sound reproducing equipment (Sch. 76, TVs, radios, VCRs, and so on), for example, is a major deficit group, $15.6 billion in 1987 (Table 8–3). U.S. consumption of consumer electronics is now supplied primarily by imports. Much of the U.S.-owned production has moved offshore to Taiwan and Mexico, countries whose real exchange rates have not moved enough against the dollar to return production to the United States.

Thus U.S. dependence on foreign production will likely not change quickly. To illustrate, about 12.4 million VCRs were sold in the United States in 1987. Only 230,000 were "made in USA"(assembled from imported parts), resulting in a total import bill of over $3 billion. Although by 1989 nearly 900,000 VCRs were expected to be U.S. made, they were expected to represent less than 7 percent of estimated sales, and they relied heavily on imported parts and com-ponents. Large deficits in VCRs will continue for the foreseeable future.[4]

Importance of the Motor Vehicle Deficit

A number of product groups are important to U.S. trade performance, but motor vehicles is by far the most critical. In 1986 the United States took 36 percent of world motor vehicle exports (Table 8–5). In 1987 U.S. motor vehicle and parts imports were nearly $75 billion, and the $53 billion motor vehicle deficit was equivalent to about 1.2 percent of GNP.

Table 8–5
Road Motor Vehicles World Exports and U.S. Trade, 1981–86*

| | Billions of U.S. Dollars | | | | Percent | |
| | | | Change | Annual Growth | Share of Total Mfrs.** | |
	1981	1986	1981–86	1981–86	1981	1986
World Exports:						
To World	125.8	194.3	68.5	9.08	12.3	14.3
To Non-U.S.	96.3	120.8	24.4	4.63	11.1	11.3
U.S. Trade:						
U.S. Exports	16.5	19.0	2.4	2.79	17.2	15.7
Imports	29.5	70.3	40.8	18.95	23.5	36.2
Balance	-13.0	51.3	-38.3	n.a.	n.a.	n.a.

* Corresponds to SITC 78
**Explanation of Terms:
   Percentage Share of Total Mfrs. Exports
      To World: The % share of this component in total manufactures
      exports to the world including the U.S.
      To Non-U.S.: The % share of this component in total world
      manufactures exports to non-U.S. destinations.
   U.S. Trade:
      U.S. Exports: The U.S. share of total world exports of this
      group to non-U.S. destinations.
      U.S. Imports: U.S. imports as a % share of total world exports
      in this product group to all world destinations, including the
      U.S.

It is difficult to overemphasize how critically the location of motor vehicle production for the U.S. market affects U.S. trade performance. Indeed, a major trimming of the motor vehicle deficit appears essential to a significant improvement in U.S. trade balances. Auto production is high in value added and does not require unique skills or processes. It is very unlikely that there is a lasting Japanese comparative advantage in Japan-based auto production that can sustain such large net Japanese auto exports to the United States. Indeed, Japan-based auto production must overcome a transportation disadvantage of about $500— the cost of moving a vehicle from Japan to a U.S. port of entry—as well as a small tariff to compete in the United States. These factors, together with increasing U.S. quality and productivity in the industry, should make U.S.-based auto production competitive against foreign-based production well ahead of many other U.S.-made products. This reasonably good and improving cost competitiveness of U.S.-based motor vehicle production, as well as the huge size of the motor vehicle deficits (the 1987 motor vehicle deficit with Japan was $30.4 billion), dictate that reducing the motor vehicle deficit will be a key element in narrowing the trade and current account deficits. Moreover, trimming the motor vehicle deficit will occur primarily by moving a major portion of Japanese motor vehicle production to the United States.

Japanese auto production capabilities in the United States have been rising rapidly but may not reflect longer term global market realities. There are signs that Japanese planners foresee capturing an expanding share of the U.S. market and that they see their U.S.-based production primarily as supplementing, rather than replacing, exports from Japan. At the beginning of the 1990s, Japanese companies planned to increase their U.S.-based production to 2.2 million units per year by 1991.[5] But even to keep their existing share in a relatively strong U.S. automobile market, Japanese producers would have to supplement this planned U.S.-based 1991 production with exports of about 1.4 million automobiles from Japan to the United States. A decline to 1.4 million units would represent a more than one-fourth reduction from the 2.2 million units shipped from Japan in 1987. There would, however, not necessarily be an equivalent decline in the U.S. automotive deficit because the 1991 exports would be higher on the luxury and price scale than shipments during the 1980s. The higher unit prices, together with increased shipments of parts and components for expanding U.S.-based Japanese assembly operations, might well produce a total value of exports from Japan little smaller than the $30.4 billion 1987 level. The 1989 U.S. motor vehicles deficit with Japan, however, improved by $1.8 billion.

There is also strong evidence that the major Japanese auto companies can profitably export to the United States at dollar exchange rates well below the 145–150 yen to the dollar range of early 1990. As their strong productivity gains and low inflation rates continue, Japan's auto makers will be able to compete at even stronger yen-dollar rates. But if the U.S. current account continues to show inadequate improvement—the likely outcome—further significant dollar declines could put extreme cost pressures on automobile and other exports from Japan. This would ultimately make much of the Japan-based production for the U.S. market a losing proposition. In fact, to achieve major improvements in the U.S. current account, the dollar exchange rate and other factors must combine to force movement to the United States of the major portion of foreign motor vehicle production for the U.S. market.

Thus, in the end, Japanese auto producers cannot win in a continuing race of cost cutting of Japan-based production against a declining dollar. Indeed, if the U.S. current account deficit is to shrink to modest levels, further dollar devaluations will likely be necessary to ensure that by the mid-1990s exports of Japanese automobiles to the United States will be only a fraction—perhaps half or less—of the nearly 2.3 million units shipped in 1986. Even a reduction of this size would leave a large dollar value of imports from Japan, since the surviving exports would likely include a larger proportion of the more expensive upscale units.

Although further declines in the exchange rate ultimately will force more foreign production to the United States, the U.S. auto industry in no small measure will affect the volume of auto imports in the early 1990s. First, many lower-priced U.S. nameplates are now imported from abroad. U.S. producers at some point could move to supply this market with U.S.-based production.

Second, as further dollar declines put increased pressures on Japanese and other auto exporters, U.S. producers can either relieve this pressure by raising their own prices and going for short-term profits, or they can choose to hold their own prices down and attempt to win back market share.

Estimates vary, but adding foreign-owned U.S.-based production of foreign nameplate autos to existing U.S. production could raise the U.S. auto industry to as much as 25 percent excess capacity by the early 1990s. Initially, Japanese auto production in the United States will be primarily assembly operations, with major components imported from Japan. The value-added component from U.S. operations will be a relatively low portion of the value of the finished product. But as the dollar sinks lower, more and more components will be produced in the United States. Given their preference for working with their own suppliers, an influx of Japanese parts and component manufacturers is likely, adding to supplies in this sector. The result will likely be significant industry restructuring and perhaps increasing controversy about foreign direct investment in the United States in the auto sector. The resulting intense competition, however, should help hold down prices and inflationary pressures in this important industry.

OUTLOOK FOR THE DOLLAR

Cutting the U.S. government budget deficit and the resulting reduction in U.S. aggregate demand are by themselves unlikely to eliminate U.S. trade and current account deficits. Dollar exchange rate changes must also occur. To the extent that reduced U.S. aggregate demand falls on U.S. imports, the trade deficit will narrow without further decline of the dollar. To the extent that reduced aggregate demand lowers auto sales, for example, automobile imports would be reduced somewhat. But in an orderly global adjustment concurrent with continued U.S. and foreign economic growth, the major portion of the adjustment is likely to occur through enlarged U.S. shares of U.S. and foreign markets, that is by switching both foreign and U.S. demand from foreign to U.S.-based production, rather than from a reduction in U.S. aggregate demand.

For the most part, price is likely to be the dominant motivation in switching to U.S.-based production. More competitive U.S. prices through productivity increases that exceed those of foreign competitors or price advantages as a result of U.S. wage restraint are unlikely to be significant factors. Instead, the price advantages needed to cause such a switch will probably occur primarily via the dollar exchange rate. Decisions by manufacturers to switch to U.S.-based production—particularly decisions of foreign companies to relocate production from the home country to the United States—will likely require a supercompetitive dollar and a firm conviction that the dollar will not experience an early recovery.

Most econometric analyses in early 1990 did not foresee significant further trade balance improvement in 1990 and beyond without further dollar decline. Some saw the deficit beginning to expand again. The disaggregated analysis of recent U.S. trade performance in this chapter leads to a similar conclusion:

forcing the return to the United States of much production for the U.S. market and switching U.S. and foreign expenditures to U.S.-based production will require additional dollar devaluation.

Thus although essential to an orderly adjustment, a decline in the budget deficit is not an alternative to further dollar depreciation. Indeed, because it will lower federal government borrowing, most expect that a decline in the budget deficit will lower U.S. interest rates. In turn, these events are expected to lower the demand for foreign capital and the dollar exchange rate.

In early 1989, however, policymakers were in a difficult position about the dollar exchange rate. Some industries were apparently near capacity output, causing a rise in the price of their output. In that environment, a further dollar decline was seen as adding to inflationary pressures, perhaps without contributing significantly to further export increases because of capacity constraints. Hence the administration continued to support a "stable dollar," that is, a policy of maintaining the dollar around early 1989 levels.

In the short term, resisting further dollar decline may appear desirable. But to the extent that U.S. firms do not invest in U.S.-based production and foreign firms do not move production to the United States because they see the dollar stabilizing, it is counterproductive and will hinder a long-term solution to the global trade imbalance problem.

A decline in the dollar exchange rate, rather than import restrictions or other government actions, is the most efficient method of deciding which particular segments of U.S. industry should expand its U.S.-based production. As the dollar declines further, the market mechanism will most effectively sort out and select those sectors in which new capacity and new investment are most desirable in moving the United States toward balance in its external accounts.

In making global production location decisions, both U.S. and foreign corporate planners targeting the U.S. market should recognize three key factors: (1) the United States cannot pay its way in the global economy while continuing to run very large manufactures trade deficits; (2) in fact, sizeable U.S. manufactures trade surpluses will be needed to balance U.S. external accounts, implying a major resurgence of manufacturing in the United States; and (3) as part of the coming adjustment process the dollar must sooner or later decline to whatever level is required to restore and reinvigorate U.S. manufacturing and generate those surpluses. In short, the dollar must decline to whatever level is necessary to give U.S. manufacturing price competitiveness leading to large U.S. manufactures trade surpluses. Recognizing these facts may lead to investments in U.S. production capacity that would otherwise be made elsewhere.

SUMMARY

• A $200 billion improvement from 1987 performance in U.S. manufactures trade, thus changing large manufactures deficits to substantial surpluses, would be required to balance the U.S. current account by 1992. This is highly unlikely.

• Major reductions in global manufactures trade imbalances will likely disrupt global trade because the large U.S. deficits cannot be eliminated without off-setting reductions in the complementary surpluses of others, primarily Japan, the Federal Republic of Germany, Taiwan, and Korea. There are no alternative creditworthy borrower countries capable of absorbing the large export surpluses that had been absorbed by the United States during the 1980s.

• In an orderly world with continuing good economic growth rates, U.S. current account deficits will decline gradually but are unlikely to be eliminated by 1992. A gradual decline, however, implies continued significant growth of the U.S. debtor position and foreign direct investment in the United States.

• U.S. trade deficits grew during the 1981–87 period primarily by foreign production capturing an enlarged share of the U.S. market, to a lesser extent because of lagging U.S. export performance. Narrowing the U.S. trade deficits will reverse these trends.

• Import substitution—the substitution of U.S.-based production for foreign production in supplying the U.S. market for manufactures—will likely dominate in major reductions of U.S. trade deficits. U.S. export expansion will play an important but more modest role.

• A drastic reduction in imports of foreign-made autos will be a critical factor in reducing U.S. trade deficits.

• Supplying recaptured U.S. markets and a growing portion of foreign export markets will require a significant expansion in U.S. manufactures output. At the end of the 1980s U.S. capacity utilization was already high, even as large deficits continued. The increased output needed to balance U.S. trade will require sig-nificantly increased investment in new capacity in some industries.

• Continued growth of foreign direct investment in the United States will likely play a key role in the resurgence of U.S. manufacturing but could generate controversy, particularly in an auto industry already with excess capacity.

• A gradual reduction and elimination of U.S. budget deficits is an essential element in a smooth adjustment of global trade and current account balances. But eliminating U.S. budget deficits is unlikely to obviate the need for further decline of the dollar exchange rate. Further dollar decline will be required both to lower total U.S. expenditures and to switch U.S. expenditures from foreign-made to U.S.-made products.

• Further significant dollar exchange rate declines—particularly against some Asian newly industrialized countries with large current account surpluses—will also be needed to increase U.S. exports and to motivate increased investment in U.S. manufacturing and movement of foreign-based production to the United States.

• The Reagan and Bush administrations have supported a "stable dollar," viewing further dollar depreciation as adding to inflationary pressures without major near-term effects on the trade balance. However, if creating expectations that the dollar will remain at current or higher levels inhibits new investment by

U.S. industry or inhibits the movement of foreign production to the United States, a "stable dollar" policy is counter to a long-term solution.

• Further declines in the dollar exchange rate will be an effective market mechanism for sorting out which areas of U.S. manufacturing require additional new investment. Import substitution by quotas and other forms of import restrictions and domestic production subsidies should be avoided. Such measures would be an inefficient means of replacing foreign production for the U.S. market with U.S.-based production for the U.S. market.

• Both U.S. and foreign corporate planners targeting the U.S. market should recognize that as a part of the coming adjustment process the dollar must sooner or later decline to whatever level is required to generate manufactures trade surpluses. These factors should weigh heavily in global manufacturing investment and plant location decisions.

NOTES

1. Allen J. Lenz, "Narrowing the U.S. Trade and Current Account Deficits: How It Will Occur" (Unpublished paper, April 1988).

2. Much of the trade data in this chapter is on an imports, cif basis. The analysis was done on this basis because world trade data are available on an imports, cif basis.

3. The "world trade" data in Tables 8–2, 8–4, and 8–5 are based on United Nations data. Because available international trade data do not include recent information for a number of countries, world manufactures exports were calculated as the sum of the following:

• The manufactures (SITC 5–9) exports of twenty-one industrialized reporting countries to all world destinations, plus

• The manufactures imports of the same twenty-one industrialized reporting countries from all other non-reporting countries, that is, other industrialized countries, LDCs, Communist countries, and other non-reporting countries

This method somewhat understates actual world manufactures exports in that it does not capture exports *among* the non-reporting group, for example, exports from one LDC to another or among Communist countries or between LDCs and Communist countries. The amount of this trade, however, is relatively small and for the most part does not represent markets with significant potential for the United States and its industrialized country competitors.

The data are in current dollars and include the effects of inflation and nominal dollar exchange rate movements. The 1981–86 period, however, on which the analysis is based, was not one of high inflation, and although the dollar fluctuated widely during the 1981–86 period, by 1986 it had returned to a relationship with key currencies close to that of 1981.

These limitations are important and should be kept in mind in evaluating the results. There is, however, no other practical alternative methodology in a disaggregated analysis of this type.

The "U.S. Trade" data appearing in Tables 8–4 and 8–5 reflect the SITC revision 2 values reported to the United Nations by the United States. The "World Exports" data in these tables, however, are based on trade as reported by both the United States and other countries. As a result of a translation of data in the data base from revision 1 to revision 2 to achieve other comparabilities and as a result of other reporting differences, subtracting world exports to "non-U.S." from world exports to "world" may yield a slightly different value than shown for U.S. exports, the value reported by the United States to the United Nations.

4. Nancy Broderick, "Consumer Electronics," in *1988 U.S. Industrial Outlook* (Washington, D.C.: U.S. Department of Commerce, January 1988), 47–7.

5. Estimate of Albert Warner, Office of Automotive Industry Affairs, International Trade Administration, U.S. Department of Commerce.

Chapter 9

Trading Partner
Adjustment Problems

The coming narrowing of U.S. trade and current account deficits is likely to impose difficult adjustment problems on U.S. trading partners, particularly on the major surplus countries: Japan, the Federal Republic of Germany (FRG), Taiwan, and South Korea. Though shrinking U.S. deficits will alter global trading patterns in many ways, a major narrowing of U.S. deficits is unlikely to be accomplished without major reductions in the surpluses of these countries.

The natural tendency of surplus countries will be to delay and resist the difficult, domestically controversial actions that would reduce their surpluses. This is because the reductions will require substantial industrial restructuring, typically a painful process.

GENERAL ADJUSTMENT ISSUES

Four factors concerning the narrowing of global trade imbalances that are common to the major surplus trading partners are reviewed in this section. Sections providing details about the adjustment problems and progress of each of the major surplus trading partners follow.

Importance of the U.S. Export Market

The most obvious similarity of the major surplus countries is their reliance on U.S. markets. For each of the surplus countries, the United States is the first or second most important market for their exports. More importantly, the United States has been the major source of growth in export markets for these countries. The importance of the United States as a source of growth in export markets leads to the second item common to the surplus countries.

Export-Led Growth

Each of the major surplus trading countries has relied to a greater or lesser extent on export growth to fuel growth in its domestic economy. The rapid increase in the demand for foreign goods created by the large U.S. trade deficits of the 1980s was filled by an expansion in the export sectors of the major surplus countries. This expansion of their export sectors in response to increased demand from the United States fueled their domestic economic growth. The surplus countries' reliance on export growth to power the expansion of their domestic economies leaves them especially vulnerable to reductions in the demand for their exports. Thus each of these countries will instinctively be reluctant to cooperate in measures that would reduce their trade surpluses, especially measures that would reduce their exports.

Need to Stimulate Domestic Demand

A corollary of the reliance of the surplus countries on export growth to fuel expansion of their domestic economies is the need for them to implement policies to stimulate domestic demand. As is argued in Chapter 8, U.S. adjustments to reduce its trade deficits will most likely result largely in import substitution rather than increases in exports. Therefore, trading partners with large trade surpluses with the United States are likely to experience a sharp decline in the demand for their exports as the United States brings its current account toward balance. To avoid a sharp decline in their domestic economies, the surplus countries will need to find new outlets for their production. Since there is no other country or region likely to be able to absorb the large trade surpluses enjoyed by these countries, they will need to look more to internal markets to absorb much of the production now shipped to the United States.

Real Currency Appreciation

Unless the imbalances are narrowed by growth in demand in the surplus countries that lowers their saving rates and increases their consumption, dollar devaluation will inevitably be a part of the narrowing of the imbalances and elimination of U.S. current account deficits. Domestic policies designed to stimulate demand for domestic and imported goods are unlikely to be entirely successful in reducing the current surpluses of U.S. trading partners. In that event, the remaining imbalances will be closed by a real appreciation of the currencies of the major surplus countries against the U.S. dollar.

The major surplus trade countries will be reluctant, however, to allow their currencies to appreciate against the U.S. dollar. This reflects their concern about the potential loss of export markets and disruptions to their economies. We can expect to see the central banks intervene in currency trading in attempts to stem any large real appreciations of their currencies. In the end these efforts will be futile. At best, the central banks will be able to prevent rapid changes in real exchange rates. In the long run foreign central banks will be unable to sell enough of their own currency (or, accomplishing the same thing, buy enough U.S. dollars) to prevent a real appreciation of their currencies against the U.S. dollar.

Importance of Manufactures in Exports

Manufactures dominate each of the surplus country's exports. For each country, well over 95 percent of the value of its exports to the United States is in manufactures. This indicates that the effects of reducing the U.S. trade deficits will fall primarily on the manufacturing sectors of the surplus countries. Thus whereas their manufacturing sectors expanded to fill the opportunities created by the large U.S. trade deficits, these same sectors will now be required to bear the brunt of adjustments forced by reductions in the U.S. trade deficits. The important role of manufactures trade for each of the five countries is summarized in Table 9–1, which provides detailed data tracing U.S. manufactures trade with each of the surplus countries. Because the adjustments will affect primarily the manufacturing sectors of the surplus countries, the following discussion of the adjustment problems of individual countries focuses on their manufactures trade.

JAPAN'S ADJUSTMENT PROBLEMS

In many ways, the adjustment problems facing Japan are archetypical of those facing all of the major surplus countries. During the 1981–89 period, Japan's current account surpluses totaled $426 billion, averaging 2.5 percent of GNP (see Table 7–1). Japan's current account surplus peaked as a percentage of GNP in 1986 at 4.4 percent of GNP. By 1989 the surplus was down to $57 billion and 2.0 percent of GNP.

The United States is Japan's single most important export market, absorbing roughly 37 percent of Japan's manufactures exports (Figure 9–1). Indeed, during much of the 1980s Japan's trade surplus with the United States has represented roughly 70 percent of its total trade surplus. The U.S. trade deficit with Japan was $56 billion in 1987 (imports, customs basis). It fell slightly to $52 billion in 1988 and to $49 billion in 1989 (Table 9–1).

The U.S. deficit on its manufactures trade with Japan in 1988, however, was $67.2 billion. Japan's imports of U.S. manufactures increased nearly 40 percent between 1981 and 1988 but at $22.0 billion remained modest compared to exports to the United States of $89.2 billion. Japanese exports of manufactures to the United States grew even faster during the same period, increasing by 139 percent between 1981 and 1988. While Japanese imports of U.S. manufactures increased $5.9 billion during the 1981–88 period, Japanese exports to the United States grew by $51.9 billion, adding substantially to the U.S. trade deficit with Japan. The U.S. manufactures trade deficit with Japan peaked at $67.6 billion in 1987, declining only modestly to $67.2 billion in 1988.

Table 9–1

U.S. Trade with Major Surplus Countries, 1980–89 (in Billions of Dollars, Imports, Customs Basis)

		1980	1981	1982	1983	1984	1985
Japan							
U.S.	Exports	20.8	21.8	21.0	21.9	23.6	22.6
	Imports	30.9	37.7	37.7	41.2	57.1	68.8
	Deficit	10.1	15.8	16.8	19.3	33.6	46.2
of which mfrs.							
	Exports	8.9	16.1	10.0	10.8	12.1	12.3
	Imports	30.5	37.3	37.4	40.7	56.6	68.1
	Deficit	21.5	27.2	27.4	29.9	44.4	55.8
Germany							
U.S.	Exports	11.0	10.3	9.3	8.7	9.1	9.1
	Imports	11.9	11.4	12.0	12.7	17.0	20.2
	Deficit	0.9	1.1	2.7	4.0	7.9	11.2
of which mfrs.							
	Exports	8.0	7.6	7.1	6.5	7.3	7.5
	Imports	11.5	10.9	11.5	12.1	16.3	19.5
	Deficit	3.5	3.3	4.4	5.6	9.0	12.0
Taiwan							
U.S.	Exports	4.3	4.3	4.4	4.7	5.0	4.7
	Imports	6.9	8.1	8.9	11.2	14.8	16.4
	Deficit	2.6	3.8	4.5	6.6	9.8	11.7
of which mfrs.							
	Exports	2.9	2.7	2.8	2.8	2.9	2.9
	Imports	6.7	7.8	8.6	10.9	14.4	16.0
	Deficit	3.8	5.1	5.7	8.1	11.5	13.0
South Korea							
U.S.	Exports	4.7	5.1	5.5	5.9	6.0	6.0
	Imports	4.3	5.2	5.6	7.1	9.4	10.0
	Deficit	−0.4	0.1	0.1	1.2	3.4	4.1
of which mfrs.							
	Exports	2.2	2.4	3.0	3.3	3.5	3.6
	Imports	4.1	5.1	5.5	7.0	9.2	9.8
	Deficit	1.9	2.7	2.5	3.7	5.7	6.2

Unlike the case with the other major trade surplus countries, Japan's manufactures exports to the United States are concentrated in a relatively few key industries. These industries have become highly efficient and dependent on export markets. Fifty-nine percent of Japan's 1987 manufactures exports to the United States were in four product groups: motor vehicles, 32 percent; telecommunications equipment, 11 percent; automated data processing equipment and office

Table 9–1 (*continued*)

		1986	1987	1988	1989	Sum 81–89
Japan						
U.S.	Exports	26.9	28.2	37.7	44.6	248.3
	Imports	81.9	84.6	89.5	93.6	592.1
	Deficit	55.0	56.3	51.8	49.0	343.8
of which mfrs.						
	Exports	16.9	16.3	22.0		116.5
	Imports	81.2	83.9	89.2		494.4
	Deficit	64.4	67.6	67.2		383.9
Germany						
U.S.	Exports	10.6	11.7	14.3	16.9	100.0
	Imports	25.1	27.1	26.4	24.8	176.7
	Deficit	14.6	15.3	12.0	8.0	76.8
of which mfrs.						
	Exports	8.8	9.7	12.2		66.7
	Imports	24.3	26.4	25.8		146.8
	Deficit	15.6	16.6	13.7		80.2
Taiwan						
U.S.	Exports	5.5	7.4	12.1	11.3	59.4
	Imports	19.8	24.6	24.7	24.3	152.8
	Deficit	14.3	17.2	12.6	13.0	93.5
of which mfrs.						
	Exports	3.6	5.2	9.2		32.1
	Imports	19.3	24.0	24.3		125.3
	Deficit	15.7	18.9	15.2		93.2
South Korea						
U.S.	Exports	6.4	8.1	11.2	13.5	67.7
	Imports	12.7	17.0	20.1	19.7	106.8
	Deficit	6.4	8.9	8.9	6.3	39.4
of which mfrs.						
	Exports	4.0	5.0	7.3		32.1
	Imports	12.5	16.6	19.9		85.6
	Deficit	8.5	11.7	12.6		53.6

Source: U.S. Department of Commerce.

machines, 9 percent; and electrical machinery, 7 percent (Figure 9–2). Exports to the United States in these four categories alone expanded by almost $44 billion during the 1981–86 period.

If U.S. manufactures deficits are narrowed by U.S. import cuts, these key export-oriented Japanese industries are likely to suffer from a significant diminishing of their markets.

Figure 9–1
Destinations of Japan's Manufactures Exports, 1987

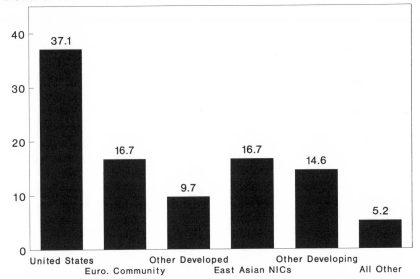

Source: U.S. Department of Commerce.

The Motor Vehicle Sector

The large U.S. motor vehicles and parts deficit is a key factor in the U.S. trade situation. The worldwide U.S. motor vehicle deficit widened from $12.6 billion in 1980 to $53.3 billion in 1987 (cif basis) and improved to $49.2 billion in 1988. A major improvement in the overall U.S. trade balance almost certainly will require a further major narrowing of the automotive deficit. The major portion of the U.S. motor vehicles and parts deficit—more than 60 percent—is with Japan, although the FRG is also an important factor.

The Japanese automobile industry relies heavily on export markets. Some 57 percent of Japanese automobile production was exported in 1987. Roughly half of Japan's auto exports, 2.2 million units, went to the United States that year. About 2.1 million units were sent to the United States in 1988 and 2.0 million units in 1989. A significant narrowing of the U.S. current account deficit could result in a reduction of Japanese auto exports to the U.S. of 50 percent or more from the 1987 level. (The critical role of auto trade in the U.S. deficit and the potential effects of deficit narrowing on auto imports from Japan are discussed in more detail in Chapter 8.)

Without offsetting increases in exports to other markets—an unlikely prospect—a cut in exports to the United States of that order would have a devastating

Figure 9–2
Concentration of Japanese Manufactures Exports to the United States, 1987

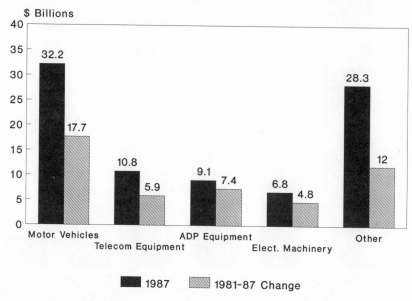

Source: U.S. Department of Commerce.

effect on the Japanese automobile industry. Some of Japan's auto companies are relatively small and may well fail if exports to the United States shrink dramatically. Moreover, there would be major repercussions on supplier industries, for example, steel, glass, chemicals, plastics, and virtually every other manufacturing sector.

Adapting from Export-Led Growth

Japan is a good example of a country that has, as a matter of policy, exploited expanding export opportunities to fuel domestic growth. Japan has had "export-led" growth for decades in that the export sector has grown faster than the rest of the economy and has propelled it forward. Moreover, the entire increase in Japan's trade balance in the six years between 1979 and 1985 came in manufactures trade, particularly in competition with U.S. producers. From 1979 to 1985 Japan's manufactured exports shot up 73 percent to $173 billion, while its manufactures imports increased by a third to $36 billion.[1]

Japan's success is the result of a concentration on, and strong investment in, manufacturing. Export expansion has consistently been a key to Japan's growth. Restructuring of the Japanese economy during the 1980s involved deemphasizing some industries when competition from lower cost producers began to hurt. But Japan has always been able to switch to other, higher technology industries and to maintain its manufactures export surpluses. A narrowing of U.S. deficits during the 1990s, however, will likely require a different—and probably more difficult and painful—kind of restructuring in Japan's manufacturing sector.

Thoughtful Japanese analysts recognize the difficulties ahead. The 1985 Maekawa report noted the need to reduce import barriers and to move away from export-led growth. If aggressively implemented, the recommendations of the Maekawa report would benefit both consumers and export industries. The effect on urban consumers would be direct, since more open trade and a more competitive distribution system should lower prices in Japan, bringing them closer to world market prices. The effect on export industries would be more indirect but also significant. Japan's large trade surpluses put upward pressure on the yen, thereby forcing export industries to make painful adjustments to maintain their sales. Increased imports would relieve upward pressure on the yen. Indeed, eliminating Japan's surplus by import expansion could allow Japan's exports to continue without the penalty of a higher valued yen.[2]

Japan's imports increased markedly in 1988 and 1989. Nevertheless, the prospects for an import expansion that would eliminate Japan's current account surpluses during the next few years without the pressure of a markedly stronger yen than the rate of around 150 to the dollar prevailing in early 1990 are dim. An archaic internal distribution system that resists imports and a host of cultural factors, laws, and policies that motivate excessive saving make it unlikely that Japan's imports will continue to grow long enough or rapidly enough to eliminate or sufficiently reduce Japan's surpluses. Policies and events may be moving in the right direction, but they may well move too slowly. Indeed, those preparing Japan's new Five-Year Plan have projected the current account surplus to remain as high as 2 percent of GNP in 1992. Coupled with other plan projections, that implies a surplus of $70 billion at an exchange rate of 125 yen per dollar.[3] At the beginning of 1990, the Organization for Economic Cooperation and Development (OECD) projected current account surpluses of $61 billion in 1990 and $69 billion in 1991 for Japan.[4]

Japan's Strategy

Given that Japan is unlikely to increase imports sufficiently to narrow its trade surplus, how will it adapt to U.S. attempts to narrow its trade imbalance? Japan will likely employ a multifaceted approach. First, it will search for new, expanding markets. China is one alternative but not one likely to allow Japan to maintain large current account surpluses. The potential market may appear huge, but near-term export market prospects are limited. China's imports, like those of any country, are limited to the sum of the earnings from what it can export plus what it can borrow. Chinese export capabilities are growing but limited. The Chinese are cautious borrowers and will not import in amounts much greater than their exports. Moreover, they tend to emphasize bilateral relationships and are unlikely to import a great deal more from Japan than Japan is willing to import from them. The Soviet Union and Eastern Europe are other potentially large customers but have similar purchasing power limitations. Nor is Japan likely to find other markets that would allow it to keep large global surpluses in the face of shrinking surpluses on its trade with the United States.

Second, in efforts to stay price competitive in the face of a strengthening yen, Japanese industries will continue to engage in strenuous cost cutting, high rates of research and development, and strong investment in plant and equipment. Automation will increase, productivity gains will be extracted, price cuts will be demanded from the captive subcontractors of larger firms, and some component manufacturing will be subcontracted to lower cost LDCs, including, for example, South Korea.

But without a massive increase in its imports, Japanese efforts to maintain exports through expansion to new markets and cost-cutting measures are, in the end, doomed to failure. Thoughtful Japanese planners understand that the market mechanism, via exchange rate movements, will sooner or later force Japan to give up its huge surpluses. They also recognize, however, that the longer the adjustment is delayed, the larger will be the Japanese holdings abroad and future income from the acquired foreign assets. As recognition of Japan's long-term inability to maintain large export surpluses grows, Japanese firms will move with increasing speed to "globalize" their production; more and more, manufacturing will take place in the foreign markets in which Japan wishes to sell. Principally, this means movement of manufacturing operations to the United States and to the European Community. Thus almost inevitably, the major factor in narrowing Japan's surpluses will be an extensive globalization of its production, with particular emphasis on movement to the United States and the European Community.

As recently as 1984, only 3.4 percent of Japan's manufacturing output was in Japanese plants abroad, compared with a U.S. ratio of about 20 percent in 1986. Japanese planners project, however, that continued direct investment abroad will raise Japan's ratio to about 20 percent by the year 2000.[5] The portion of Japan's foreign sales derived from manufacturing in Japan will decline dramatically in the years ahead.

This seemingly inevitable "hollowing" of Japanese manufacturing will pose tough challenges for Japanese planners. Because of the export boom of recent years, Japan has proportionately more people in manufacturing than do other countries.[6] An expansion of domestic demand may increase the domestic sales of some manufactures, but any increase in demand will more likely occur mostly in the "services" area and is unlikely to boost domestic consumption of manufactures sufficiently to compensate for large export declines.

Thus there is the prospect of thousands of redundancies in blue-collar jobs in the steel, automotive, consumer electronics, and machinery industries. Peter Drucker, an internationally recognized author and management consultant, projected

The steel industry will lay off one-third. Similarly, with the shift of automobile production for the export market from Japan to plants in the United States and Spain, the automobile industry—Japan's largest single industrial employer—may face forced reductions of up to 50 percent.[7]

Changes of this magnitude could cause massive social disruption and threaten, if not destroy, the Japanese concept of lifetime employment, an important element in the social compact between blue-collar workers and industry.

Japan clearly has difficult adjustment problems ahead. It has successfully made other difficult adjustments in recent decades, but they were adjustments within the basic export-led growth strategy. During the 1990s Japan must carry out a different strategy, one that will require it to prove that it has a strong, self-sustaining economy when it is unhooked from the life-support mechanisms of export-led growth and huge manufactures export surpluses. Japan's immediate self-interest lies in slowing the necessary adjustment, a strategy that will allow it more time both to make internal adjustments and to enlarge its holding of foreign assets. Slowing adjustment, however, risks rising difficulties in relations with the United States and spillover problems for an integrated world economy and its efficient trade system on which Japan is so dependent. In late 1989, the staff of the International Monetary Fund made the following assessment concerning Japan:

The pace of external adjustment appears to have slowed, and the staff is projecting a widening of the current account surplus in 1990. . . . Beyond the near term, policies should aim at maintaining adequate growth of domestic demand, particularly if substantial fiscal correction in the United States were to reduce demand for Japanese exports. . . . it is now essential to accelerate the pace of structural reform in a number of important areas, including agriculture, land regulations, and those aspects of the distribution system that add to domestic costs and prices and inhibit market access. These reforms would not only improve domestic resource allocation and enhance consumer welfare, they would also promote international adjustment and reduce protectionist pressures in other countries.[8]

GERMANY'S ADJUSTMENT PROBLEMS

U.S.-FRG trade is large and has produced substantial U.S. deficits. The bilateral imbalances, however, are not of the same order of magnitude as those with Japan. The U.S. merchandise trade deficit with the FRG was $15.3 billion (customs basis) in 1987, $12.0 billion in 1988, and $8.0 billion in 1989 (Table 9–1). The United States took 9.5 percent of the FRG's 1987 exports; 6.3 percent of the FRG's 1987 imports came from the United States. Eight percent of 1987 U.S. manufactures imports were provided by the FRG and 4.8 percent of U.S. manufactures exports went to the FRG. The U.S. manufactures trade deficit with the FRG was $16.6 billion in 1987 and $13.7 billion in 1988.

The FRG relies much less on the United States for export markets than do the other major trade surplus countries. The FRG's importance in the coming adjustment process derives not so much from its bilateral trade balance with the United States as from its global surpluses and its critical role in the European economy, a region producing roughly 30 percent of world output.

The FRG is the world's leading exporter. Since 1985 it has exported more than the United States. But it has imported only half as much as the United States. The result has been trade surpluses that totaled about $200 billion during the 1982–87 period, averaging about 4 percent of GNP. Current account surpluses for the period totaled about $121 billion (Table 7–1). New record current account surpluses were set in both 1988 and 1989, however, at $48.5 billion and $52.7 billion. The 1989 current account surplus was equivalent to 4.5 percent of GNP, significantly above Japan's 1989 figure of 2.0 percent and higher even than Japan's 4.4 percent record of 1986. Moreover, OECD projections see continued growth in the FRG's surpluses, both in dollar terms and as a percentage of GNP, with the current account surplus perhaps reaching 5.5 percent of GNP in 1991.[9] These surpluses are a significant factor in global current account imbalances. Given the FRG's continuing large surpluses and foreign exchange reserves that were over $75 billion in 1988, it has a major role to play in reducing global trade imbalances.[10]

Like the case with Japan, the dollar's real appreciation over the first half of the 1980s accounted for much of the FRG's growing trade surplus with the United States. The growth in the trade surplus accounted for almost half of the growth of its economy in this period. Dollar depreciation, however, has eroded FRG price competitiveness against the dollar and has probably played an important role in the decline of the U.S. bilateral trade deficit with Germany. Nevertheless, the German export machine continued to roll, piling up growing global surpluses. Both these surpluses and forecasts of future performance indicate that, as it entered the 1990's, the FRG's currency was still undervalued both relative to the dollar and on a global basis.

Pivotal Role of the FRG

The FRG is often described as the "linchpin" for Europe, its rate of growth by and large determining growth rates for the entire region. The close economic ties between the European economies, brought about in large part by the European monetary system, have reduced the freedom of the individual states to pursue independent economic policies. Because of the size of its economy, the FRG's fiscal and monetary conservatism have set the pace for the region in recent years. When the FRG's neighbors have tried to use expansionary policies to stimulate growth and reduce unemployment, they have usually experienced outflows of capital, downward pressures on their currencies, and increased inflation. This has made it difficult for them to continue such efforts.[11]

Growth in real German GNP was strong in 1989, at a seasonally adjusted annual rate of 6.75 percent based on first half-year performance. The main driving forces in this growth were buoyant international demand and a competitive exchange rate.[12] Increased German domestic demand could stimulate growth elsewhere in Europe. Moreover, continued slimming of U.S. current account deficits and the likely accompanying decline of the U.S. dollar can be expected to reduce exports and economic growth of the other European countries, independent of their effect on the FRG. The likely contraction of European economies, caused directly by a reduction in U.S. imports, and the FRG's strong economic position highlight the need for German leadership in the development of a European growth strategy.

At the end of the 1980s several observers believed that Europe needed to launch a coordinated growth strategy and was in a good position to do so. European inflation rates were low; unemployment rates were high, near 9.0 percent of the OECD European labor force in 1989;[13] and rates of return on capital have risen significantly from their depressed levels following the oil price shocks of the 1970s. At the beginning of the 1990s, however, there had been no spontaneous growth of private consumption and investment in most European countries and no assumption of a leadership role by the FRG. German growth has continued to be primarily a function of export growth, prompting the comments that "the West German economy, Europe's largest, is more caboose than locomotive, since it was other European countries, with their healthy appetite for German goods that helped to pull it along so fast," and "Germany's sluggish domestic consumption and recent interest rate increases, are holding back growth for all of Europe."[14]

A relatively smooth transition of the global economy from unsustainable imbalances to a sustainable situation will be very difficult—probably impossible—without strong growth of domestic demand and imports in Europe, especially the FRG. Absent such increases in demand, further real dollar declines will ultimately choke off German and other European exports, further dampening European growth prospects and, perhaps, triggering a downward growth spiral.

The FRG appears to prefer the current situation—large current account surpluses, low inflation, and relatively high unemployment—to the uncertainties of more aggressive action on its part. On the one hand, it surely must recognize that the current imbalances cannot continue indefinitely and that, without stimulative action in Europe, reduction of U.S. deficits will have significant negative effects on the German and European economies. These effects will force difficult structural changes.

But on the other hand, the FRG has an overriding fear of the inflation it believes might result from stimulating European economies. This fear probably motivates German leadership to downplay the country's potential as a European "locomotive." In its "World Economic Outlook" of late 1989, the International Monetary Fund staff also downplayed the role of expansionary policies for Germany but made other recommendations:

In the current situation there is clearly little scope for expansionary monetary and fiscal policies to reduce Germany's current account surplus. But there is now an urgent need to

reduce structural distortions and rigidities that seriously impair efficiency, raise unemployment, and hinder the reallocating of resources from tradable to nontradable goods.
Trade liberalization, deregulation, and the reduction of subsidies would benefit the German
economy by enhancing its flexibility in adjusting to exchange rate changes, helping to
reduce price pressures, and improving the rate of return on domestic investment.

Germany will likely continue to resist actions to stimulate its domestic demand
and to revalue its currency. Aggressive action will probably be taken only when
further dollar decline has had a sufficiently damaging effect on FRG exports and
employment to override their concerns about potential inflation.

The rapid movement toward reunification of the two Germanys—the Federal
Republic of Germany and the German Democratic Republic (GDR)—injects new
uncertainties in the FRG's role. If reunification proceeds satisfactorily, large
amounts of capital will flow from what is now the FRG to what is now the
GDR, in effect raising the new Germany's domestic investment level and perhaps
lowering its external current account balance. The eastern portion of the country,
however, has only about 17 million people and cannot absorb new investment
at rates that would substantially pare German current account surpluses, projected
by the OECD to grow to $76 billion in 1991.[15]

TAIWAN'S ADJUSTMENT PROBLEMS

Relative to the size of its economy, Taiwan's current account surpluses have
been larger than those of any other country, totaling $58 billion during the 1981–
87 period (Table 7–1). Taiwan's surplus in 1987 was $17.9 billion, an amount
equivalent to almost 18 percent of its GNP. The 1989 surplus was $10.5 billion,
about 7 percent of GNP. Continued huge current account surpluses represent net
lendings that have allowed Taiwan to accrue net foreign assets that by the end
of 1988 totaled about $73 billion, equivalent to about 60 percent of its 1988
GNP.[16]

U.S. imports from Taiwan in 1988 totaled $24.7 billion (customs basis), more
than triple the 1981 level of $8.1 billion (Table 9–1). Manufactures imports
from Taiwan in 1988 were $24.3 billion, 98 percent of the total. The 1989 U.S.
deficit on trade with Taiwan was $13.0 billion, up from $3.8 billion in 1981.
In 1987, 7.6 percent of total U.S. manufactures imports were supplied by Taiwan,
just short of the FRG's 8.1 percent. U.S. imports from Taiwan in 1989 at $24.3
billion remained almost at the 1987 level. The 1988 U.S. deficit with Taiwan,
however, declined to $12.6 billion, largely as a result of Taiwan's imports of
gold from the United States. It remained almost constant in 1989, at $13 billion.
The U.S. manufactures deficit with Taiwan was $18.9 billion in 1987, $15.2
billion in 1988.

Taiwan is more dependent on U.S. markets for its exports than any of the
other major surplus countries, though its dependency is decreasing. The United
States took 44 percent of Taiwan's total 1987 merchandise exports and about

36 percent in 1989, down from 48 percent in 1986. Taiwan's exports to the United States are spread over a wide array of low unit value products. The largest single category, shoes, provided 9.7 percent of Taiwan's total 1987 exports to the United States and 9.4 percent in 1988. The second-ranking item, baby carriages and toys, provided another 7.3 percent in 1987 and 6.2 percent in 1988.

Taiwan's Adjustment Process

Taiwanese officials realize that they can no longer depend on continuing growth of export surpluses to stimulate economic growth and employment and that existing surpluses must shrink. To play its role in a smooth reduction of global imbalances and to avoid domestic economic stagnation, Taiwan must follow essentially the same prescription as Japan and the FRG. It must reduce its dependence on export surpluses by increasing domestic demand and imports, while simultaneously switching much of its export capacity to satisfying an increasing domestic demand.

Because its manufactures export surpluses are so large relative to the size of its economy, adjustment may be even more difficult for Taiwan than for Japan. It will be very difficult to increase domestic demand enough to absorb the export-oriented production that will become redundant if Taiwan's exports to the United States decline. Adjustment will likely entail extensive changes in Taiwan's industrial structure. The inability to increase import demand sufficiently to eliminate the large trade surpluses will put upward pressure on the value of Taiwan's currency. Some manufacturing facilities will be modernized, allowing them to compete internationally in the face of a real appreciation of the currency. It is unlikely, however, that all of existing capacity can survive a major narrowing of U.S. current account deficits.

There are important political obstacles to the major structural adjustments that will be needed. In particular, much of Taiwan's manufacturing is made up of many small and medium-sized firms that are now among Taiwan's leading exporters. These firms are often undercapitalized and may have trouble reorienting to meet increased domestic demand, much of which may be for services rather than for manufactures.

Important self-interests should move Taiwan to reduce its unsustainable surpluses. The large accumulation of reserves growing out of continuing surpluses threatens inflation. The persistent undervaluation of its currency has helped cause a chronic misallocation of resources. With too many resources going to net exports and too few to domestic uses, Taiwan has foregone internal investment in long-term productive ventures such as new plants and equipment and improved infrastructure. Moreover, domestic consumption and the standard of living are well below those merited by national output. The excessive accumulation of foreign reserves is at the expense of current living standards—and, perhaps, future living standards. Indeed, a decrease in net exports would permit both more domestic investment and more domestic consumption.

The Role of Taiwan's Exchange Rate

The value of Taiwan's currency—the New Taiwan Dollar (NTD)—is carefully controlled by the Taiwanese central bank (Bank of China) through a system of managed floating. This management has effectively undervalued the NTD relative to the U.S. dollar and has played a central role in the export-oriented economic development strategy that Taiwan has employed so successfully.

Movement toward a more market-oriented exchange rate will likely be a critical component in an orderly narrowing of Taiwan's surpluses. Largely in response to U.S. pressure and the threat of protectionist retaliation by the United States and the European Community, Taiwanese officials allowed the NTD to appreciate significantly beginning in 1985. From late 1985 to January 1988 the NTD appreciated 40 percent against the U.S. dollar. This was a major movement, but the NTD rose considerably less than the Japanese yen (79 percent) and the FRG mark (72 percent) against the dollar over the same period. Moreover, Taiwan's current account surplus continued to increase through 1987, though it did begin to decline in 1988. By early 1990, the NTD had appreciated about 50 percent against the U.S. dollar from early 1985 levels. Although no one can accurately forecast the current account equilibrium exchange rate of the NTD, most observers expect the U.S. deficit with Taiwan to narrow further, partly due to aggressive efforts of the Taiwanese to purchase from the United States. Nevertheless, it is also widely expected that Taiwan's global trade surplus will remain near 1989 levels, perhaps indicating the need for significant further appreciation of its currency.

Taiwan's Strategy

Taiwan has taken some steps to narrow its huge surpluses. In 1988 Taiwan significantly reduced its surplus with the United States by gold purchases. But although such efforts indicate an awareness of their problems, gold purchases are a temporary phenomenon and do nothing to accomplish the required structural adjustment. More constructively, Taiwan made a number of tariff cuts, and, as noted above, the NTD has appreciated significantly. Restrictions on credit availability have been eased, mortgage lending is expanding, the real estate market is beginning to revive, and even consumer credit is becoming available.[17] Moreover, in early 1989, perhaps partly to avert U.S. action under the "Super 301" provisions of U.S. trade law, Taiwan announced a "Trade Action Plan" for eliminating most of its trade barriers by 1992. The Plan includes timetables for tariff reductions, removal of some non-tariff barriers, improved market access for the service industries, and improved intellectual property protection. The plan will also promote macroeconomic adjustments and diversify Taiwan's exports toward non-U.S. markets. But it remains to be seen whether these promised actions will be adequate. Required additional actions include lowering of agricultural tariffs, reduction or dismantling of export incentives, and reduction of tax law incentives biased toward saving.

An orderly adjustment without a major domestic recession will require significant measures to stimulate domestic demand. Domestic demand's share of the GNP grew from 81 percent in 1987 to 89 percent in 1989, and this trend was expected to continue in 1990. Notwithstanding these favorable changes, however, further appreciation of the NTD may well be required. In late 1989, the OECD view was that the appreciation that has been accomplished would likely be overcome and that Taiwan's exports would resume strong growth.[18] Taiwanese officials will be loathe to give up the export surpluses that have played a key role in their remarkable economic growth and, without continued external pressure, will likely mute domestic demand growth and make only moderate and carefully controlled real exchange rate appreciations of the NTD. They will probably continue to try to buy time to allow their mostly small manufacturers to adjust to a strengthening currency.

They will also be hesitant to appreciate further the NTD without a parallel appreciation of the South Korean won, since South Korea is a major competitor for key markets. As with other surplus countries, Taiwanese officials will find it politically difficult to change a strategy that has proven successful simply to protect against projected future problems of uncertain timing.

SOUTH KOREA'S ADJUSTMENT PROBLEMS

South Korea's current account surpluses are of recent vintage but have grown rapidly, reaching $9.9 billion in 1987, about 8 percent of GNP (Table 7–1). In 1988 the surplus rose to $14.2 billion. Reflecting currency appreciation, a large increase in imports, and internal labor strife that restrained export growth, Korea's current account surplus fell to $5.0 billion in 1989. South Korea's recent surpluses have been used to reduce outstanding external debt and to build up currency reserves. Nevertheless, external debt at the end of 1988 was estimated at $11 billion (Table 6–1), just over 6 percent of GNP.

U.S. goods imports from South Korea totaled $19.7 billion in 1989 (customs basis), up from $5.2 billion in 1981 (Table 9–1). In 1987 and 1988 U.S. trade deficits with Korea were $8.9 billion each year, falling to $6.3 billion in 1989. Almost 98 percent of U.S. merchandise imports from South Korea are manufactures. As with Taiwan, U.S. imports from South Korea are spread over a wide variety of products. Automobile imports have been growing rapidly, however, and represented one-eighth of the 1987 total. South Korea's rapid penetration of the U.S. motor vehicle and parts market has been little short of phenomenal, rising from only $6 million in 1985 to $2.2 billion in 1987 and about $2.6 billion in 1988, despite production-disrupting labor problems early that year.

Like Taiwan, South Korea is heavily dependent on U.S. markets, which in 1987 took about 37 percent of South Korea's merchandise exports. South Korea ran a large $5.2 billion trade deficit with Japan in 1987, concurrent with a surplus on U.S. trade of $9.9 billion. Japan supplies 31 percent of South Korean imports, the United States only 21 percent.

South Korea's need to reduce its large international debtor position somewhat mitigates its recent accrual of large current account surpluses. But it faces the same compelling need to unhook from dependence on trade surpluses for economic growth as do the other surplus countries. The large U.S. current account deficits are unlikely to narrow significantly with South Korea's surpluses unimpaired. Particularly, competition for the U.S. auto market is likely to become extremely tough, and the spectacular growth rates of South Korean exports to the United States will be difficult to maintain.

South Korea's Adjustment Process

Like the other surplus countries, South Korea is reluctant to take steps to reduce its current account surpluses. An often cited reason for delay is its outstanding foreign debt. South Koreans are very anxious to eliminate foreign debt. Their eagerness, however, appears to reflect domestic political concerns that foreign debt creates dependency rather than sound economic principles.

South Koreans also argue that adjustment is not required because the existing surpluses are the result of favorable "shocks": the fall in oil prices, the decline in world interest rates, and the recent appreciation of the Japanese yen. The implication is that these effects are only temporary and that South Korea needs to maintain large surpluses in case conditions take a turn for the worse.

These arguments have been weakened, however, as large surpluses continued and as South Korea's economy strengthened and its foreign debt has declined. South Korean leadership has become increasingly aware of the risks of inflation from large surpluses and the opportunity costs of exporting capital (implicit in large current account surpluses) while the nation's living standards remain low and while additional domestic investment could still offer high financial and social returns. Moreover, there is increasing awareness that continuing large current account surpluses are unsustainable and that they raise the threat of foreign retaliation.[19]

As is the case with Taiwan, the adjustment process for South Korea should be multifaceted. Removal of import barriers and export incentives are important steps. Progress has been made in these areas, but much remains to be done. The more that import restrictions are lowered and the more that imports increase, the less pressure there need be to revalue the won.

Importance of the Exchange Rate

Nevertheless, as with other surplus countries, growth in imports and domestic consumption sufficient to avoid further real appreciation of the domestic currency is unlikely. South Korean exports stagnated in 1989 but are projected to recover. Unless domestic wage growth further stimulates import demand, South Korea's current account surplus will stabilize near 1989 levels, perhaps begin to grow again. Continued external pressure will likely be required to move Korea to an exchange rate that will eliminate large surpluses.

Like Taiwan, South Korea controls the exchange rate of its currency, in effect tying it closely to the U.S. dollar. South Korean authorities officially claim their currency is pegged to some combination of a trade-weighted multicurrency basket. The won's movements during the past few years, however, suggest that, in practice, its value is determined at the Ministry of Finance's discretion.[20]

From early 1985 (the dollar's peak against most major currencies) through mid–1986, the won remained loosely linked to the U.S. dollar. Although the dollar depreciated around 26 percent against the yen and most European currencies during this period, it actually gained about 5 percent against the won. In real terms, from 1986 the U.S. dollar fell only about 8 percent vis-à-vis the won through the end of 1987. Although the won further appreciated in 1988, most analysts considered it still to be undervalued. At the beginning of 1990, the won-dollar nominal exchange rate (around 683 won per dollar) was little changed from a year earlier but had appreciated some 22 percent from early 1985 levels. Nevertheless, the International Monetary Fund (IMF) projected continued large surpluses for South Korea, anticipating that "current account adjustment—after the significant reduction of the Korean surplus in 1989—is likely to be modest."

Although it is unlikely that South Korea's current account surplus will narrow adequately without further won appreciation, more appreciation may come only slowly. Powerful business interests in South Korea have argued against further "excessive" appreciation on grounds that it could undermine the country's manufacturing base. Moreover, the Korean government recognizes that, for domestic political reasons, it must carefully avoid the impression of giving in to American demands.

SUMMARY

• Other than in the United States, the effects of the coming narrowing of global trade imbalances will be felt most strongly in the major surplus countries: Japan, the FRG, Taiwan, and South Korea.

• Issues common to the situation of the major surplus countries include reliance on the United States as a major export market; domestic growth, which has been fueled by rapid increases in exports to the United States; the need to stimulate the demand for domestic and imported goods to replace U.S. demand for exports; reluctance to allow domestic currencies to appreciate relative to the U.S. dollar, and the concentration of any adjustment effects on the manufacturing sector.

• Japan's exports are concentrated in a relatively few product groups. Japan's motor vehicle industry is particularly dependent on the U.S. market. Some 28 percent of total Japanese automobile production was exported to the United States in 1987.

• Japan's manufacturing sector is highly developed as a result of continued strong investment. But without major increases in Japan's imports, narrowing global imbalances will probably require a substantial "hollowing" of Japanese manufacturing, with Japanese firms forced by an appreciating yen to move production to the major markets to be served, primarily the United States and the European Community.

• Japan's current account surplus in 1986 was equivalent to 4.4 percent of GNP, 2.8 percent in 1988. A major trimming of that surplus—generated in manufactures exports—will have a significant effect on Japan's manufacturing sector, whose output is about 30 percent of the GNP.

• There are significant political and cultural impediments to markedly increased Japanese imports, which is the alternative to a hollowing of Japanese manufacturing. If U.S. deficits are narrowed primarily by U.S. import cuts, some Japanese industries will be seriously affected.

• Japanese imports have been increasing and the economy is moving toward reduced reliance on export-led growth. Progress, however, is slow, and it remains to be seen whether it will continue.

• The FRG economy plays a pivotal role in Europe, and German failure to compensate for declining export surpluses with the United States by stimulating domestic demand could lead to further economic slowing in Europe, with undesirable effects on the world economy.

• Concerns about inflation are an important factor in restraining FRG actions to speed its growth and reduce its reliance on export surpluses.

• Relative to the size of its economy, Taiwan's imbalances are the world's largest, equivalent to nearly 20 percent of GNP for some years, leaving it with huge reserves and a very large international creditor position relative to its GNP.

• Taiwan has generated huge export surpluses by a carefully controlled, consistently undervalued currency. The new Taiwan dollar has appreciated markedly and Taiwan's current account surplus may have stabilized, but significant further appreciation will likely play a necessary role in trimming Taiwan's still very large surpluses.

• Taiwan is highly dependent on manufactures exports to the United States and shrinking its surpluses will put very strong pressures on the manufacturing sector to downsize.

• Taiwan needs to undertake major steps to increase consumption and living standards and to reduce its dependency on unsustainable current account surpluses as a source of economic growth. Some actions have been taken, but much remains to be done.

• South Korea has also amassed very large current account surpluses, but they are of recent vintage, and South Korea has a modest, though shrinking, foreign debt.

• South Korea is overly dependent on manufactures export surpluses with the United States, which in 1987 took 37 percent of South Korea's exports.

• Like Taiwan, South Korea must take steps to reduce its reliance on export-led growth. It should increase domestic consumption and investment not related to export expansion.

• The South Korean won has been tied to the dollar, and its undervaluation has been a key factor in Korea's export success. The won has appreciated significantly since 1987, and South Korea's current account surpluses have declined but remain high and may begin to grow again. Further appreciation of the won will likely be a necessary factor in constraining, if not narrowing, South Korea's large surpluses.

NOTES

1. Joint Economic Committee, Congress of the United States, *Restoring International Balance: Japan's Trade and Investment Patterns*, Staff study (Washington, D.C., July 1988), 5.

2. Ibid., 40.

3. Ibid., 3.

4. Organization for Economic Cooperation and Development, *Economic Outlook* (Paris, December 1989), 35.

5. "Overseas Investments by Japan Seen Soaring," *Journal of Commerce*, 26 March 1986, 5A.

6. Peter Drucker, "Japan's Choices," *Foreign Affairs*, Summer 1987, 937.

7. Ibid., 937

8. International Monetary Fund, *World Economic Outlook* (Washington, D.C., October 1989), 40.

9. International Monetary Fund, *World Economic Outlook*, 35, 36, 64.

10. Joint Economic Committee, Congress of the United States, *Restoring International Balance: The Federal Republic of Germany and World Economic Growth*, Staff study (Washington, D.C., June 1988), 1.

11. I am indebted to Dan Bond for this point.

12. International Monetary Fund, *World Economic Outlook*, p. 60.

13. Ibid., 23.

14. "West Germany's Export Irritate Its Trading Partners," *New York Times*, 19 September 1988, D12.

15. International Monetary Fund, *World Economic Outlook*, 35.

16. A comprehensive review of Taiwan's trade situation can be found in Joint Economic Committee, Congress of the United States, *Restoring International Balance: The Taiwan Economy and International Trade*, Staff study (Washington, D.C., 30 October 1987).

17. Bela Balassa and John Williamson, *Adjusting to Success: Balance of Payments Policy in the East Asian NICs* (Washington, D.C.: Institute for International Economics, June 1987), 62.

18. International Monetary Fund, *World Economic Outlook*, 40.

19. Ibid.

20. Martin R. Veeger and James W. Fatheree, *Exchange Rate Management in the East Asian NICs: Issues and Prospects* (Washington, D.C.: International Trade Administration, U.S. Department of Commerce, August 1988), 7.

Chapter 10

Implications for LDC Debtors

International capital flows—and the resulting trade flows—are influenced by the *relative* economic policies and performance of national economies. Investment capital moves to those countries that offer the best combination of risk and return. The economic policies, performance, and prospects of LDCs, especially those in Latin America, have had and will continue to have, important effects on international capital flows and, in turn, on U.S. trade and current account balances. Moreover, a narrowing of U.S. trade deficits may cause significant problems for LDC debtor countries.

For most of the 1970s, banks overflowing with funds recycled from cash-rich Organization of Petroleum Exporting Countries (OPEC) countries were eager to lend money to sovereign nations, often buttressing shaky credit evaluations with the rationale that "nations are immortal" and hence acceptable credit risks.

Many developing countries seized the borrowing opportunity, and their debt grew rapidly. The growing debt fueled an unsustainable surge of imports by some LDCs. U.S. exporters benefited, expanding their exports to LDC debtors, particularly in Latin America. But in the early 1980s the borrowing bubble burst. Many LDC debtors are no longer considered creditworthy and are experiencing negative real resource transfers; that is, to service debt they are exporting more goods and services than they are importing, handicapping their development.

Latin American debt increased not only by reason of trade deficits but through "capital flight." As the economies of some Latin countries deteriorated, holders of wealth in those countries became fearful of a drastic devaluation of national currencies that had been propped up by governments. They converted their wealth to foreign currencies and moved it to "safer havens." Much of the conversion was into U.S. dollars. Billions of dollars moved from Latin America to the United States, raising the dollar exchange rate and helping to fund U.S. deficits. In turn, the governments of those countries experiencing capital flight had to borrow dollars to support the exchange rate of their currencies. In effect, they borrowed dollars to finance the flight of capital from their countries. The amount of capital flight was very large. It has been estimated that by 1987 capital flight from fifteen troubled debtors totaled $295 billion, about 61 percent of their $484 billion external debt.[1]

The fact that many LDCs have exhausted their credit, can no longer run trade deficits, and must now run merchandise trade surpluses to service existing debt has important effects on world trading patterns and complicates narrowing the current account imbalances of the United States and the major surplus countries. As long as Latin American economic policies and performance do not motivate new foreign lending to them and the return of flight capital by their own citizens, Latin American countries will not be an attractive investment market for international investment capital. This shrinks the pool of alternatives for investors and makes it easier for net capital inflows to the United States to continue. In short, earlier mismanagement of LDC debtor economies contributed to net capital flows to the United States and the U.S. trade and current account deficits. Continued mismanagement prevents net capital inflows to the underdeveloped economies of Latin American debtors and hinders the ability of the United States to narrow and eliminate its net capital inflows and trade and current account deficits.

The heavily indebted position of LDC debtors also leaves them vulnerable to adjustments in trade flows among the United States and the major surplus countries. A disruptive narrowing of global imbalances would clearly cause major problems for LDC debtors who, among other problems, are vulnerable to trade slowdowns and interest rate rises.

But even a gradual, relatively smooth narrowing of global imbalances may pose difficulties for troubled LDC debtors. The United States has absorbed the great majority of the growth in LDC exports that has allowed a number of LDCs to continue servicing their debts. As U.S. deficits contract, LDCs could be adversely affected. The origins of the LDC debt problem are examined in some detail in this chapter.

WHY BORROWING OCCURS AND HOW IT GOES ASTRAY

Developing countries presumably become net borrowers to speed their development. Many less developed countries have low saving rates, with a very high portion of their incomes required to maintain their low levels of consumption. Net inflows of capital (borrowing) can allow a country to increase its domestic investments and its productive capacity more rapidly than it could by relying on only its own saving. Theoretically, as productive capacity rises so do exports, thereby enabling the debtor to meet debt servicing payments. The remaining added production funded by borrowed capital then provides a net increase in the output of the economy that would not have been available without borrowing.

Sometimes it has worked that way, but too often it hasn't. South Korea is an example of success. Argentina, Brazil, and Mexico are prominent examples of borrowing that went awry. Poland, although not an LDC, has also borrowed unsuccessfully.

Borrower nations can stray from the path of success in many ways. Poor investment decisions abound. In retrospect, some Polish steel projects and a number of other Polish investments never were viable for a variety of reasons.

Projections of the future are often wrong. Supply-demand situations and prices may change dramatically after investment decisions are made; some oil drilling and mining investments made when prices appeared headed ever upward went sour when prices turned down. Loans from commercial banks are at interest rates that "float"; that is, they are adjusted periodically to reflect international market rates. Thus loans taken out when real interest rates were low (or even negative because of the effects of inflation) may become impossible to service when nominal interest rates rise well above inflation rates.

Since international borrowers must export to earn the foreign currency to service their debt, they are subject to global economic conditions that may unexpectedly affect export markets. Global recessions, for example, not only may cut the volume of LDC exports but may lower the unit prices of many primary commodity export items. Protectionist actions may close anticipated export markets. It is also possible that, for any number of reasons, the borrower may be unable to make imported equipment and technology work properly. The labor force or infrastructure of a developing economy, for example, may not be able adequately to support new production technologies.

Moreover, borrowing has often been to fund consumption rather than investment. Still more often, borrowing has been to compensate for capital flight. Unlike the United States, LDCs cannot borrow in their own currencies; most LDC borrowing is denominated in dollars, and the borrowers may be adversely affected by changes in the exchange rate. If their currencies depreciate against the dollar, larger amounts of earnings in the domestic currency and larger quantities of goods in real terms may be required to buy a given amount of dollars.

Borrowing and debt servicing follow an inevitable resource flow cycle. In the beginning, international lending allows trade deficits and real resource transfers to LDC borrowers and employment-generating surpluses to developed country creditors. But as debt grows larger and interest payments increase, a larger and larger portion of new borrowing may be needed to fund interest payments. Real resource transfers to the borrower diminish, as do the export surpluses of creditor countries. Then at some point creditors may lose confidence in the borrower, and new loans dry up. Borrowers must then run trade surpluses to service their debt. Real resource transfers are from borrower to creditor, and creditor nations must then accept trade deficits.

In those instances in which the borrower successfully develops its industrial capacity, new borrowing narrows and then ceases, with the result that debt servicing and debt reduction also force trade deficits on creditor nations.

CAUSES OF THE DEBT BUILDUP

The rapid rise in petroleum prices during the 1970s was a key factor in the emergence of the LDC debt problem. The large oil price hikes, particularly those in 1973 and 1979, created both the need and the means for much LDC borrowing. Rising petroleum prices dramatically increased the oil import bills of non-oil LDCs, who were left with the choice of borrowing or cutting back their development to meet higher oil prices.

At the same time, borrowing by non-oil LDCs was made possible because Western banks—flush with cash deposited by newly rich OPEC countries—were eager to "recycle" these funds to borrowers. Eagerness to lend was also initially fueled by a contraction in loan demand in many industrialized country markets caused by the global recession.

Many non-oil LDCs chose to increase their borrowing to meet their current problems. Some oil exporting LDCs—for example, Mexico, Nigeria, and Venezuela—also went on borrowing binges, attempting to speed the development of their economies and more rapidly boost living standards. In large measure, their willingness to borrow was based on a belief that oil price rises would continue and would provide them with ever-increasing oil export income in later years.

Another factor in the LDC debt buildup was expansive OECD monetary and fiscal policies implemented to counter the depressing effects of oil price hikes on economic growth. These policies fostered excessively optimistic projections of LDC debt servicing capacity, encouraging lenders and borrowers alike to engage in credit excesses. These policies also lowered interest rates to a point where "real"—that is, inflation-adjusted—interest rates were well below nominal rates and sometimes negative, making borrowing more attractive.

THE BEGINNING OF THE DEBT CRISIS

Rapid growth of LDC debt from a relatively low base posed few problems as long as world interest rates remained low and OECD economies continued their strong growth. By the late 1970s, however, global inflation rates were rising and industrial countries began to tighten money and credit to cool off an overheated world economy. Real interest rates escalated and turned sharply positive; that is, nominal interest rates rose well above rates of inflation.

Rising interest rates slowed OECD economic growth. An OECD recession beginning in 1981 depressed demand and prices for many LDC non-oil exports, especially primary products important in LDC exports.

Meanwhile, spending by some oil-rich LDCs had gotten out of hand. The need for foreign exchange—fueled by excessive government spending and the printing of money—increasingly outstripped oil revenues. Some LDCs, mostly in Asia, implemented belt-tightening actions to restrain demand for foreign exchange and to strengthen exports. Most notably, local currencies in some Asian countries were devalued sharply against industrial country currencies in order to constrain import demand, discourage capital flight, and promote a shift of domestic production away from local consumption and toward exports.

But many other LDCs—both hard-hit non-oil LDCs and free-spending oil rich nations—were reluctant, for political reasons, to squeeze consumption. Instead, these countries sought to defer adjustment by escalating borrowing from commercial banks.

Industrialized country banks—hoping for some improvement in the world economic climate and clinging to the belief that "countries, unlike companies, can't go bankrupt"—initially accommodated growing LDC loan demands. Growth of the already large debt continued to accelerate. External obligations of the principal debtor countries grew dramatically from 1979 to the end of 1981, reaching $532 billion.

A key factor fueling debt growth was attempts by many LDCs to keep their exchange rates unrealistically high in the face of strong domestic inflationary pressures. Imports were kept as cheap as possible to benefit domestic consumption. But overvalued currencies discouraged exports, sucked in imports, and drained foreign exchange.

Some LDCs squandered billions of dollars in efforts to support their currencies through exchange market interventions. As the real cost of dollars expressed in LDC currencies continued to fall, capital flight—a long-standing problem—accelerated, adding to borrowing requirements and future interest payments without contributing to either industrial capacity or higher per capita living standards.

By mid-1982 banker confidence was beginning to crack. The LDC debt was spiraling out of control, growing at unsustainable rates. Creditor banks increasingly realized that much new LDC borrowing was for non-productive purposes—mainly to finance interest payments or capital flight. New debt was being piled on top of old without augmenting export capacity—the key to future export earnings and debt repayment.

With creditor confidence waning, an increasing number of LDCs found it more and more difficult to arrange new borrowings. As credit dried up, LDCs were forced to draw on remaining foreign exchange reserves to sustain import levels and keep up interest payments. Their liquid reserves plummeted. The stage was set for crisis.

Mexico in August 1982 became the first major LDC to announce that it could no longer meet its debt service obligations. Over the ensuing year, Mexico's lead was followed by Brazil, Argentina, and most of the rest of Latin America. Other LDCs—The Philippines, Nigeria, Yugoslavia, and others—also ran into payment problems.

DEBT CONTROL STRATEGY

The prospect of massive LDC defaults sent shock waves through the global banking system, spurring unprecedented international cooperation among all affected parties—commercial banks, LDC governments, industrial country governments and central banks, and the International Monetary Fund and World Bank. The result was a flexible, case-by-case international debt management strategy that was applied, with some modifications, to virtually every LDC financial emergency from 1982 until implementation of the Brady Plan in 1989. In "conventional" approaches to debt management, debt is not forgiven. Rather, debt payments are restructured in a way that preserves the original value of bank claims on the borrower but recognizes the debtor's current inability to meet prior payment schedules. In situations in which LDC debtors have exhausted their credit and face default, "involuntary loans" from commercial banks have been arranged under pressure from industrial governments. These loans are often supplemented by various forms of IMF lending or other forms of official credits.

The Baker Plan, which surfaced in 1985, basically institutionalized and made more explicit the earlier ad hoc U.S. government procedures. It sought internal adjustments by debtor countries to aid economic growth (for example, trade and investment liberalization and reduced government regulation of economic activity) in exchange for continued financing by commercial banks and international financial institutions. Thus the goal of the Baker Plan and its ad hoc predecessors was to slow the rate of debt accumulation of LDCs while they built export capabilities. The idea was to buy time so that debtor export earnings could catch up with their debt service obligations.

The theory was that as debt service payments once again became manageable, lender confidence would return and LDCs would gradually regain normal access to international bank loans. In addition, improving conditions would motivate the return of flight capital to debtor countries and new investment in their economies. Similarly, improving conditions would attract foreign direct investment. The strategy recognized that until debtors can regain access to normal market-oriented voluntary bank lending, a return of flight capital, and increased foreign direct investment, LDCs would have to be kept afloat with involuntary bank loans arranged by industrial country governments.

Accomplishments of the Debt Strategies

In March 1989 the Baker Plan was, in effect, supplanted by the Brady Plan. The Brady Plan, for the first time in any official scheme, set a role for limited debt forgiveness for some of the biggest and some of the poorest borrowers. Under the plan commercial banks would simultaneously pare down the borrowers' obligations on some loans and lend new money, easing the burdens of some borrowers and providing them new credit. As with the Baker Plan, creditors' actions were to be conditioned on economic reforms by the debtors.

Aided by declining global interest rates and a pickup in OECD economic growth, the international debt management strategies have scored some important successes. First, the global economic and financial systems have been tested by the LDC debt problem, but major difficulties have been averted. Although growth

Table 10–1
Total 1987 External Debt, Selected Market Borrowing Countries and Highly Indebted Countries

Market Borrowing Countries		Highly Indebted Countries	
Country	$ Billion Debt	Country	$ Billion Debt
Algeria	23.5	Argentina	59.2
Cameroon	5.2	Bolivia	5.1
Ger. Dem. Rep.	20.8	Brazil	121.0
Greece	20.3	Chile	21.8
Hungary	17.7	Colombia	17.1
India	55.8	Costa Rica	4.5
Indonesia	52.6	Ecuador	10.7
Korea	35.6	Ivory Coast	12.4
Malaysia	22.9	Jamaica	3.9
Peoples Republic		Mexico	107.6
of China	36.2	Morocco	19.8
Pakistan	16.6	Nigeria	29.2
Portugal	19.2	Peru	17.5
Thailand	18.9	Philippines	28.7
Tunisia	7.4	Uruguay	5.5
Turkey	38.3	Venezuela	33.5
		Yugoslavia	22.9
Total	390.9		520.7

Source: The Institute of International Finance, Washington, D.C.

in a number of debtor countries contracted sharply in 1982 and 1983, most have returned to positive economic growth since then. Also, agricultural output in some key debtor countries has responded to economic reforms, reducing dependence on food imports. Finally, current account deficits have been cut substantially and debt growth has slowed appreciably since 1982.

Nevertheless, severe problems remain for a number of LDC debtor countries, which differ greatly in their financial situations. Some are coping successfully and can obtain further voluntary credit from banks. The World Bank terms these nations "market borrowing countries" (Table 10–1). Others, which the World Bank classifies as "highly indebted," continue to obtain new credits only through special arrangements and usually on the condition that they will implement further economic reforms.[2]

Restraining LDC debt growth has required sharp and sustained reductions in LDC current account deficits, the combined balance on interest payments, other services, and merchandise trade. This has been essential to reducing the rate of debt accumulation because annual current account deficits continuously pile new debt on top of existing debt. Slashing LDC current account deficits means that LDCs must run sustained, unprecedentedly large merchandise trade surpluses. No other component of their current accounts can be squeezed enough to achieve a marked slowdown in debt growth.

The debt strategy intended that LDCs should increasingly achieve required trade surpluses through export expansion, not by import contraction. This would allow them to maintain the imports they require for growth but continue to restrict debt growth. For this strategy to be successful, markets in industrial countries must accept steadily expanding LDC exports.

Debt Strategy Problems

Despite some accomplishments, the various international debt management strategies have not met their original goals and face continuing difficulties. Economic reforms have lagged in many debtor countries. The current account balances of many have been improved primarily by import cuts, not by export expansion. Domestic investment has generally been below requirements for strong economic growth. Most have not experienced a substantial return of flight capital, and direct investment inflows have fallen far short of expectations. Moreover, debt strategies are highly vulnerable to an industrial country recession or an increase in interest rates. Either could quickly trigger serious problems in meeting debt servicing requirements.

A narrowing of U.S. trade deficits also poses potential difficulties for LDC debtors. Shrinking U.S. deficits could cut LDC exports to the United States, and the complementary shrinking surpluses in some other countries could lead to cuts in their imports from debtor LDCs.

Exports of most of the highly indebted LDCs grew only modestly during most of the 1980s.[3] Exports in 1986 of seventeen "highly indebted" LDC debtor countries to Industrial West (IW) countries were only 1 percent above the 1982 level, and estimated exports for 1987 were only about $4 billion above 1980.[4]

Export performance by most of the debtor group has been more unfavorable than indicated by group summary statistics. This was despite steady economic growth in the IW countries after 1983. Moreover, this weak performance contrasts sharply with that of the Asian NICs, who have posted very strong export growth. When Mexico and Brazil are separated from the other debtors in the group of seventeen highly indebted countries, the weak performance of remaining countries is revealed. In 1986 exports to the IW countries by the other fifteen debtor countries were almost 6 percent below 1982 and 27 percent below 1980.

Disappointing export performance has, in most cases, prevented a significant recovery in imports by most of the seventeen highly indebted LDCs. Their imports from IW nations were down in 1986 by 14 percent from 1982 and were 23 percent below 1981. The imports of these LDCs from the United States in 1987 were about 2 percent below 1982 and 23 percent below 1981.

Falling earnings from oil exports—a key source of revenue for countries like

Mexico, Venezuela, and Nigeria—had been an important factor in poor performance by the oil-exporting countries during much of the 1980s. Lackluster demand for other non-oil commodities during much of the decade was also important for several debtors. Though price recovery occurred in some commodities, a key factor depressing commodity export earnings has been sustained weakness in commodity prices, stemming from both slack demand and excess global supplies of many commodities. Persistent weak demand, especially for metals and other raw materials, stems partly from technological advances that are causing some displacements of traditional LDC exports by synthetics and other substitutes.

One bright spot for high debt country exports has been escalating sales of manufactured goods. During 1982–86 debtor country exports of manufactures to the IW countries rose from $20 billion to $33 billion. This growth was impressive, but the improvement was mostly by Brazil and Mexico. Together they accounted for 79 percent of the growth. High debtor country exports of manufactures grew by 68 percent during the 1980–86 period, while those of Eastern Europe (Bulgaria, Czechoslovakia, the German Democratic Republic, Hungary, Poland, and Romania) remained essentially unchanged. Exports of the Asian NICs to the IW during the same period, however, increased by 106 percent.

As was the case with the major trade surpluses among developed countries, LDC exports to the IW countries have been highly dependent on the U.S. market. In 1986 the U.S. market absorbed about 49 percent of total high debt LDC exports to the IW, $44 billion compared with $33 billion by the European Community (EC) and $7 billion by Japan.

The high debt LDCs' dependence on the United States as a market for their manufactures exports is even greater. Between 1980 and 1986 U.S. imports of manufactures from the high debt LDCs rose by 119 percent, or $11 billion. During the same period, the EC increased its imports by only 23 percent, or $1.8 billion, while Japan's imports from the group declined modestly, to a total of only $1.6 billion. Put another way, the U.S. market absorbed 80 percent of the 1980–86 growth in the exports of high debt LDCs to the IW countries.

The heavy dependence of LDC debtors on the U.S. market means that large reductions in the U.S. trade deficit could have a major impact on the exports of Mexico, Brazil, and other debtors. With LDC exports to third countries also coming under pressure, many LDC currencies are tied to the U.S. dollar. Thus to the extent that U.S. trade performance improves as a result of dollar depreciation against the currencies of other developed countries, LDC exports to those countries would also seem to gain the advantages of a relative depreciation. But this assumes that these developed country markets would be open to increased LDC exports.

The worst case scenario would be one in which the U.S. trade deficit is narrowed by deep U.S. import cuts. In this scenario, debtor exports to the United States—as well as exports of the industrialized countries—would likely decline. Moreover, debtor exports to Europe and Japan could be hurt because those

industrial economies—themselves somewhat reliant on American import demand—would be struggling to overcome the dampening effects of U.S. import
cutbacks, possibly taking measures to preclude a surge in imports from the LDCs.

Industrial country protectionist actions against imports from LDC debtors,
however, would be counterproductive. Industrial country restraints on imports
from debtor countries simply force those debtor countries to make parallel one-
for-one reductions in their imports from industrialized countries. Thus the effect
of protectionist actions is to depress total trade levels—as well as global economic
growth—without correcting trade imbalances.

OUTLOOK FOR THE LDC DEBT PROBLEM

There is no realistic chance of an early resolution of the LDC debt problem.
For the foreseeable future, to service their debt, most problem LDC debtors must
continue to run trade surpluses while their external debt continues to grow. Some
countries—mostly in Latin America—are so deeply in debt and their economies
are performing so poorly that they will have great difficulty even in paying
interest on still accumulating debt. Their problems are well beyond the solution
of some kind of "jump start" that could be provided by modest additional loans.

Neither is any kind of debt forgiveness likely to be a solution. Debt forgiveness
for one country would increase the pleas of others for similar treatment and
would do little to increase the credit available to any. The Brady Plan is not
likely to trigger either significant debt forgiveness or new lending by commercial
banks who see pouring good money after bad as foolish and costly. Voluntary
lending by private-sector sources occurs largely based on favorable evaluations
of the performance and prospects of borrower economies. Involuntary lending
by banks reflects unfavorable analyses of performance and prospects that will
not be fundamentally improved by debt forgiveness.

Return to Latin America of the billions of dollars of flight capital sent abroad
by its nationals could provide a major source of new investment in several Latin
LDC debtor countries. But economic policies, performance, and prospects in
the debtor countries are not motivating a return of such capital.

Nor does there appear to be any source of major new official lending to the
most troubled debtors. Neither developed country governments nor international
organizations have large amounts of loan capital available. The United States
could make a substantial contribution to LDC debtors by pursuing policies that
would reduce U.S. interest rates. Such reductions would, in turn, lower the
interest rates faced by the LDCs. In fact, however, the growth and creditwor-
thiness of LDC debtor countries now depend primarily on their own economic
policies and their willingness to take on difficult economic reforms. But unfortunately, economic reforms usually require years to show effects, and the normal
course is for things to get worse before they get better. Even when reform
programs are successful, they are usually prefaced by increased austerity, a
difficult prospect for fragile governments.

Without the ability to borrow significant amounts to finance internal investment, the only alternative for debtor countries is to pay for needed investments
by further reducing their private and public consumption—to make short-term
sacrifices for the prospect of long-term gains. This is the same prescription the
United States has so far been unable to implement to stop its trade deficits and
external borrowing. But it is an even more difficult prescription in nations that
are poor and have experienced negative or low economic growth for several
years.

The outlook then is for continued difficulty, with some modest portions of
debt swapped for equity, continued "writing down" (but not forgiveness) of the
original value of loans by banks, some debt sold off by banks (sometimes to the
debtors) at market values well below face value, and continued, but shrinking,
involuntary lending by banks. The hope is one of "muddling through" or, at
least, buying more time for banks to strengthen their balance sheets against
further write-offs.

In the meantime, rising U.S. interest rates or increasing international protectionism will remain as potential threats to the ability of debtors to meet their
payments. Probably the most important contribution the United States can make
is to cut its budget deficit in a manner that increases U.S. saving. This, as
mentioned earlier, would tend to lower the U.S. interest rates that so directly
affect interest rates on LDC debt. At the same time, however, declining U.S.
trade deficits will likely impede LDC exports, both to the United States and to
third countries whose trade accounts may be squeezed. Declining oil prices would
help the balances of some LDCs but hurt those of others. Major debt defaults
and escalating crises are continuing threats. Yet there appears to be no opportunity
for a major breakthrough—no more viable strategy than "muddling through."
In such an environment, LDC debtors are unlikely to become rapidly expanding
markets for U.S. or other industrialized country exports in the foreseeable future.
They must continue to restrict imports and push exports to service their debts.
Neither the Baker Plan nor the successor Brady Plan can markedly change these
fundamentals in the near term.

SUMMARY

• International borrowing by LDCs can speed the pace of their growth and
development, but there are many ways in which plans can go awry.

• The rapid rise in petroleum prices in the 1970s was a key factor in the
development of the LDC debt crisis that matured in the early 1980s. High oil
prices provided a need for non-oil LDCs to borrow more. Expectations that oil
prices would continue to increase provided a rationale for some oil rich LDCs
to borrow to develop oil resources and to speed the growth of their economies
in other areas.

• The extreme liquidity of financial markets resulting from the large earnings
of many oil rich countries created a need to "recycle" oil earnings. It also

created the means to finance loans to LDCs that might not have been considered good credit risks had financial markets been less liquid.

• The LDC debt crisis came to a head in 1982 after high interest rates had raised the cost of debt servicing, and a global recession had impaired LDC exports.

• Overvalued currencies were a key factor in the failure of several LDCs to use their borrowings effectively. Overvalued currencies stimulated imports of many LDCs, held back their exports, and motivated capital flight.

• Much LDC debt growth was caused not by imports used to develop production capabilities, but by imports used to support high levels of consumption and to finance capital flight—the flight of capital from the home country to safe havens, where owners could preserve the value of their capital.

• Capital flight from LDCs was one important source of the large flows of capital into the United States during the 1980s and thus helped finance U.S. trade deficits and keep U.S. dollar exchange rates high.

• The fundamental debt control strategy has been a case-by-case approach of restructuring payments and extending some new credit to distressed debtors in exchange for an agreement to lower trade and investment barriers and reduce government regulation in attempts to improve economic performance.

• Where debtors have exhausted their credit and face default, involuntary loans by commercial banks have been arranged under pressure from industrial country governments, often supplemented by various forms of official lending.

• The fundamental goal of the debt strategy has been to slow the rate of LDC debt accumulation while debtors build their export capabilities; that is, to buy time so that debtor export earnings can catch up with debt service obligations.

• The coming narrowing of U.S. trade and current account deficits could hit LDC exports. Many LDCs are highly dependent on U.S. markets. As industrial country surpluses with the U.S. narrow, their imports from LDCs could also be restrained.

• There is no realistic chance of an early resolution of the LDC debt problem. Debt relief plans implemented at the expense of banks would probably result in curtailing new loans. On the other hand, government-financed reserve plans may be seen as bailouts of the lending banks and as rewarding selected debtors.

• "Muddling through" will continue. Some modest portions of debt will be swapped for equity, writing down of the book value of some debt will continue, and some debt will be sold off at discounted rates. Debt forgiveness, however, will not be a widely accepted or a particularly helpful alternative.

• Significantly improved U.S. trade balances with troubled Latin American debtors are an unlikely source of the improved U.S. trade performance required to narrow U.S. current account deficits.

NOTES

1. See "LDC Debt Reduction: A Critical Appraisal," *World Financial Markets* (Morgan Guaranty Bank, New York City), December 1988, 9. Capital flight cannot be precisely

quantified. Earlier, in 1986, Morgan Guaranty estimated total capital flight for eighteen debtor countries at $198 billion for the 1976–85 period, a large portion of their $451 billion increase in gross debt over the same period. See "LDC Capital Flight," *World Financial Markets* (Morgan Guaranty Bank, New York City), March 1986, 13.

2. *World Debt Tables, 1987–88* (Washington, D.C.: World Bank, 1988), Table 12.1.

3. This section draws heavily on the data and thoughts contained in William F. Kolarik, *Exports of Financially Distressed LDC Debtors to the United States and Industrial West: Trends, Outlook, Implications* (Washington, D.C.: International Trade Administration, U.S. Department of Commerce, July 1988).

4. "Industrial West," as defined in this chapter, is a twenty-two country group that consists of Australia, Austria, Canada, Finland, Japan, New Zealand, Norway, Sweden, Switzerland, the United States, and the twelve-nation European Community.

PART IV

COPING WITH THE FUTURE

The years ahead promise many difficult problems for U.S. policymakers. Reducing and eliminating U.S. current account deficits and trading partner surpluses while maintaining good world economic growth rates will pose difficult challenges. Actions to improve U.S. productivity and competitiveness are likely to be even more difficult. Successfully coping with these and many more critical international economic issues will require a number of major policy changes.

Chapter 11 outlines the basic policy alternatives for dealing with the trade deficit and international competitiveness problems and the bias toward the use of trade policies to solve problems resulting more fundamentally from flawed U.S. macroeconomic policies.

Dealing effectively with the plethora of difficult international economic issues in the 1990s will strain U.S. abilities. Chapter 12 notes shortcomings in the organization of the U.S. government for international economic policy making and suggests changes.

Broad-based recommendations for coping with the future are spelled out in Chapter 13.

Chapter 11

Policy Alternatives

The United States in the 1990s faces an imposing array of very tough international economic problems. At the forefront of these problems are the trade deficits and international competitiveness. The trade deficits pose an immediate, difficult and risky problem. The challenge is to gradually narrow the U.S. trade deficits and the complementary surpluses of some trading partners without major disruptions of the world economy and without triggering increased protectionism that could invite trade wars. U.S. trade deficits must be narrowed because continued large deficits and foreign borrowing could, in time, lead foreign lenders to see U.S. investments as less attractive. A sudden change in lender attitudes could trigger rapidly rising U.S. interest rates, a U.S. recession, and major disruptions for the world economy. Even a more gradual withdrawal of foreign lending could lead to a U.S. recession and global economic problems if foreign lending shrinks more rapidly than the U.S. need to borrow. Major global economic disruptions are risky because they provide a climate in which protectionism is more likely to escalate and trade wars may begin.

The challenge then is to gradually reduce U.S. borrowing needs while maintaining good U.S. and foreign economic growth rates. But even if U.S. policies are successful in gradually trimming the need for imported capital there will still be risks. A slowing of the U.S. economy, increased concern about the accumulating foreign debt, and other factors could result in increased protectionism in the United States, perhaps including a resort to managed trade. Retaliatory actions by trading partners could follow, leading to "trade wars" that could do very serious damage to the trading system and the world economy.

Trimming the U.S. trade deficits will also cause problems for trading partners. A shrinking of their trade surpluses with the United States will require difficult adjustments in their economies. These problems also could lead them to protectionist actions that would increase the risk of trade wars.

Simultaneously, the United States must also take steps to improve its international competitiveness. Thus the task of U.S. policymakers is not simply one of achieving a "soft landing"—a gradual decrease in trade deficits. Rather, it is doing so while achieving sufficient economic growth and productivity gains to permit rising, rather than declining, U.S. living standards. The alternatives—closing the trade deficit through a recession or slowed economic growth or a reliance on continuing depreciation of the dollar—would result in a politically and economically costly decline in U.S. living standards and international competitiveness.

Simultaneously improving U.S. international competitiveness while narrowing U.S. trade deficits and the complementary surpluses of some trading partners is a difficult problem. Maintaining an open world trading system and good global economic growth also pose unparalleled challenges. American political leadership will be hard pressed to sort out and implement those policies that are in the best long-term interests of the nation. Refraining from actions that may have popular appeal but would be counterproductive will be difficult. It will be tempting, for example, to seek quick fixes for trade and competitiveness problems by "managed trade" or through other actions that do not address the root causes of U.S. problems. Some trading partners will likely have difficulties in adjusting to a shrinking of their trade surpluses, and their reactions to aggressive U.S. trade policy initiatives may pose great risks. In this difficult environment successfully transiting the 1990s will require informed policies that deal with the root causes of U.S. trade deficits and competitiveness—not just the symptoms of both problems.

TRADE DEFICITS AND COMPETITIVENESS: DIFFERENT PROBLEMS

Trade deficits and international competitiveness pose related but different problems for policymakers. Understanding the differences and linkages between the two is essential to effective policy making.

The trade deficits are a dangerous problem but one that is, nevertheless, transitory. No nation can borrow indefinitely at rates that raise debt relative to its GNP. If the United States does not act to reduce its large budget and trade deficits, international capital markets will—sooner or later—shrink lending to the United States, forcing an involuntary reduction in the trade deficits. The temporary, self-correcting nature of U.S. trade deficits does not imply, however, that there is no cause for immediate concern and action. A narrowing of the trade deficits forced by foreign unwillingness to continue lending could cause major U.S. and global recessions, recessions that would severely damage the U.S. and world economies, with lasting effects on U.S. international competitiveness. Moreover, extended borrowing will continue to enlarge the U.S. debtor position and result in growing debt servicing costs, impairing future U.S. living standards.

The United States and its trading partners should adopt policies that will prevent the precipitous changes in international capital movements and rapid shrinking of the U.S. trade deficits that market forces otherwise might bring about. The right policies will help to narrow U.S. trade deficits sooner and more smoothly than would otherwise be the case. They could also slow the U.S. accumulation of foreign debt, hold down its negative effects on future U.S. living standards and international competitiveness, and lessen the risks of severe global adjustment problems.

The international competitiveness problem—maintaining rates of advance in U.S. living standards that compare favorably with those of other advanced nations—differs from the trade deficit problem in several ways. First, declining competitiveness is neither temporary nor self-correcting. Though staying abreast of foreign competition is a relatively new challenge for the United States, it is not just a temporary difficulty but one that will endure and intensify. More and more nations—many of them low-wage developing countries—are saving and investing at rates that outpace those of the United States. They are acquiring modern technology and manufacturing skills. In this new, increasingly competitive environment, it will be ever more difficult for the United States to generate the export surpluses needed to service accumulated foreign debt and pay for growing oil imports and other vital import needs. It will be especially difficult to do so while trading on terms (dollar exchange rates) that will allow strong gains in real per capita incomes.

The U.S. competitiveness problem is not likely to precipitate a sudden U.S. or global crisis. By way of analogy, the United States is less likely to suffer a competitiveness "heart attack" than an industrial "hardening of the arteries." Declines in U.S. competitiveness will be slow and imperceptible on a day-to-day basis. There will be no monthly accounting of competitiveness performance similar to the monthly trade balance figures.

The trade deficit and competitiveness problems also differ in their tractability. A relatively few macroeconomic policy actions, which lie mostly within federal government control, will probably eliminate the trade deficits. The task may require only a few years and will be measured, year-to-year, by an improving trade balance.

Unfortunately, however, improving the nation's productivity and living standard growth rates is a much more difficult and longer-term task, requiring a complex set of interrelated actions. Many of these actions lie outside the norm of federal government involvement. There are few "quick fixes" that will have any significant near-term effect on the nation's productivity and competitiveness. Not only may steps to improve international competitiveness take a long time to take effect, but results will be more difficult to link to policy initiatives taken many years earlier. Moreover, success will require sustained efforts, not only by the federal government but by state governments, labor unions, businesses, and other segments of U.S. society. Patience, a consensus on the need for action, agreement on policies, and long time horizons—elements often scarce in the

U.S. political environment—will be essential if the nation is to implement policies and practices to enhance productivity, improve living standards, and strengthen U.S. competitiveness.

These differences of visibility, time horizons, and tractability are not, however, the most important reasons for separating the trade deficit and competitiveness problems. Distinguishing between them is important because they require policy prescriptions that differ. Some actions will clearly help both to shrink the trade deficits and to improve international competitiveness. Others may affect one problem but have little influence on the other. Most importantly, some policies may ease one problem but exacerbate the other. That is, some actions that could shrink the trade deficits in the short term may actually reduce U.S. international competitiveness in the longer term.

The difficulties of dealing with the competitiveness problem make it an issue that policymakers are not eager to grapple with. Without a clear but hard-to-achieve understanding of the more insidious and difficult competitiveness problem, it may well be neglected, with attention and policies being directed primarily to trade balances. Indeed, given the less visible and more difficult nature of the competitiveness problem, there is significant risk that the trade deficits will be eliminated without improving—and perhaps at the expense of—the U.S. competitiveness position.

Thus how competitiveness is defined and perceived is important. It affects how the U.S. trade and competitiveness problems will be identified, the remedies that will be sought, and the policies that will be applied.

AVAILABLE POLICY TOOLS

The trade deficit and competitiveness problems are different but interrelated. Policies applied to affect one will almost always affect the other to some degree. Nevertheless, categorizing the major policy tools applicable to each is useful.

The key policy tools in dealing with the trade deficits, conceptually illustrated in Figure 11–1, include U.S. fiscal and monetary policy, progress on resolution of the LDC debt problem, and better coordination of monetary, fiscal and economic growth policies among the industrialized countries. Fiscal policy determines the size of the government budget deficit and influences the critical relationship between national saving and investment. Monetary policy influences interest rates and hence domestic demand and the dollar exchange rate. Together, monetary and fiscal policy have powerful effects on the direction of net international capital flows. These flows make a nation a net borrower or lender, a net goods and services importer or exporter.

Resolving the LDC debt problem could encourage capital outflows to debtor countries—both the return of flight capital and new outflows from creditor countries—and help expand U.S. exports to debtor countries. Resolution of the LDC debt problem, however, is primarily dependent on debtor country macroeconomic policies, not on U.S. and other developed country actions. The macroeconomic

Figure 11–1
Relevant Policy Tools for the Trade Deficit and International Competitiveness Problems

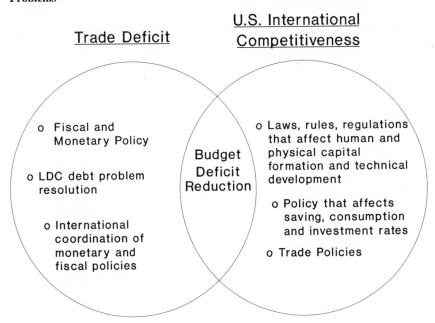

Trade Deficit

U.S. International Competitiveness

o Fiscal and
   Monetary Policy

o LDC debt problem
   resolution

o International
   coordination of
   monetary and
   fiscal policies

Budget
Deficit
Reduction

o Laws, rules, regulations
   that affect human and
   physical capital
   formation and technical
   development

o Policy that affects
   saving, consumption
   and investment rates

o Trade Policies

policies of developed country trading partners also influence the growth rates of their economies, their saving and investment patterns, and the resulting size and direction of their net international capital flows. They also affect their demands for U.S. exports.

Less important to immediate international trade and capital flows, but crucial to longer term U.S. international competitiveness, are those U.S. laws and regulations that affect human and physical capital formation and technology development in the United States. Effective trade policies also play an important, though more limited, role in enhancing competitiveness.

Both problems will be ameliorated by sensibly achieved reductions in the U.S. budget deficit. The budget deficits have been a critical factor in generating the trade deficits. Continuing trade deficits not only pose immediate risks but are impairing future competitiveness by accumulating debt that must be serviced in the future. They also increase current interest rates to levels that restrain current investment.

The effects of tax policy on the trade deficits and international competitiveness may differ. Some actions that could shrink the budget and trade deficits would hurt—rather than aid—long-term competitiveness. For example, tax law changes that increase tax revenues but discourage private-sector saving and investment in human and physical capital will impair international competitiveness.

Similarly, budget cuts that reduce government-financed research and development and investment in the nation's infrastructure and human capital could quickly narrow the current budget and trade deficits but jeopardize future international competitiveness.

Improved U.S. trade performance and international competitiveness cannot be achieved by a few simple policy actions. Instead, many significant and difficult changes will be required. Several key policy alternatives are examined in this chapter. There are, however, many impediments to effective policy making.

COMPETITIVENESS AND NATIONAL POLICY MAKING

Although important, microeconomic factors, such as foreign trade barriers in individual product lines, "dumping" in U.S. markets, and other foreign and U.S. trade practices, are not the fundamental causes of either the huge U.S. trade deficits of recent years or the relative decline of U.S. international competitiveness. Differences in U.S. and foreign macroeconomic policies are primarily responsible. For a number of reasons, however, U.S. policymakers have not focused on the macroeconomic factors that determine trade flows and enhance productivity growth and competitiveness. Instead, attention has focused on trade policy issues. In effect, policymakers have sought easy, popular, but ineffective solutions.

The Limitations of Trade Policy

Trade policies—the laws, regulations, procedures, practices, and international agreements that govern U.S. and foreign participation in international trade—include:

- General Agreement on Tariffs and Trade (GATT) negotiations
- Market access initiatives
- Antidumping and countervailing actions
- Export incentives and disincentives

The vast majority of trade analysts agree that trade balances are not determined by trade policy actions but primarily by other macroeconomic factors (Chapter 4). Trade policy actions are often justified as a means to improve trade performance. In fact, they normally have little impact on trade balances.

Over the longer term, however, trade policy initiatives may improve the efficiency of the international trading system. GATT negotiations, for example, can reduce barriers to exports of both goods and services. All parties can benefit by arriving at more efficient trading patterns not distorted by tariffs and other protective devices. It is also possible that the outcome may marginally improve U.S. performance relative to its major competitors. This may improve U.S.

international competitiveness. But major U.S. competitiveness or trade balance gains will not result from successful GATT negotiations, since agreements normally involve concessions by all parties. Typically, U.S. concessions will be traded for foreign concessions, usually with the goal of neutralizing effects on trade balances.

Similarly, although potentially important, the likely effects of bilateral market opening or market access initiatives, such as reducing specific individual foreign trade barriers, should not be overrated. In a fast-changing world of new technologies and products, slow-paced bilateral negotiations directed at lowering barriers in individual products can generate much publicity. They often cause a great deal of animosity but have little effect on trade balances and the U.S. competitive position.

It has become widely accepted that foreign trade barriers may account for as much as 10 to 15 percent of recent U.S. trade deficits. Even that amount would represent only a relatively small portion of the deficits. There is, however, no identifiable source of empirical data or research behind this statistic. Nor is there any practical way of quantifying accurately the effects of foreign trade barriers, if any, on U.S. trade balances. When foreign barriers to imports are removed, the benefits may go to other competitors, not the United States. Moreover, the United States has imposed its own barriers in several products, including autos, textiles, apparel, steel, machine tools, and sugar. Statistics purporting to quantify the effects of foreign barriers on U.S. exports ignore the effects of similar U.S. import barriers.

Effective enforcement of antidumping and countervailing duty regulations is desirable. It can protect individual U.S. firms and industries from "unfair" competition. International viewpoints on what is unfair may vary, however. Also, the estimates and calculations made to quantify foreign producers' costs and foreign government subsidies are, at best, highly tenuous and the methodologies arguable. In the end, the effects of these kinds of actions on trade balances are likely to be minimal and the long-term effects on U.S. competitiveness uncertain. Effective policy making should accept the limitations of trade policy actions directed at foreign behavior.

U.S. firms are often said to be "not export oriented" but preoccupied with the large U.S. market. A series of government-sponsored export exhortation programs have tried to make U.S. producers more export aware. In time, these programs, such as the Commerce Department's recent "Export Now" program, may have some effect on U.S. exports. But export awareness programs can be only marginally effective. A relatively few large multinational firms make up the dominant portion of U.S. exports, a fact unlikely to change. These companies are thoroughly familiar with foreign markets. Their trading decisions are based on economic factors little influenced by export promotion rhetoric. Major increases in exports depend on changing the economic incentives to export, not on government cheerleading.

There are, however, several U.S. laws and regulations that disadvantage or discourage U.S. exporters. Export control regulations and antitrust constraints are two examples. Minimizing these disincentives could have significant, favorable long-term effects on competitiveness.

Why Trade Policy Is Overemphasized

Changes in trade policy do not offer a significant means of improving U.S. trade performance or international competitiveness. U.S. and foreign macroeconomic policies are the primary determinants of both. Nevertheless, just as lemmings are drawn to the sea, U.S. policymakers are driven to concentrate on microeconomic trade policy issues rather than on macroeconomic factors. Why this predilection to trade policy? There are several reasons.

U.S. international competitiveness is a concept seldom clearly defined and one readily open to confusion. It is not widely understood in the macroeconomic, national living standards terms applied in this book. Instead, there is a natural tendency for most persons to use recent U.S. trade performance—the trade balances—as a measure of competitiveness.

There is also a tendency to measure competitiveness anecdotally, that is, on the basis of the performance of individual firms and industries. Decline or difficulty in a particular industry is equated with declining national competitiveness. Too often this leads to microeconomic solutions designed to help specific firms and industries. The short-term interests of individual firms and industries, however, may differ from the long-term best interests of the nation. How may industry interests differ from those of the nation, and why are policies frequently responsive to shorter term individual industry needs rather than longer term national needs?

The reasons are not hard to identify. The national interest is essentially one of increasing the nation's total income and wealth, of maximizing long-term economic growth and competitiveness for the benefit of all present and future members of the economy. Individual firms have narrower interests and shorter time horizons. They must be concerned about their immediate survival and profitability. From a U.S. firm's perspective, international competitiveness is its ability to sell and profit in international markets or, at a minimum, to compete successfully against foreign firms in the U.S. market. Individual industries— groups of firms in the same kind of business, for example, autos, steel, computers, machine tools—perceive international competitiveness in much the same way. That is, they see themselves as competitive when most firms in the industry are able to compete successfully and to prosper in U.S. and international markets. Since firms and industries must get through today—meeting their payrolls and satisfying creditors and stockholders—to be in business tomorrow, their primary concerns naturally are their own immediate survival and welfare rather than the longer term future of the national economy.

The distinction is important. The survival and profitability of individual firms and industries—their own competitiveness—may be aided in several ways that do not benefit the nation's competitiveness. For example, dollar depreciation, cutting or holding down employee wages, overseas sourcing of production, government subsidies, import quotas, "voluntary" restraints on exports to the United States, and other kinds of import restrictions all may enhance the profits of individual firms and industries and their ability to meet foreign competition, at least in the short term.

These kinds of actions, however, do not normally make the nation as a whole better off. Dollar depreciation increases the cost of imports and means the nation must, in real terms, export a larger amount of goods to pay for a given amount of imports, lowering the purchasing power of U.S. consumers and raising the costs of U.S. producers that depend on imports. Wage cuts also lower the purchasing power of workers. Both actions put downward pressure on the nation's living standards.

Similarly, subsidies granted to weak industries are at the expense of individual taxpayers and other, stronger industries. Likewise, the burden of higher prices generated by quotas and import restrictions must ultimately be borne by other industries and by consumers.

Quotas, subsidies, and other forms of import restrictions are usually only short-term palliatives. They benefit particular industries by reallocating the nation's production, income, investment, and consumption differently and less efficiently than would market forces. Ultimately, this reduces total national output and consumption and lowers the nation's competitiveness. Dollar depreciation benefits all industries competing against foreign-based production and spreads the costs of declining competitiveness widely across the economy. It does not artificially distort the allocation of resources and production within the economy. In itself it does not, however, improve the nation's productivity or its competitiveness as defined in this book.

In short, several kinds of actions taken in the name of competitiveness are most unlikely to improve the nation's overall economic position. To be internationally competitive, the United States must have industries that compete successfully in U.S. and foreign markets without subsidies or special protection. At the same time they must pay good wages, concurrent with a relatively strong dollar and sustainable balances in external accounts.

From a national viewpoint, maintaining and improving international competitiveness requires continuing structural change to stay abreast of never-ending global changes. Indeed, it can be argued that in tomorrow's world economy the most competitive nations will be those that best facilitate and adapt to the continuing process of structural change. This implies that at any time some U.S. industries will be growing. Inevitably, however, others will be shrinking. Maintaining international competitiveness thus can be pleasant for those in expanding industries but a painful process for those in shrinking fields.

Understandably, declining industries and firms are unlikely to welcome a "national" view of international competitiveness that accepts structural change as inevitable. Because change is usually difficult and painful, industries in trouble resist decline. It is natural for them to equate their need to survive with national competitiveness. Typically, hard-pressed industries organize to make their case effectively to the government. Seldom, however, is a strong countering case made for the potential longer term negative effects of protectionist actions on consumers, other producers, and the nation's competitiveness.

From a national viewpoint, the aim of international trade is to increase the nation's total wealth and its living standards. But the trade policy actions needed to deal with foreign competition by individual firms and industries will all too often differ from those needed to enhance the nation's competitiveness. In such situations we might conclude that policymakers would focus on the nation's overall interests, on longer term national welfare, not on the narrower, shorter term interests of individual industries or sectors.

In fact, however, U.S. policy making does not focus on the nation's competitiveness but on the problems of individual industries. There is undue U.S. reliance on trade policy actions that may benefit some groups but that are unlikely to improve either the nation's trade balance or its international competitiveness. Executive and legislative branch trade policy actions that purport to aid the U.S. position are more likely to aid individual industries at the expense of national competitiveness.

Why Competitiveness Is Neglected

Among the factors determining U.S. international competitiveness, "trade policy" is not unlike the tip of an iceberg. An iceberg's tip is visible, gets attention, and catches the prevailing winds. The mass beneath the surface, however, is several times larger and bears the forces of the underlying currents most important in setting the course and speed of the iceberg's flow. In this analogy, the broad range of policies and other factors that influence the development of human and physical capital are the unseen mass beneath the surface—the driving forces in determining the nation's competitiveness.

Nevertheless, policymakers neglect the factors influencing human and physical capital and productivity growth rates. Trade policy issues dominate U.S. international economic policy making, consistently drawing a great deal more attention than the macroeconomic policies that much more strongly affect international competitiveness. Policy making too often involves responses to the complaints of individual firms or industries. Their problem—survival—is easy to understand. It is easier to identify with, is more visible, and attracts more attention than the more complex and seemingly less urgent issues of saving, investment, and capital formation.

Initiatives that would affect human and physical capital are less appealing to policymakers because they are unlikely to show immediate effects. As elected or appointed officials, policymakers typically feel a need to show quick results. Steps to improve productivity have long gestation periods. The results may be hard to measure and to link with specific earlier actions. Moreover, competitiveness expressed in terms of productivity gains and living standard advances is a complex, difficult concept to convey to constituents. Although critically important, productivity gains and capital formation rates are dull and dreary stuff compared to stories about workers displaced by imports. Blaming "foreigners' unfair trade practices" for U.S. problems is likely to be politically more appealing than calling for more U.S. saving and investment.

Immediate, crisis-driven situations also draw more media and public attention than problems with long-time horizons. Actions to deal with foreign trade barriers or to ease the problems of individual industries are likely to involve directly the individuals who have voting power. Active grass-roots movements to raise saving and investment or letter writing campaigns expressing concern about the long-term national interest are unlikely. The changes required to increase investment in human and physical capital and research and development are inherently controversial, and their supporting constituencies are diffused and mostly business oriented. Even though programs to increase capital formation serve a broader national interest, advocacy of policies by business to raise saving and investment will be labeled self-serving by other interest groups with other agendas.

There are, then, many incentives for government policymakers to dwell on microeconomic, industry-oriented trade policy actions that give the appearance of dealing immediately and directly with well-identified, visible trade problems. Without an immediate competitiveness crisis, it will be difficult to stir support for actions that deal with the underlying determinants of international competitiveness.

Most trade policy actions are likely to be ineffective—even counterproductive—in addressing the real determinants of U.S. competitiveness. The greatest cost of the overemphasis on trade policy, however, is that it diverts time and attention away from effective action. Dealing with the tangential, but more immediately visible, issues draws attention away from and substitutes for dealing with the tougher, less visible, but more important issues. For example, enactment of the recent 500-page Omnibus Trade and Competitiveness Act of 1988 consumed two years of legislative and executive branch effort. It has been widely heralded as a major step in improving U.S. competitiveness. In fact, however, the act is dominantly a series of trade policy mandates directed at foreign trade barriers. If successful, it could contribute to modest improvements in the U.S. position. There is, however, very little in the 1988 law that is relevant to the underlying elements that determine the nation's international competitiveness.

FOCUSING ON
MANUFACTURING COMPETITIVENESS

Improving U.S. international competitiveness will require a wide range of actions by the private sector and every level of government. New measures to increase investments in human and physical capital will take a long time to produce results. This makes it very important that programs to improve competitiveness begin by focusing on those elements that offer the fastest and most significant potential payoffs. Although improving human capital and other factors are at least as important as physical capital improvement—perhaps more important—the focus of this book is on the contribution of physical capital. To be most effective and to provide results as rapidly as possible, policies directed at increasing U.S. international competitiveness through physical capital improvement and growth should focus strongly on goods production, particularly on the manufacturing sector.

The manufacturing sector should be at the top of the competitiveness agenda because international trade is now and will continue to be predominantly an exchange of manufactured goods among nations. The United States competes in the world economy primarily through its manufacturing sector. U.S. manufacturing has borne the brunt of increasing foreign competitiveness. Manufacturing is the "swing factor"—the sector in which changes in the size and direction of net international capital flows inevitably are manifested. The huge deterioration during the 1980s in the U.S. trade balance occurred almost entirely in the manufactures trade account. Service industries are not unimportant to the nation's trade performance, and some service industries are affected by changing capital flows. The nation's trade and current account deficits, however, were manifested predominantly in manufactures trade deficits. The United States cannot pay its way in the world economy and continues to run large manufactures trade deficits. The current account deficits will have to be narrowed primarily through an improvement in manufactures trade performance. Indeed, elimination of current account deficits and cessation of foreign borrowing will require substantial manufactures trade surpluses (see Chapter 4).

Improved trade performance by U.S. manufacturers will come about not primarily by the growth of foreign markets but by increasing the U.S. share of U.S. and foreign markets. Gaining an increased share of these markets will require improved price and quality competitiveness. The potential sources of improved price competitiveness are declining wage levels, a declining dollar exchange rate, and productivity gains at rates that compare favorably with those of competitors. Productivity gains—the most desirable means of improved competitiveness—are largely determined by a nation's flow of new investments. But not all new investments are equally beneficial to U.S. competitiveness.

Any investment that improves the productivity of human and physical capital helps to increase U.S. living standards and, to some extent, U.S. international competitiveness. Many service industries, for example, provide inputs to goods-producing industries. Productivity gains in service industries lower the costs of services provided to goods-producing industries. This aids the international price competitiveness of U.S.-based goods production, even if only modestly and indirectly. Improvements in the infrastructure that supports manufacturing and other goods production, such as roads, bridges, communications, and service industries, are also beneficial. They increase the efficiency with which various goods and services are delivered to consumers and thus contribute directly to living standard improvements. They also indirectly enhance the efficiency and competitiveness of U.S. manufacturing. On the other hand, many infrastructure improvements, including more efficient communication and transportation networks, may prove as beneficial to the sales of imports as they are to the sales of domestically produced goods.

Thus all new investment is expected to benefit the economy. The contributions of new investments to international competitiveness vary, however. Some forms of new U.S. investment—for example, those in the housing and retail sectors—do little or nothing to enhance the ability of U.S. manufacturing and other U.S. producers of tradeable goods and services to compete in U.S. and world markets. New shopping malls may increase the efficiency with which the retail sales sector delivers its services and hence improve U.S. living standards, but they do not raise the international competitiveness of U.S.-based goods production. Shopping malls do, however, consume scarce financial capital and may increase consumption, lower savings, and raise interest rates and the cost of capital. Tax and other laws that stimulate investment in non-tradeable goods and services sectors may actually harm the tradeable goods sectors by siphoning off scarce investment capital. In fact, tax law changes of the early 1980s stimulated investment in housing and other types of construction but did so at heavy costs to U.S. manufacturing (see Chapter 5).

To summarize, steps that increase saving should improve U.S. competitiveness by increasing the total supply of domestically generated saving, lowering the cost of capital, and leading to increased investment. Yet the goal of new competitiveness initiatives should not be simply to increase investment. There are many kinds of investment. Not all of them contribute significantly to the ability of U.S.-based goods production to compete against foreign production. Increasing investments that will enhance—not damage—U.S. international competitiveness should receive top priority.

TAX POLICY AND INTERNATIONAL COMPETITIVENESS

Effects on Saving and Investment

The effects of tax policy on international competitiveness merit further exploration. Chapter 4 noted the significant effects of fiscal policy in creating a U.S. saving-investment gap, resulting international capital flows, and the U.S. trade deficits. With private-sector saving rates too low to both offset government dissaving and fund private-sector investment, the government's fiscal policy and budget deficits have been a very important factor in the growth of large trade deficits. Fiscal policy—the balance between the government's tax collections and its expenditures—is also critically important to U.S. international competitiveness. It determines the government's saving or dissaving, which, in turn, affects interest rates, the cost of investment capital, and capital formation rates.

But tax policy—the kinds, levels, and incidences of taxes levied in executing a given fiscal policy—is also critical. U.S. international competitiveness very much depends on new investment in human and physical capital and on a high level of investment in research and development. Tax policy is not the only determinant of these investments, but it is very important in determining the supply of investment capital (saving), the demand for it, and its price. Tax and other policies that increase gross U.S. savings, for example, will tend to lower interest rates and encourage more investment.

Tax policy is also important in that it is an instrument that governments can alter quickly if there is a will to do so. Unfortunately, however, very little attention has been given to international competitiveness in forming U.S. tax policies. Instead, in designing taxes to obtain given amounts of revenue, there is a preoccupation in the United States with the initial incidence of tax burdens; a tendency to focus on the use of tax policy to influence the initial distribution of income among recipients, rather than on the formation of capital so critical to growth of the nation's output. Influencing income distribution and issues of fairness and equity in distribution of the initial incidence of tax burdens are clearly important and useful goals of tax policy. Too unequal a distribution of a nation's income will ultimately raise both political problems and economic disarray. But income distribution goals should not be pursued to the exclusion and detriment of the capital formation required to create new wealth. Tax policy should focus not just on influencing the initial distribution of income—how to divide the existing economic "pie" among members of the economy—but also on how to make it grow; that is, policy should also focus on the division of national income between investment and consumption. Moreover, policy making should recognize that some uses of tax policies designed to serve income distribution goals will inhibit the growth of national income.

Much recent tax legislation has been devoted to changes intended to ensure that corporations pay their "fair share" of taxes. Corporations, however, do not pay taxes. They are simply legal creations. They are not themselves the ultimate recipients or consumers of income. Rather, the owners of the corporation and its employees bear a part or all of the first incidence of corporate taxes in the form of lower profits and wages. In the end, however, all members of the economy must bear the burden of taxes levied on corporations. These burdens are transmitted not only through their effect on prices and profits but also via their effects on capital formation, productivity, and U.S. international competitiveness.

The populist and mythical view of tax policy presumes that the portion of the nation's taxes levied on "business"—primarily on corporations—somehow does not much affect the economy and all its members. Populist arguments reflect a presumption that taxes can be shifted from consumers to corporations without significantly lowering capital formation and economic growth rates. In essence, additions to business taxes are popularly seen as tapping excess profits rather than affecting levels of investment.

When the United States enjoyed economic dominance, some sectors of the

U.S. economy that faced international competition may have been so strong that they could absorb new taxes without important effects on investment. This is no longer the case, however. We live now in an integrated, highly competitive world economy. Today's world is one in which the United States has few unique products and processes, most goods can be produced in many competitor nations, and there are few inherent advantages in U.S.-based production. As more and more nations industrialize, we should expect intensifying competition and a global glut of manufactures. In such a world, excess U.S. business profits— profits that exceed those needed to motivate investment in new products, processes, and technology adequate to stay ahead or abreast of foreign competition— are unlikely to persist long in any industry. In this new environment, competition for U.S. and foreign markets will hold down the profits of U.S.-based production. There will rarely be ongoing pools of excess U.S. business profits that can be tapped without affecting costs, wages, prices, and investment.

Although all taxes are in the end borne by members of the economy—not by inanimate corporate organizations—the initial incidence of taxes can have potent effects on the nation's choices between consumption and investment. Tax policy can retard or enhance capital formation rates. This has always been true but the significant effects of tax policy on saving, investment, and U.S. international competitiveness must be more carefully considered now than in the earlier period of U.S. economic dominance.

Some may see an increase in business taxes, for example, as a means of reducing the budget and trade deficits or, perhaps, as a popular means to redistribute income by lightening the taxes levied on individuals. Such shifts, however, will produce other longer term effects. Increasing business taxes may help to decrease the federal deficit but will not improve gross U.S. saving to the same extent because it will decrease business saving. Additions to business taxes that discourage investment in the United States will also ultimately lower U.S. productivity. In turn, this imposes burdens on the individual members of the economy in various forms, such as higher prices, lowered competitiveness of U.S.-based production, reduced employment, downward pressures on real wages, and a lower dollar exchange rate.

To illustrate, it has been estimated that the shift of taxes from individuals to corporations effected by the Tax Reform Act of 1986 transferred some $125 billion in taxes to corporations over the ensuing five-year period. This transfer, it is estimated, will raise the rate of return required to motivate a new investment by 0.5 percent and reduce domestic investment by U.S. corporations by as much as 8 percent.[1]

In short, the initial incidence of taxation is increasingly important in a more integrated and competitive world economy. In today's world, U.S. tax policy must turn away from its traditional focus on apportioning the initial incidence of taxes between business and individuals and among income groups as a means to influence income distribution. There must be increased examination of the effects of tax incidence on capital formation.

Peter Drucker argued persuasively about the effects of tax incidence on competitiveness. He saw the Japanese competitive advantage as coming from the fact that the Japanese economy is saving driven, whereas the U.S. economy is consumption driven. Indeed, the focus of U.S. macroeconomic policy has been primarily on demand creation, certainly not saving and investment. In fact, a recent survey revealed that many Americans regard saving as bad for the economy because it slows demand for business.

In Drucker's view, however,

the enormous competitive disadvantage we suffer vis-à-vis the Japanese [is] through our prohibitive cost of capital. It is not structural; it is the result of an inadequate savings rate caused in the main by our clinging to the belief in the consumption driven economy against our own experience and against all the evidence.[2]

Drucker argued against the popular notion that "to penalize saving 'soaks the rich.' And to promote consumption 'spreads the wealth.' " He argued that to promote saving does not favor the rich, but that

Any country that has given a tax exemption or tax deferment to saving has had the same experience as Japan: Middle- and lower-income earners take the most advantage of these opportunities. . . . We also know that a consumption-driven economy does not "spread the wealth." There is far more equality of income in investment-driven Japan than in consumption-driven America or Britain. . . . We know, in other words, how to jack up America's dismal savings rate and how to bring down America's prohibitively high cost of capital. It is less a matter of the level than of the "incidence" of taxation—which is economists' doubletalk for a chance legally to avoid taxes.[3]

Tax Policy and Manufacturing

Specifically, there must be new tax policy making attention given to capital formation in the goods-producing sector. Why should tax policy give specific consideration to one sector of the economy? "Neutrality" has been an important goal of U.S. tax policy; that is, taxes should not distort the allocation of resources from that which would occur without taxes. The concept is good. But what is *neutrality*? When one sector is the primary interface of the U.S. economy with the world economy, taxes can significantly affect international competitiveness of that sector and the economy. When the juxtaposition of U.S. and foreign tax policies results in a lower U.S. saving rate than that of U.S. competitors, triggers large net capital inflows and trade deficits, or discourages investment in U.S. capital-intensive goods-producing industries, tax policy is not neutral. It is actually biased against the manufacturing sector in ways that significantly inhibit investment in manufacturing and its ability to compete in the world market.

Microeconomic trade policies that purport to respond to foreign actions receive much attention in the United States. Tariffs, dumping, restrictive trade practices, foreign governments' subsidization of their industries, and other actions seen as

disadvantaging individual U.S. firms or industries have received constant attention from U.S. policymakers. U.S. and foreign macroeconomic policies that
more fundamentally—but less visibly—affect and disadvantage U.S.-based production get very little attention. The "neutrality" of U.S. taxes compared to
those of foreign competitors as they affect capital formation in goods production
needs to become a new consideration in U.S. economic policy making if the
United States is to maintain a competitive, top-notch manufacturing sector.

To avoid disadvantaging domestic production and to encourage critically
needed investment, it may well be necessary to give special tax treatment to the
manufacturing sector. Such special treatment, however, should be in addition
to a fundamental overhaul of tax and other policies that would increase U.S.
saving relative to consumption and increase investment and productivity in all
sectors of the economy. Available policy options for changing the saving and
investment ratios would include major changes such as eliminating double taxation of corporate income, increasing the use of consumption taxes, eliminating
taxes on interest income, and eliminating or reducing deductibility of some
interest expenses.

The neutrality of U.S. tax policy needs to be reexamined in light of new
conditions in today's world. Tailoring tax policy to meet the international competitiveness needs of the tradeable goods and services sectors will be difficult
but not impossible. The indirect taxation levied on U.S. industry through regulatory policies and the consequent disadvantaging of U.S.-based production by
such policies must similarly be given new consideration. Reflecting international
competitiveness considerations in regulatory policies will also be difficult.

Precisely how tax policy can best focus on the needs of those sectors that
must compete internationally is beyond the scope of this book. Some examples,
however, can be cited. Canada recognizes the importance of its manufacturing
sector and that sector's interrelationship with the world economy through its
corporate tax rate, which by 1991 will be about 6 percentage points lower on
manufacturing and processing income than on other corporate income.[4] Other
tax policy alternatives include more favorable tax treatment of investments in
research and development and plants and equipment. International competitiveness considerations, for example, can be factored into tax credit and depreciation
schedules for individual sectors.

To lower the costs of pollution abatement expenditures to industry, immediate
"expensing" of those costs could be allowed. Generating an increased portion
of total federal government revenue from consumption taxes would also help to
parry the negative effects of similar foreign taxes on U.S. export competitiveness.

Certainly, imposing new taxes on the manufacturing sector should be avoided.
An oil import tax, for example, might make a contribution to narrowing the
budget deficit, but it would certainly impair U.S. international competitiveness.
An oil import tax would immediately disadvantage U.S.-based manufacturing,
particularly the more energy-intensive industries, by raising the costs of U.S.-
based production vis-à-vis foreign production. The negative effects would be

many. The resulting changes in U.S. versus foreign price competitiveness would increase U.S. imports, decrease U.S. exports. In addition, to offset the decline in the price competitiveness of U.S.-based production, additional wage restraint or dollar decline would need to occur, and some new investments would be made abroad instead of in the United States. This would shift the burden of the tax to all members of the U.S. economy in unintended ways.

In a period of budget deficits there will be a constant search for new revenues, particularly for revenues that can claim not to violate a pledge of "no new taxes." This raises the prospect of a series of new "user fees" that imply taxing the user of various services. U.S.-based manufacturing would, in fact, be further handicapped by new fees that are in reality new taxes. For example, there has been talk of levying fees on emissions from manufacturing plants. One stated goal of such taxes would be to discourage pollution. The fees, however, would be in addition to regulations that set emission standards plants must already meet. The effect would be not so much to tax users of the environment but rather to tax U.S.-based production and discourage new investments in the latest emission reduction technologies. Consumers could avoid the tax by using imported items, which would not include U.S. emission fees. U.S.-based production would be disadvantaged, again with unintended effects on the nation's international competitiveness.

Many alternatives to avoid penalizing U.S.-based goods production through tax policies should be considered. The key point, however, is that tax policy—both as it relates to saving and to investment—must in the future consider its effects on the nation's international competitiveness. The potential effects of two major policy changes—consumption taxes and capital gains taxation—are reviewed in sections that follow.

Consumption Taxes

Fundamental changes in U.S. tax policy are needed to increase U.S. investment in human and physical capital without resorting to foreign borrowing. The value-added tax (VAT) and other forms of consumption taxes now widely used by competitor countries deserve careful consideration. The VAT is rebated on exports, collected on imports. A VAT increases the motivation toward saving compared to consumption. Also, VATs—and other forms of taxes that do not apply to exported goods (for example, excise taxes)—give an advantage to those countries that export vis-à-vis those countries that produce a higher portion of their total taxes in ways that cause the taxes to be included in the prices of exported goods.

Rates vary among European Community (EC) countries, but about 30 percent of total EC tax revenue is now derived from consumption taxes (principally the VAT) that are not included in the costs of exported goods. This compares with about 17 percent of total U.S. revenues obtained from consumption taxes (mostly state retail sales taxes and excise taxes). Thus U.S. exports to the EC are disadvantaged in that costs of production of the U.S. goods include taxes comprising about 83 percent of U.S. tax revenues. By contrast, EC products exported to the United States on average would include costs equivalent to only about 70 percent of total EC taxes.

U.S. exports to third countries are similarly disadvantaged against those of the EC. That is, at third-country ports of entry, U.S.-produced goods on average reflect 87 percent of U.S. taxes; EC goods, however, reflect only 70 percent of the EC tax burden. The EC's heavier reliance on consumption taxes thus subtly disadvantages U.S.-based production, whether the market be the United States, the EC, or third countries.

The 1992 evolution of the European Community to a full customs union will create the world's largest trading unit. Current EC 1992 proposals would allow individual countries to set standard VAT rates within a 14 to 20 percent band that will likely maintain the consumption tax portion of total collections at about 30 percent. This difference in U.S. and EC taxation approaches will significantly disadvantage U.S.-based production in competition against EC-based production. Similarly, in 1990 Canada implemented a 7 percent "goods and services tax" (GST) that will be rebated on exports, collected on imports. A stated objective of enacting the GST was "to ensure that Canada can compete effectively in the world economy."[5] This will cause border tax adjustments (GST rebates to Canadian exporters, GST collections on imports) favoring Canadian production on trade that moves across the U.S.-Canada border, which is approximately one-fifth of total U.S. trade.

The United States is already disadvantaged against countries that employ the VAT and other consumption taxes. The increased size and importance of the EC market, however, and the increased competitiveness of EC producers that will come when the EC achieves full customs union status will make the EC's VAT a more important competitive factor. This, as well as the adoption of the equivalent of a VAT by Canada, and the modest new Japanese value-added tax means that U.S. businesses in a few years will be facing border tax adjustments by countries that together count for more than 60 percent of all U.S. trade.[6]

Countering the significant competitive disadvantages of U.S.-based production caused by foreign consumption taxes is an important reason to consider a greater reliance on consumption taxes in the United States. A still more important reason for increased reliance on consumption rather than income taxes is that consumption taxes encourage savings and discourage consumption relative to income taxes. Consumption taxes are one potential means of nudging the private sector consumption-saving relationship toward higher saving rates.

Capital Gains Taxation

Changes in the 1986 tax act removed the preferential tax treatment formerly accorded long-term (over six months) capital gains. New consideration has been given, however, to legislation that would provide more favorable tax treatment to capital gains, partly on grounds that it will increase "investment" and, hence, improve U.S. international competitiveness. In fact, any effect of capital gains tax benefits on international competitiveness is likely to be modest. Indeed, depending on what kinds of transactions benefit from capital gains treatment, the effects on international competitiveness may be negative.

Not all kinds of investment improve the nation's international competitiveness (Chapters 2 and 11). Increased investment in residences, the retail trade sector of the economy, office buildings, domestic service industries (for example, health spas, restaurants, and gambling casinos), and some other sectors may be desirable for other reasons but will do little to enhance the competitiveness of U.S. goods production. Indeed, such investments may actually impair investment in manufacturing by increasing the demand for, and driving up the cost of, investment capital.

Most capital gains tax proposals would extend the benefits to all forms of investment. This would probably provide greater incentive to investment in other sectors, such as housing and real estate, than it would to manufacturing.

The capital gains tax would likely benefit most those investments in which asset values tend to rise with inflation or by reason of changing supply-demand relationships. Residential and commercial real estate prices, for example, tend to move upward with inflation. Prices on real estate also rise when, for some reason, demand rises against a relatively fixed supply within a particular geographic area. Manufacturing establishments, on the other hand, are much less likely to profit from these factors. Existing plant and equipment depreciate through wear and technological obsolescence and then often must be replaced at prices pushed up above original costs by inflation. Manufacturing industries will benefit from a capital gains tax primarily through higher stock market prices or lower borrowing costs. A capital gains tax may make industrial company shares somewhat more attractive, putting some upward pressure on their prices. The effect, however, is likely to be greater on those businesses and investments that can benefit more directly from favorable treatment of capital gains.

In short, a reduction in the tax on capital gains would benefit U.S. international competitiveness only if it increased gross U.S. saving more than it increased the demand for investment funds by the non-manufacturing sector. It would aid manufacturing only to the extent it acted to reduce the cost of capital for the U.S. goods-producing sector and only if it did not increase the net inflow of foreign capital, since such inflows inevitably negatively affect the manufacturing sector. Most forms of capital gains tax reduction seem unlikely to meet these tests. Instead, they seem more likely to raise the cost of capital for U.S. manufacturing and to stimulate inflow of foreign capital.

REGULATORY POLICIES, SOCIAL PROGRAMS, AND INTERNATIONAL COMPETITIVENESS

The role of government regulation continues to increase as society becomes more complex, and more government programs with social objectives (for example, universal health insurance, child care, and pension programs) are advocated. Although many of these regulations and programs may be desirable, their potential effects on international competitiveness are not widely recognized. Federal and state government regulatory policies and programs can be carried out in ways that impose substantial indirect taxes on U.S. businesses and may impair U.S. international competitiveness.

Regulation of industry and programs that mandate business to provide specific benefits to employees are increasingly favored tools of elected officials in achieving various social objectives. This is because regulation and mandated programs provide a means to implement new programs without levying new taxes directly on individual taxpayers. Instead, they can provide a means of hiding new taxes. That is, the public gets the benefit of the particular program but business appears to bear the burden. In the end, the public bears the burden of these hidden taxes because costs of new regulations and new programs are passed through to the customers and to the public in a variety of ways. The increased costs, however, are far less visible to individuals than if paid for by direct tax taxation.

The effects of increased costs of regulation and other programs imposed on business in today's competitive world economy need to be considered carefully. They seldom have been. When additional costs are imposed on businesses that do not face foreign competition, the costs of individual U.S. firms and their U.S. competitors increase together. All competitors are burdened equally. If the costs fall on particular kinds of businesses or industries (for example, a new program imposing strict regulation on beauty parlors and pool halls) those businesses and industries may suffer because, as their costs and prices rise, consumption of their output will decline. In such instances, the costs of meeting new regulations serve to alter domestic U.S. production and consumption patterns. The benefit of the new regulatory program to American society may or may not be worth its cost, and the judgment may hinge on whether one likes or dislikes beauty parlors and pool halls. The increased costs of regulation do not, however, disadvantage U.S.-based production relative to foreign production because foreign production cannot provide beauty parlor and pool hall services.

The results are different, however, for those sectors of U.S. industry that must face international competition—principally manufacturing industries. For these industries regulatory and social measures can become major cost burdens that impair their ability to match foreign competition. Actions to maintain and enhance the environment, for example, are becoming more and more costly, increasing both capital expenditures that do not contribute to productivity gains and annual operating costs. The costs of environmental improvement fall primarily on the manufacturing sector. When the costs of U.S.-based production of internationally tradeable goods rise, foreign production may replace U.S. production.

Most U.S. service industries are much less burdened by environmental costs. Moreover, most service industry firms compete only against other U.S. firms bound by the same laws and regulations. Thus environmental regulation costs and the costs of health care programs, pensions, and other social programs can more readily be passed on by service and other industries that do not face international competition.

Mandated child care and parental leave programs are examples of programs that may—or may not—be desirable on a societal cost versus benefits basis. They will, however, more likely be legislated if, in the populist view, they are seen to be paid for by "business." In the end, however, the costs of these programs will not be borne by business. Programs that raise the costs of production will raise the prices paid by consumers. In those industries that face international competition, higher costs will lower U.S. competitiveness and displace U.S. jobs. These costs, however, will be invisible to most persons.

It should be emphasized that these facts are not arguments against the desirability of environmental and social programs. Rather, they highlight a growing need, when designing new domestic programs, to consider how such programs affect domestic firms vis-à-vis their foreign competitors and the attendant effects on the workers in domestic firms that face foreign competition.

Social and regulatory programs should be examined from two aspects. First, there is a need to examine their costs versus their benefits. Even health and environmental programs, for example, may be carried to such extremes that alternative uses of national income would yield higher societal returns. To illustrate, a national health care system that provides no incentive to users to restrict their demands and allows suppliers to set their own prices without benefit of significant competition will likely lead to continual escalation of health costs as a percentage of the GNP. Costs may rise to levels where spending becomes excessive in that alternative uses of part of the spending would provide more benefit to the nation's health and living standards.

Similarly, environmental standards can be raised to levels of such purity that further small incremental gains become exceedingly expensive and provide little or no added benefit. When this happens, spending should be shifted elsewhere to achieve greater increases in health and safety. But as long as the costs of environmental and other regulatory and social programs are popularly thought to be borne by "industry" or "corporations," there will be little incentive for legislators and other policymakers to restrain the growth of these programs. No matter how marginally beneficial or grossly expensive new measures may be, there is likely to be inadequate consideration of their cost-benefit merits or their effects on capital formation and the nation's competitiveness.

Indeed, it may be politically tempting to impose punitive regulations and requirements on U.S. industry. Punitive environmental cleanup measures, for example, might seem to some to be justified on the presumption that corporations, rather than the society as a whole, have benefited from production that created pollution. It might then seem logical that corporations must therefore now bear the costs of environmental cleanup, whatever they may be. It may be good politics to advocate that "they" (U.S. industry) should pay. But who is "they"?

There are no corporate persons to bear the costs of taxes, be they direct or indirect, imposed by various regulations and mandates. There are stockholders, who are members of the economy and may be seen as a wealthy class that can readily absorb the effects of reduced profits. The ownership of U.S. business is, however, more widely dispersed and integrated into the economic and social fabric of the nation than is widely understood. Employee pension funds and insurance company premiums for annuities and life insurance, for example, are invested in a variety of financial instruments, including corporate stocks and bonds. These holdings comprise a large portion of the total ownership of U.S. industry. At the end of 1988, private pension funds' ownership of stocks was equivalent to 20.8 percent of the New York Stock Exchange's total market value. State and local pension funds owned another 9.1 percent of the New York exchange's total market value of stocks. About 50 percent of the total assets of U.S. life insurance companies is invested in corporate stocks and bonds.[7] Pension funds and institutional investors are now by far the most significant players in U.S. financial markets and the greatest beneficiaries of corporate profits.

In fact, the future viability of pension funds and the ability of insurance companies to meet their obligations is in large measure a function of the profitability and growth of private-sector industry. Tax and other policies that lower profitability and inhibit the profits and growth of "business" raise the contributions that must be made to achieve a given level of pension and insurance benefits and lower the future ability of pension funds, insurance companies, and other institutions to meet their obligations. Thus actions that inhibit or jeopardize the long-term growth of U.S. industry lower its earning power and valuation.

There are manifold effects on capital formation, productivity, competitiveness, and so on that result from profit reductions. They affect the society as a whole. The end result of regulatory measures that impose punitive levies that markedly raise costs and lower the profits on U.S.-based production may be simply to drive production from the United States. Such actions will not "punish" a particular group of persons so much as they will punish the economy as a whole. In the end, individuals—all members of the economy, including pension fund beneficiaries and not just corporations or business—must absorb the costs of regulatory and social programs. Lower profits ultimately translate into lower saving, a higher cost of capital, lower investment in new plant and equipment that would raise productivity, reduced investment in research and development that would speed the rate of technological advance, lower U.S. productivity, and diminished international competitiveness.

Regulations and social programs should therefore be judged on their cost-benefit merit, not on the erroneous presumption that costs will not be borne by individual members of the economy. There is no free lunch—no way that costs can be finally lodged with corporations or particular groups of the population. Any failure to make the most effective use of limited national income and resources, whether by government or business, lowers U.S. living standards below levels that could be achieved by more efficient use. In the real world, however, societal cost-benefit analyses are difficult and uncertain. Seldom will opposing interests agree on the calculations. The analyses can shed light on the issue and help to focus the debate but are unlikely to overcome emotional predilections.

The negative effects of increased regulations on U.S. international competitiveness suggest there must consistently be a second path of analysis in evaluating new programs. In an integrated, highly competitive world economy, particular attention must be paid to the international effects of new programs that add to industry's costs. Regardless of the national balance of costs and benefits, U.S.-based production will be disadvantaged and U.S. living standards will be unfavorably affected to the extent that environmental, social, and other program costs hinder the competitiveness of U.S.-based production. Despite the importance of the nation's international competitiveness, there has been essentially no consideration of the competitiveness effects of new regulatory and social programs that constitute indirect taxation. Indeed, in efforts to hold down the federal budget, there is a growing tendency to impose new programs on U.S. businesses. Many of these programs might better be funded by general revenues, rather than impose costs more directly on the business sector.

The trend toward imposing the initial cost of new regulatory and social programs on U.S. business, thus obscuring the visibility of their costs, is dangerous. In a world of scarce resources, where not all problems can be solved simultaneously, better decisions are likely when the costs of new proposals are visible to those who will bear them—all members of the economy—rather than hidden from them by indirect taxes levied on business.

Generating new revenues without directly affecting individual taxpayers and funding new social programs without adding to the federal budget may make good populist politics. But actions that result in greater costs than benefits or unnecessarily disadvantage U.S.-based production are bad economics. They are a sure way of the nation "shooting itself in the foot." In an increasingly integrated and competitive world economy, the trend should be toward less indirect taxation through regulations and mandated programs—not more. Taxes on consumption may be unpleasant but are likely to be far less damaging to the economy than taxes on production. It will often be less damaging to the economy to fund desirable programs by means other than direct or indirect taxes on business that raise the cost of production.

Federal antitrust laws are among a range of existing regulatory activities that should be thoroughly reviewed. Antitrust concerns remain, but in an integrated world economy in which many types of U.S. businesses face foreign competition, the opportunities for monopoly control are very much diminished, and many of the concerns are less relevant than they were in earlier times. The effects of U.S. laws and regulations on the nation's international competitiveness must be considered in light of the existence of global competition.

SUMMARY

• Trade deficits and U.S. international competitiveness are interrelated but essentially different problems. They in part, however, stem from common causes.

The trade deficits are a visible, transitory problem that can be dealt with relatively quickly in a few years. Competitiveness, however, is an enduring, much more insidious and intractable problem.

• Some actions that would help narrow the trade deficits would actually impair long-term U.S. competitiveness.

• Policy making to deal with international competitiveness is complicated by a lack of public understanding of the problem. Attention tends to focus on the immediate problems of individual firms and industries, rather than on actions to improve the nation's productivity and competitiveness.

• Policymakers are disposed to focus on trade policy—the laws, rules, procedures, practices, and international agreements that govern U.S. and foreign participation in international trade. They purport to do so in an effort to solve U.S. trade and competitiveness problems. In fact, however, trade policy actions have only a limited ability to affect either. Moreover, there are opportunity costs involved. The attention given to trade policy issues detracts from, and substitutes for, attention that should be given to the real determinants of trade balances and competitiveness.

• Tax policy is an important way of influencing capital formation and productivity gains. Unfortunately, however, tax policy has been primarily focused on the incidence of taxes—on how to divide the income pie—rather than on capital formation—how to make the pie grow larger.

• Improving U.S. capital formation rates and enhancing international competitiveness will probably require basic changes in U.S. tax laws that will be controversial and difficult to achieve.

• Consumption taxes merit serious consideration. U.S.-based production is disadvantaged when compared to production in those countries that rely on consumption taxes to provide larger portions of their total tax revenues. In addition, a consumption tax could be an important means of encouraging increased saving.

• It is not enough simply to adopt policies that encourage capital investment. Many forms of investment—for example, shopping malls—do nothing to enhance the ability of U.S.-based goods production to compete internationally. In fact, increased investment that causes net capital inflows to the United States will likely be to the detriment of the manufacturing sector.

• Tax and other policies must focus increasingly on their effects on international capital flows and the goods-producing sector—primarily manufacturing—that faces international competition.

• Reduction of the federal budget deficit is a logical first step to improve both the trade deficits and U.S. international competitiveness. However, tax policies that increase revenue but discourage capital formation in the goods-producing sector could decrease the budget and trade deficits but in the long run would be to the detriment of U.S. international competitiveness.

• Regulatory policies and other social programs can impose significant indirect "taxes" on U.S. business. These indirect taxes can seriously affect the ability of the manufacturing sector to meet foreign competition, a fact that must be considered in the design of regulatory and social programs.

• The trend toward increased use of regulation and mandated social programs that impose indirect taxes on businesses is dangerous. In a world of limited resources where not all problems can be solved simultaneously, better decisions are likely when those who will bear the costs—all members of the economy— are aware of both the costs and the benefits of new proposals.

NOTES

1. William A. Niskanen, *Reaganomics: An Insider's View* (New York: Oxford University Press, 1988), 104.

2. Peter F. Drucker, "Japan's Not-So-Secret Weapon," *Wall Street Journal*, 9 January 1990, A–10.

3. Ibid.

4. *Corporate Taxes: A World Wide Summary, 1989 Edition* (New York: Price Waterhouse, 1989), 64.

5. *Tax Notes* (Arlington, VA: Tax Analysts, 23 October 1989), 483.

6. Ibid., 488.

7. *Institutional Investor Fact Book, 1990* (New York: New York Stock Exchange, January 1990), 6; *Life Insurance Fact Book Update*, 1989 (Washington, D.C.: American Council of Life Insurance, 1989), 4.

Chapter 12

Making U.S. International Economic Policy: In God We Trust?

An increasingly integrated and sophisticated world economy holds promise for dramatic advances in global living standards. But there is ample opportunity for things to go awry. The world economy is in uncharted waters, with difficult, risky times ahead. Narrowing unsustainable global trade and current account imbalances while maintaining good world economic growth rates, keeping protectionist forces in hand, and avoiding triggering an LDC debt crisis will be critical problems well into the next decade. Successful completion of the GATT Uruguay Round negotiations and halting a trend toward increased bilateralism will be difficult. Other knotty problems include increased volatility in international capital movements, fluctuating oil prices, intensifying competition for world markets driven by a global oversupply of manufactures, and an increasing pace of technological and structural change within economies.

Successfully steering the world economy through the troubled waters ahead will require foresight, increased cooperation, and more effective coordination of economic policies among governments. But setting and staying on the right course are unlikely, if not impossible, without strong, effective leadership.

Since World War II, the United States has filled the role of global economic leader. At the beginning of the 1990s, however, many difficult problems—including large trade and budget deficits and declining international competitiveness—have revealed flawed U.S. policy making. Even though it remains the world's strongest economic power, U.S. dominance has waned and, with it, the ability to orchestrate the institutions and processes that guide the global economy. No other nation is yet ready or able to assume economic leadership, a role that promises to be more difficult as power is shared among a growing number of participants.

Looking ahead, international economic leadership and policy making will need to be particularly enlightened, compelling, and effective. Are U.S. policymakers up to the task? This chapter discusses shortcomings in U.S. international economic policy making and how it could be improved.

MANAGEMENT OF U.S. INTERNATIONAL ECONOMIC POLICY

Preoccupied with managing Western defense, enlarging trade deficits, and rising protectionist sentiments, the U.S. Congress and more than one administration have given too little attention to the dramatic changes occurring in the global economy. Little thought has been given to implications of the relative decline of the economic power and dominance that long provided the basis for U.S. military, political, and economic leadership.

Responsibility for formulation and execution of U.S. international economic policy lies primarily with the government's executive branch. The routine microeconomic tasks of international trade policy—export licensing, administration of the U.S. laws concerning foreign trade practices, and bilateral trade relations—are highly visible issues that attract public attention. Increasingly, Congress intervenes on these matters through oversight hearings and new laws that try to micromanage the formulation and execution of trade policy. Executive branch policy making responds to these public and congressional interests by allocating a great deal of time and attention to them.

But microeconomic trade policy issues are generally not the crucial matters of international economic policy; they will not usually have important, lasting effects on the U.S. or world economies. In fact, they divert attention and resources from more important matters.

Formulation and execution of the more important U.S. policies too often have been improvised—ad hoc, reactive, and lacking in foresight and analysis. The root causes of problems often are not addressed because policies to deal with them are controversial, and the problems will not yield to quick solutions. Sometimes driven by short-term political considerations, cosmetic public relations-oriented programs that do not deal with the real issues are adopted. "Strike Force" was touted to the public during the Reagan administration as a major market opening initiative but inside the bureaucracy was known as "Strike Farce." Amazingly little thought, analysis, and expertise lay behind some U.S. government pronouncements and actions that purport to deal authoritatively with critically important issues.

Examples drawn from trade performance and competitiveness issues—one segment of U.S. international economic policy making—illustrate the lack of focus on important matters:

- There was no Reagan administration major interagency executive branch examination of (1) expansion of the trade deficits during the 1980s, their causes, expected duration, and potential effects on U.S. industry and the world economy; (2) the problems of narrowing global imbalances—the unprecedentedly large U.S. trade deficits and complementary trading partner surpluses; and (3) long-term implications of a rising U.S. international debtor position and growing foreign direct investment in the United States.

- Notwithstanding the 1985 report of the Presidential Commission on Industrial Competitiveness and two years of deliberation before the 1988 passage of a trade bill purporting to deal with U.S. competitiveness, there was no enduring interagency examination of U.S. international competitiveness. A 1986 task group did not deal with the basic issues, instead degenerating into a search for politically attractive legislative options. Even as the 1990s began, neither executive nor legislative branch policymakers had addressed saving and investment as the primary determinants of productivity growth and international competitiveness.

- There is no evidence that meaningful executive or legislative branch consideration was given to effects of the Tax Reform Act of 1986 on U.S. international competitiveness. Indeed, when questioned about potential effects, Treasury staff working on the legislation reportedly indicated competitiveness was a criterion outside their assignment. Nor has there since been any major examination of the effects of tax policy on international capital flows and domestic savings and investment.

In short, there has been very little recent use of the full resources of the executive branch to examine many of the major international economic policy issues. There has been essentially no systematic, coordinated effort to identify long-term trends and the problems that lie ahead for the U.S. and world economies. The focus has been primarily on responding to congressional and public concerns about narrow trade policy issues. Executive branch resources for assessing broad international economic policy issues have not been adequately harnessed.

Improvised, reactive policy making was not unique to the Reagan administration. Most administrations have not focused on international economic policy, and deeply imbedded forces probably ensure continuing underemphasis. Costs of neglecting this policy area will continue to rise for the United States, its trading partners, and the global economy.

Reasons for inadequate attention include lack of public and policymaker focus on increasingly important international economic issues, inadequate expertise in the government, and poor organization.

LACK OF FOCUS ON INTERNATIONAL ECONOMICS

One reason that difficult, controversial international economic issues are often not broadly examined inside the U.S. government is that a low level of public understanding makes reviews politically risky. It is virtually impossible to prepare studies of controversial issues—even national security issues—without leaks to the press. In addition, the results are likely to be used against incumbent administrations. Assessments of international economic problems—let alone the solutions—are seldom clear-cut. Interpretations are likely to differ. The press, ever looking for attention-grabbing stories, tends toward shallow analyses that emphasize specific shortcomings, rather than provide overall, in-depth evaluations.

Given the public's modest understanding, incumbent administrations can probably expect to lose from a public airing of difficult international economic issues.
In 1985, for example, internal assessments of the trade situation that accurately
projected continuing expansion of the trade deficits were not welcomed by the
administration but were rejected because it was feared they might inflame protectionist sentiments in the Congress. Also, "bad news" leaks could adversely
affect critical markets (for example, the dollar exchange rate).

Comprehensive interagency reviews of difficult, long-term issues also lack
appeal because the time horizons of administration appointees who direct the
policy making process are very short. There are all too many immediate problems
to deal with and little incentive for transient officeholders to become embroiled
in difficult matters they cannot claim to have resolved before the next election.
Even less reason exists to surface impending problems that will be controversial
or require difficult, unpopular actions. There is ample motivation to "let sleeping
dogs lie."

The short time frames of policymakers and their concerns about public reactions contribute heavily to the lack of internal analyses of important problems.
Yet national security issues are widely and thoroughly examined. Why the difference? The answer is that international economic matters are not yet considered
as critical to the nation's well being as security matters.

Not fully using internal government resources narrows the information provided to policymakers, risking decisions made on inadequate information. It also
transfers policy making influence from the government bureaucracy to external
groups. In fact, competent small think tanks such as the Brookings Institution,
the Institute for International Economics, the American Enterprise Institute, and
a few others affect U.S. government policy making on many important issues
more than do the much larger executive branch resources.

Policy making that does not fully use interagency processes may work satisfactorily for a time. Indeed, it often may be faster and appear more effective
than time-consuming and inefficient interagency processes. Results may be sat-
isfactory as long as decision makers succeed in spotting oncoming problems,
get good advice on every potentially important topic from whatever outside
sources are used, are omniscient in judgments, and have time to focus that
omniscience on the key issues.

But these conditions are seldom met for long. Administrations invariably begin
with internal power struggles to determine who is "in charge" of various issues,
sometimes without establishing clear winners or lines of authority. Most importantly, those who take key cabinet and subcabinet policy positions typically
begin with very little knowledge of the issues. Frequent turnover throughout the
tenure of administrations compounds this problem.

Although private-sector organizations provide very useful analyses, it is dangerous to rely too heavily on external sources for analyses that would guide U.S.
policies. Publicly supported non-profit research foundations simply do not have

enough resources to cover adequately all aspects of every international economic issue.

Finally, the U.S. government's information collection system cannot be matched. The various departments and agencies—State, Treasury, Commerce, the Central Intelligence Agency (CIA), and a host of others—collect vast amounts of economic and political intelligence that should be fully used. Private-sector resources should play an important role, but U.S. policy making would benefit from better use of the government's international economic resources.

EXECUTIVE BRANCH EXPERTISE

Selecting Key Policymakers

Even though a growing global interdependency and evolution of the world economy has been evident for some years, few presidents assume office with any real understanding or appreciation of international economic issues. The domestic economy and national security matters traditionally have concerned voters most and have played the lead roles in getting presidents elected and staying elected.

One result has been too little emphasis on international economics when new administrations select key cabinet members, set up the White House organizations that must steer the executive branch bureaucracy, and dole out political appointments in agencies with important international economic roles.

In both the Reagan and Carter administrations, for example, White House coverage of international economic issues was primarily through a handful of National Security Council (NSC) staff. Nor has the need for an understanding of the world economy consistently been an important criterion in selecting key agency heads. Not every successful Wall Street financier necessarily makes a good Treasury secretary. To some with Wall Street viewpoints, a strong dollar may be a welcome foreign endorsement of the strength of the American economy, even in the face of huge and growing trade deficits decimating the nation's manufacturing sector. But those with a more global view may see the situation differently—as an aberrant international transfer of resources, with potential longer term costs and disruptive effects on the U.S. and world economies.

Similarly, in an increasingly integrated global economy, not every successful business executive has the national and global orientations appropriate to a good secretary of commerce. Appointees from business backgrounds are likely to view problems from the perspective of individual firms and industries; they may intuitively look to microeconomic, individual-industry solutions. But what appears best in the short term for individual firms and industries may not be best in the longer term for the nation. Many problems manifested in individual industries actually require macroeconomic, not microeconomic, solutions.

The opportunities for imperfect staffing go well below the cabinet level. Cabinet officers often have little say in the selection of key subordinates but must choose from a list of individuals considered "qualified" by the White House personnel office. The qualifications, however, are often political, not technical.

Relevant experience may be easier to come by in some other fields, but there are few good private-sector training grounds for most federal government international economic positions. Notwithstanding success in their private-sector occupations, very few appointees to international economic assignments have much experience applicable to the jobs they take.

Instead, most come to their positions not to dispense expertise but to acquire it. Most work in relatively narrow areas in their government assignments and do not understand the international economy or the U.S. role in that economy. Tenures are relatively short, seldom lasting the full four years of a presidential term. Incumbents soon move on to market their brief government experience, making room for additional appointees to pass through the government accreditation turnstile.

The Impact of Inexperienced Leadership

A low level of entry expertise and high turnover among policymakers leads to excessive time spent educating new leadership. The wheel is continually reinvented, frequently reemploying cast-off ideas that are new only to new managers. There are continual reorganizations and reshufflings of staff in a never-ending search for organizational solutions to more basic problems.[1]

Inexperienced, constantly changing leadership can foster other, deeper problems. Uncertain in its role and unable to interpret confidently the information presented by career bureaucrats, inexpert management will likely follow without question the party line emanating from above. Assessments containing bad news and those not buttressing administration positions may not be delivered to higher levels. In today's world, messengers delivering bad news may not be shot, but they will certainly be unwelcome and unrewarded.

Inexperience and rapid turnover also affect international negotiations. Foreign negotiators invariably are career professionals who have spent most of their lifetimes working on the subject under negotiation. They soon recognize the lack of expertise and short-lived tenure of their U.S. political appointee counterparts. Foreign teams may have strong motivations to stall negotiations, knowing they will likely soon face a new U.S. negotiator, if not a new administration. Intelligence reports have confirmed that this is a conscious strategy used by some key trading partners.

Effects on the Career Force

Political appointments have been encroaching on positions farther and farther down in the executive branch career force. Both Democratic and Republican administrations, with the knowledge and consent of the congress, have increased the number of political appointments to more than 3,000. Roughly half are in jobs that might otherwise be filled by senior career personnel. One result is to block promotion of career staff to positions of responsibility.

This growing incursion of political appointees is in startling contrast with other mature democracies. West Germany has a grand total of 50 to 60 "political" appointees—political in that the jobs are vulnerable to a change in government. But in fact about half of the incumbents in those positions were promoted from the civil services.[2] The United Kingdom has about 150 political jobs; France has about 400, again with about half drawn from the civil service. Japan has even fewer, essentially none.

In the U.S. system, all appointee positions usually change simultaneously at the end of an administration, often leaving vacancies for several months. There is also frequent, continuing turnover during administrations. Because international trade positions are particularly sought after, the ratio of political appointees to career staff may be higher than in other policy areas. In the Reagan administration, however, there were five layers of political appointee supervisors between the secretary of commerce and the highest career person in the International Trade Administration.

The "value added" by these layers is minimal, often negative. Each layer provides an opportunity to alter, garble, delay, or stop the flow of information upward. On directions moving downward, each layer is an opportunity to muddle the original transmission. Some political partisans are pressing for still greater numbers of political appointees, arguing that more are needed for better, faster implementation of presidential programs. In fact, however, administrations could typically exert more effective control by reducing—not enlarging—the number of intermediaries between cabinet heads and senior career staff.

A continuing expansion of the layers of political appointees and lagging federal pay scales have caused the loss of many senior international economic career force personnel. These effects also extend to junior staff, where the limitations of career service are becoming ever more obvious. The United States does not now have an "elite" senior civil service in international economics. It is unlikely to build one as the incursion of appointees continues and career force prestige and pay scales continue to lag.

Fewer political appointments should be made to international economic policy jobs, appointees should have more relevant international trade and economic experience, their tenures should be longer, and the role and stature of the career staff should be enlarged. This is, however, highly unlikely. There is little incentive for new administrations to cut the number of jobs available to their campaign workers. Nor can new administrations increase significantly the level of relevant experience in the selections made from the pool of those politically qualified.

IMPACT OF THE LEGISLATIVE BRANCH

Responsibility for the short-term focus and sometimes less than desired performance in formulating and executing U.S. international economic policy does not rest solely with the executive branch. Although congressional staff expertise on the very broad spectrum of international issues is thin, congressional "oversight" and intervention in the details of policy making are rising and seem certain to escalate further.

The many congressional committees and subcommittees have overlapping, unclear interests and jurisdictions in international economic matters, making both duplication and omissions inevitable. Responding to constituent concerns, the Congress creates a continuing flow of legislative proposals directed at trade policy. Electorate pressures are more likely to focus legislators' attention on narrow, short-term microeconomic problems—on the immediate concerns of individual firms and industries—than on broader, more fundamental issues of greater, longer term national and global importance.

Legislators are not always seriously committed to bills they introduce. Some are simply to placate constituents. But each new bill diverts and consumes executive and legislative time, attention, and resources. The Omnibus Trade and Competitiveness Act of 1988 exemplifies massive investments of executive and legislative branch resources in response to public concerns. The act treats symptoms but fails to address underlying causes. It pursues microeconomic, sectorally oriented trade policy initiatives but ignores the macroeconomic saving-investment determinants of the trade deficit and international competitiveness problems. There is no organizational mechanism to direct congressional attention from symptoms to causes—to broader problems of the U.S. and world economies. Executive branch leadership is required.

REORGANIZING INTERNATIONAL ECONOMIC POLICY MAKING

Given growing executive branch reliance on inexperienced and constantly changing appointees, a diminishing career force role, and escalating intervention of the congress, more effective use of available executive branch resources is vitally important.

Making major policy decisions inevitably involves only a few key players at the top. They cannot be instant experts on every topic but should be well informed, basing their decisions on all of the information and arguments available. A properly organized interagency process facilitates collection and exchange of information and a venting of viewpoints and ideas. Without it, decisions may be based on incomplete information and argument. The question is, does the United States have a process that draws on the full range of agency and external expertise to provide the information needed for intelligent policy formulation? Does it ensure an exchange of viewpoints?

The answer is that formulation and execution of U.S. international economic policy has long been an organizational hodgepodge. Resources are fragmented, located in a large number of departments and agencies: State, Treasury, Commerce, Labor, Agriculture, the Office of the U.S. Trade Representative, the

International Trade Commission, the CIA, and a variety of others. Most, however, are oriented toward reacting to electorate concerns about microeconomic issues. Typically, there has been no systematic direction of agencies toward identifying or examining larger problems.

Without a clear White House prescription of policy making responsibilities and processes, both continuing neglect of important long-term problems and divisive interagency struggles for the lead roles on high visibility issues are ensured. Conflict, confusion, duplication, and omissions are guaranteed results.

The need for effective coordination has probably become even greater in international economic policy than in national security policy. The 1971 Williams Commission report found that as many as sixty different government agencies could have an interest in a given international economic policy issue.[3] The number is probably larger today and the price of flawed policy making greater.

ALTERNATIVE MODES OF ORGANIZATION

How should the executive branch manage international economic policy making? There are three basic alternatives: a cabinet mode, first-among-equals, and centralized White House control.

Most administrations have followed some version of a cabinet approach. White House coordination and control are typically minimal. No clear definition of international economic responsibilities among departments is likely; there is no organized White House level procedure for resolution of interagency differences, no coordinated interagency effort to identify important developing problems. Modest staff support for international economic issues is provided by the NSC. Other things equal, the Treasury secretary typically will dominate most of the high-visibility issues. But Treasury lacks the staff to identify and examine the full range of emerging issues and the charter to coordinate interagency examinations in fields outside its own expertise. A cabinet approach to international economic issues is likely to produce interagency turf struggles, a lack of forward planning, and improvised responses to many problems.

There are two models of a first-among-equals approach. Responsibility for various segments of international economic policy could be parceled out among a number of individual cabinet departments. The lead role in some trade matters, for example, might go to the Commerce Department, foreign aid issues to the State Department. Alternatively, responsibility for coordination of all international economic issues could be given to a single lead agency.

Both approaches have damning shortcomings. It is impractical to divide coordination responsibilities among individual agencies by subject areas because topics overlap, leading inevitably to confusion and jurisdictional disputes. The lead-agency approach is equally flawed. Individual agencies are ill-equipped to lead and coordinate the work of others. No one agency has the staff and technical competence to deal with the full range of international economic issues. Interagency differences on policy recommendations are unlikely to be resolved below the White House level in a lead-agency mode of organization. Even drafting papers that only identify policy options is more difficult and less productive when the work is coordinated by a lead agency. Inevitably, parochial interagency differences and suspicions make it tempting to escalate differences to the president for a decision. A White House headed coordinating group has a better chance of resolving differences and minimizing appeals to the president by agency heads.

HOW BEST TO ORGANIZE

Strong centralized White House coordination of executive branch agencies through the equivalent of a National Security Council for international economic policy matters is a third alternative. A White House council can provide an effective, viable means of collecting information and agency positions, synthesizing differing views into options papers, and forging decisions when agency views and recommendations differ.

Such an organization does not exist today. Although technically a White House unit, the Office of the U.S. Trade Representative (USTR) does not fill the need for a central coordination organization. Its staff has a high proportion of career personnel and is among the government's most competent and experienced. The USTR's focus, however, has always been primarily on trade policy and trade negotiations, not on longer term, macroeconomic issues and problems outside the trade area. Moreover, it is already overemployed by recent legislation and can only become more embroiled in day-to-day operations and negotiations as congressional micromanagement of trade issues expands.

A White House coordination organization—the Council on International Economic Policy—was created in 1971. It was active and effective for several years before becoming a casualty of President Nixon's exodus, disappearing when its legislated authorization expired in 1977.

A full-fledged international economic policy council would include an adviser to the president for international economic affairs and a small supporting staff. Although most of its work would be accomplished in interagency meetings at lower levels, council meetings would normally be chaired by the president. It would likely include the vice-president and the secretaries of treasury, state, commerce, and defense, the USTR, and, possibly, the secretary of labor as permanent members, with attendance by other agencies dependent on the issues involved.

The role of White House coordination organizations is frequently misrepresented by news media. The purpose is not to dominate cabinet and other agencies but rather to stimulate and coordinate the work of agencies, to ensure that important topics are addressed, and to act as catalyst, cajoler, expediter, referee, and honest broker. Typically, agency viewpoints on important issues differ, reflecting their traditional biases and the concerns of their constituents. A primary

White House coordination function is to solicit, synthesize, and present these differing views for presidential decision making.

A council staff drawn from the career force bureaucracy, think tanks, and academia offers an opportunity to put together assessments that reflect a broader national viewpoint; one that may differ from that of individual agencies that have come to dominate in particular issues. It can also divert some agency resources from daily operations to longer term assessments and planning.

A strong White House international economic coordinating organization would not be welcomed by all. The secretaries of treasury and state see themselves as the leading actors in most international economic issues. They are likely to oppose a White House coordinating unit because it could diminish their power and freedom of action. The national security advisor might also view it as diminishing his role. But agencies that lack a strong policy making voice— including the Commerce Department—would probably welcome a White House coordinating unit. Without such an organization, no structured mechanism exists to collect and assess their views, and their arguments are thus less likely to be heard.

Media and the public might also be wary, fearing White House staff domination of policy making. A naive public faith in cabinet government and concern about White House control persist, despite the impossibility of governing through cabinet meetings. The spectrum of problems that presidents must deal with has become so broad and complex and involves so many different agencies that effective management requires strong White House coordination. Cabinet government simply cannot cope effectively with the large number and variety of important issues that require presidential involvement. An institutionalized White House coordinating unit is essential, particularly in a system where there is constant turnover in the top levels of management.

Though recent events have highlighted the dangers of White House organizations exceeding their charters and crossing over into operations, poor coordination poses greater risks. Absent strong White House coordination, errors of omission—notably, the failure to take action—are much more likely. So are flawed, incomplete analyses more likely. These failures are much more dangerous than the risks of a new international economics coordination unit stepping out of bounds.

Some have suggested that the NSC be given responsibility for both national security and international economic issues. A single unit, however, would overload its head. Effective policy making requires a division of responsibilities inside the White House.

One method would divide White House control and coordination activities among three councils that together would embrace the full spectrum of issues the president must deal with: the existing National Security Council, an International Economic Policy Council, and a Domestic Policy Council (see Figure 12–1). Each would be headed by an assistant to the president and have a sup-

Figure 12–1
"Council" Method of White House Policy Making Organization

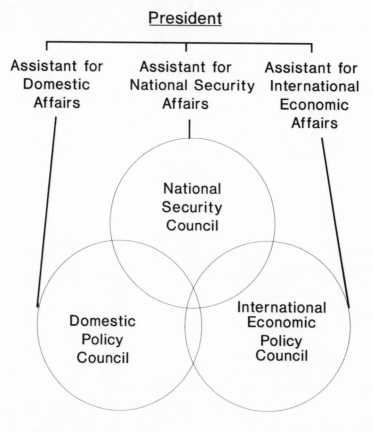

President

Assistant for
Domestic
Affairs

Assistant for
National Security
Affairs

Assistant for
International
Economic
Affairs

National
Security
Council

Domestic
Policy
Council

International
Economic
Policy
Council

porting staff. President Nixon created essentially this form of organization in his second term.

Clearly, organization alone cannot ensure good analysis and correct decisions. No form of organization can completely eliminate jurisdictional overlaps, disputes, and turf battles. Under any chartering, disagreements about responsibility for particular issues will inevitably arise.

Success would greatly depend upon the abilities of the assistant to the president for international economic affairs and his interactions with key cabinet members, other White House officials, and the president. In the end, effectiveness very much depends on the personalities involved, how they work together, and their technical competence. To be most effective, close working relationships among White House coordination organizations and their leaders would be necessary. Success, however, will be even more dependent on recognition by presidents of the importance of international economic issues and taking the time to understand and deal with them.

CONCLUSIONS

Better organization is not a panacea for flawed U.S. policy making, but some methods of organizing simply have a greater chance of being effective than others. An institutionalized, more ordered process is necessary for consistently effective management of international economic affairs. Without an institutionalized process, outcomes are even more dependent than need be on the personal knowledge, experience, skills, and chemistry of a few people at the top. Some top level teams may work effectively without a structured process, but turnover is rapid, continuity lacking, and results uncertain.

A permanent, mandated International Economic Policy Council would raise the visibility of international economic policy making, increase presidential involvement, and provide improved continuity, structure, and order to the process. It offers the best chance of informed, effective U.S. policies and leadership.

Prospects for quickly changing and improving a flawed U.S. international economic policy making apparatus and increasing its focus on longer term global economic issues are slim. In the meantime, the experience and personal skills of a few key U.S. policymakers hopefully will be adequate to the task of global economic leadership in a particularly difficult and critical period. A little luck would help too.

NOTES

1. The essence of the effects of the continuing flow of appointees through the executive branch is captured by the following apocryphal anecdote, often repeated within the bureaucracy: A new political appointee arrives for duty in his executive branch position, full of vim and vigor, ready to accomplish great works. Counsel from his tired, bedraggled predecessor is rejected by the bright, confident new arrival. The dismissed appointee, on his departure, hands his successor three sequentially numbered envelopes, advising that they be opened "when things get tough." Fully confident of his capabilities, however, the new incumbent stuffs the envelopes in a drawer and sets about his business.

For a while, all seems well, but as time passes, things begin to go wrong for the new appointee. The problems he is to solve are more complex, difficult, and intractable than he had anticipated. There is no clear bottom line measure of success, often no good options, seldom a course of action that will satisfy most critics. The new administrator becomes increasingly frustrated. Then, remembering the envelopes, he opens number one. Inside it says, "Blame your predecessor." He follows that advice, and for a time it seems to work. Soon, however, things again begin to deteriorate; pressures and criticism are mounting, and the predecessor can no longer credibly be blamed.

Turning to envelope number two, the advice inside is "reorganize." This seems an excellent idea, and the appointee follows it. Reorganization takes several months and occupies a lot of the new appointee's time, as well as much staff time. But it gives him a feeling of momentum. At last things are happening. He is moving blocks on organization charts and desks and people. He has a feeling of control and shaping events. He is leaving his imprint on the organization!

As time passes, however, more and more seemingly intractable problems appear, and the frustration level begins to rise again to intolerable levels. Finally, in desperation, he opens envelope number three. Inside, the advice, is, "Prepare three envelopes."

2. Paul A. Volcker, *Public Service: The Quiet Crisis* (Washington, D.C.: American Enterprise Institute for Public Policy Research, 1988), 11.

3. Commission of International Trade and Investment Policy, "Administering International Economic Policy," in *U.S. International Economic Policy in an Interdependent World*, Report to the President (Washington, D.C.: July 1971), 299.

Chapter 13

Conclusions and Recommendations

For most of the post–World War II period, the dominant concern of the Western world has been military security, and the United States has been the keystone of that security. With the turn of Communist countries toward more democratic and free market-oriented systems and the growth of other new Western economic powers, the world is a much different and more complicated place. The world economy is at a crucial, difficult juncture. Economic policies—both international and domestic—will be critically important in the 1990s, perhaps more so than ever before.

U.S. trade performance and international competitiveness will certainly not be the only difficult international economic problems facing the United States in the 1990s, but they will be key issues. A continuing U.S. dependence on net inflows of foreign capital and the resulting trade deficits risk a change in the attitudes of lenders that could shrink U.S. ability to borrow. This could markedly raise the cost of borrowing, perhaps forcing the United States into a major recession and disrupting the world economy. The risks are not limited to foreign actions. Continued large trade deficits, concern about jobs lost, and rising foreign debt could cause growing support for protectionist policies in the United States. These concerns could trigger U.S. trade policy actions and counteractions by trading partners, leading to trade wars and to disruption of the world economy.

The 1990s will also impose difficulties on U.S. trading partners. Reducing U.S. trade deficits requires that the surpluses of some trading partners must also decline. This will force difficult adjustment problems on them as well as on the United States. These adjustments are likely to put pressure on some trading partners to initiate protectionist trade policies that could lead to reciprocal actions by the United States and others. The adjustment problems facing U.S. trading partners increase the potential for trade wars.

Narrowing and eliminating the U.S. trade deficits, maintaining good foreign and domestic economic growth, and avoiding a series of U.S. and foreign actions that could escalate into trade wars or global recessions clearly will be difficult and risky. The need to look to the longer term and to take steps to improve U.S. competitiveness further complicates the tasks of U.S. policymakers.

Policy changes that would enhance the long-term rise in U.S. living standards and competitiveness will not seem an urgent problem to many. Declining competitiveness does not carry the near-term risks of escalating foreign debt, recession, and trade wars, all of which accompany trade deficits. Nevertheless, in a broad sense international competitiveness is the United States' number one problem, surpassing trade deficits, national security, crime, drugs, protecting and improving the environment, health care, and every other national problem. It deserves priority treatment.

Competitiveness should be given priority because the nation's economic performance is critical to dealing with its other problems. Economic strength is the basis of domestic political stability. Weak economic performance reduces the resources available for domestic programs and national security. Lagging economic performance compared to that in other developed countries undermines the electorate's willingness to assume international political, military, and economic leadership roles. An inability to deal with the nation's basic economic problems also undermines the international credibility of U.S. leadership.

The increased growth of U.S. productivity required to improve U.S. competitiveness is also the key to an ability to provide adequately for an aging population in the next century. All national retirement systems actually are income transfer payment systems and must function on a "pay as you go" basis. In essence, those working are supporting those who are not. The creation of special funds to provide for bulges of retirees in the next century is a sham, whether the funds are invested in government securities or private-sector stocks and bonds. The only way of easing the burden on future workers who must support a higher ratio of retired persons to working persons is to improve the productivity of those future workers, so that they will have larger incomes from which the transfer payments will be made. Increasing the productivity of future workers requires increased current saving and investment to increase productivity and to provide a larger output to be shared among the working and non-working populations in future years.

To provide the basis for meeting the needs of both the working and non-working segments of the population in the next century and the basis for continued U.S. global leadership in this century and beyond, the immediate tasks of U.S. policymakers are both to end U.S. trade deficits and to initiate actions that, over the long term, will improve U.S. competitiveness. But these difficult tasks must be accomplished in ways that will avoid severe global economic disruptions and will not impair world economic growth. Severe global economic problems are always costly, difficult, and unwelcome. They could be particularly difficult, perhaps disastrous, at this critical point in the evolution of the world economy. It would indeed be ironic if market-oriented economic systems experienced severe setbacks at the very time when the USSR and the countries of Eastern Europe

have rejected communism as a viable economic system and are turning to more
market-oriented systems.

BASIC STRATEGY FOR DEALING WITH THE TRADE
DEFICIT AND COMPETITIVENESS PROBLEMS

Required Action

Both the trade deficit and competitiveness problems demand immediate attention and will be difficult to resolve. As difficult as solutions will be, the trade
deficits will yield earlier and more readily to corrective policies than will the
competitiveness problem. Dealing with the competitiveness issue also promises
to be more controversial.

Although competitiveness is an immediate concern, focusing initially on reducing the federal budget and trade deficits is appropriate. Gradually reducing
the federal budget deficit by carefully reasoned measures is the fastest and surest
way to increase national saving and gradually decrease the trade deficits. At the
same time it will lessen the chances of a sudden, precipitous narrowing forced
by external market decisions. Cutting the trade deficits will also benefit future
international competitiveness by slowing and then halting debt growth and the
resulting future drain on U.S. living standards. In addition, the increase in
national saving implicit in most forms of budget deficit reduction should help
to lower interest rates and encourage new investment. Such investment is needed
to increase productivity and improve living standards.

But actions must not be limited to cutting and eliminating the federal budget
deficits. Although eliminating federal budget deficits may lead to an elimination
of trade deficits, it is unlikely alone to change national saving and investment
rates sufficiently. Major increases in saving will be needed to finance the levels
of investment required if the United States is to stay abreast of other nations
with high investment rates. In upcoming years, the saving and investment rates
of key competitor nations may decline to levels comparable to those of the United
States. Perhaps, for example, Japanese saving rates and investment in manufacturing will shrink from rates about twice those of the United States to rates
similar to those of the United States. But this is an uncertain prospect, and until
competitor rates fall, maintaining U.S. international competitiveness will require
significantly higher U.S. saving and investment rates.

Balancing trade accounts without continued dollar depreciation will doubtless
require higher saving and investment growth rates and larger productivity gains
than would result from simply eliminating the budget deficit and improving
government savings. The need for increased U.S. saving is unlikely to be met
by dealing only with government sector saving. The easiest and hence most
likely route to cutting and eliminating the federal budget deficit is a series of
piecemeal tax policy actions, not a major overhaul of the tax system. Unfortunately, significant changes in the nation's consumption-saving ratio probably

cannot be accomplished by just tinkering with tax and fiscal policies. Instead, decreasing consumption and increasing saving and investment will likely require more basic changes in tax laws. The changes needed are not simply to eliminate the federal budget deficit but to alter the distribution of both private-sector income and national income between consumption and investment.

New approaches to regulatory measures and the cost incidence of social programs, as well as a new emphasis on public sector investment in the nation's infrastructure and its human capital, are also needed. Each of these changes will be controversial and difficult. They will also take a long time to affect U.S. international competitiveness.

Prospects for Success

What are the prospects for major changes in U.S. approaches to tax and regulatory policy? Is the United States capable of needed but far-reaching and controversial changes? It is easy to find grounds for pessimism.

Assessing the costs and benefits of new tax and other initiatives designed to increase human and physical capital development will be a difficult and an uncertain process. Similarly, changes in government regulatory actions and philosophies will provoke controversy. In addition, actions to improve performance in the basic determinants of productivity will take a long time to bear fruit. Moreover, it will be difficult to link particular outcomes with specific earlier policy actions. Changes in tax policy intended to raise saving and investment rates, for example, may take several years before they have any significant effect. Measuring the effects will be difficult, and proposals to give special tax and other policy considerations to the manufacturing sector will likely be controversial. In a country of impatient voters eager for results, the consistent application of policies that will provide long-term payoffs is very difficult. There is a strong likelihood that policymakers will go for measures that seem to offer "quick fix" solutions, not waiting long enough for any program to have a real effect. It is likely that policymakers will ricochet from one alternative to another in the search for immediately visible progress.

Unfortunately, there are no one-time "quick fixes" that offer significant advances in productivity and international competitiveness. There are no permanent, decisive, visible "wins." International competitiveness is an invisible, but unending contest that takes place on many different fronts. Absolute and relative changes in living standard rankings occur only gradually, by reason of outcomes in a host of factors: saving, investment, research and development, education, government regulations, and many others. But they do change. The race will belong not to those who do well in the short dashes but to the long distance runners. To maintain and enhance its competitive position a nation must persevere in policies that enhance performance in the basic determinants of competitiveness.

There are many significant institutional barriers to making the changes needed to enhance U.S. competitiveness. One is the incentives provided by the American political system. Another is the poor image of U.S. business, particularly that of U.S. manufacturing.

In the American political system, the first imperative of elected officials is usually to ensure their reelection. The surest route to reelection is to eschew difficult, unpopular issues. That is, exercise "followership," not leadership. Read the polls, sense public option, and follow it. Do not attempt to lead it. Unfortunately, public opinion is likely to be short-sighted, not attuned to complex issues when there is no evident crisis. When effecting change requires even modest sacrifices, those who advocate "be happy—don't worry" are most likely to be heard.

The adversarial relationships between business and government and between business and labor also pose difficult barriers to implementing the kinds of changes needed. Business is seen by many Americans as an opponent, rather than as a partner, in wealth creation. In Japan, Germany, and successfully developing LDCs, business is cosseted; in the United States it is more likely to be chastised. This is particularly true of "heavy industry"—the "big business" that is much of U.S. manufacturing.

Too often, U.S. manufacturing is seen by the general population as polluting the environment while producing inferior products. Labor sees it as an adversary from which it must extract higher wages. Government sees it as a kind of "cash cow" from which it must exact the maximum amount of tax revenues to avoid more direct taxation of individuals. Curiously, for the world's leading capitalist nation, few Americans understand the linkage between business profitability and their own economic progress and security. Few understand the relationships between business profits, research and development, technological advance, capital investment, productivity, and living standards. Fewer still recognize the link between business profitability and their own individual economic welfare and security. There is an inherent public distrust of business and a widespread antagonism toward business profitability.

The existing public image of U.S. industry is a serious handicap to long-term U.S. competitiveness and must be changed if capital formation and U.S. competitiveness are to be enhanced. Government and the public must view industry as an asset, not an adversary, and policy making must reflect such a view. Government must avoid draconian, punitive measures that reflect populist notions but may impair industry's competitiveness. Tax and other policies should focus on capital formation, on making the economic pie grow, not just on how to divide the existing pie. Labor also needs to take a longer term view. It must look beyond extracting the most in current wage and benefits in contract negotiations. It must begin considering actions that raise productivity and help to make U.S. industry more viable and competitive over the longer term.

Changing the public perception of U.S. industry from adversary to asset— from a black hat to a white hat—will not be easy. It is not clear how the poor image developed, and how it might be changed is equally unclear. Neither is it certain whose job it is to try to change it. But it is certain that if U.S. industry itself does not take on the difficult task, no one else will.

Despite the many difficult barriers to improving U.S. competitiveness, there is some ground for optimism. There is a growing sense in the nation that something is amiss. As the public becomes more aware of the continuing decay in the U.S. competitiveness position, the political environment for accomplishing change will likely improve, and it may become practical for knowledgeable, effective leadership to take a number of steps that will make for long-term gains in U.S. competitiveness. The following sections review specific policy actions that will help in narrowing the global trade imbalances and in improving U.S. international competitiveness.

NARROWING GLOBAL TRADE IMBALANCES

An orderly, gradual reduction of U.S. and trading partner trade and current account imbalances poses difficult domestic and international coordination problems. Some key required actions are noted below.

Reduce and Eliminate the Federal Budget Deficits

To narrow and eliminate the U.S. trade and current account deficits while maintaining good U.S. and global economic growth, the U.S. saving-investment gap must be narrowed and eliminated. This can be accomplished in several ways, but the quickest, surest, and safest way is to undertake a step-by-step reduction of federal budget deficits. This should not be done, however, by discouraging capital formation and lowering U.S. international competitiveness. Enhanced U.S. competitiveness requires increased investment by business in research and development and plants and equipment.

Push Harder for Complementary Actions by Surplus Countries

The U.S. trade deficits are only part of a global problem. Eliminating the U.S. saving-investment gap is only part of the solution. The role of countries with trade surpluses in creating global imbalances as well as the need for their participation in the solution has been underemphasized. Inordinately high saving rates and inflexible trade surplus orientations are the ultimate foreign trade barrier. Top level negotiations must aim at macroeconomic changes by surplus countries that are complementary to U.S. changes. That is, we must increase saving, decrease consumption. Some surplus countries must do the opposite: increase consumption, decrease saving. They must take steps to increase their domestic demand and reorient their economies away from dependence on export surpluses.

Effective U.S. actions to reduce its budget deficits will put the United States in a stronger position to press for actions by surplus countries.

Accept the Inevitability of Further Declines in the Dollar

Because the surplus countries face difficult adjustment problems, there is ample motivation for them to delay actions to reduce their surpluses. It is most unlikely that the exchange rates of the early 1990s will facilitate a significant further narrowing of U.S. trade and current account deficits. The strength of the dollar may be maintained for some time, perhaps years. Significant further declines in the dollar will, nevertheless, sooner or later be a key factor in an orderly move back toward balance in U.S. external accounts.

Further dollar decline has disadvantages for the United States. These disadvantages include worsened terms of trade, a boost to inflation, and downward pressure on U.S. living standards. Some argue that further dollar declines are not a solution because the post-1985 decline did not eliminate the deficits. They argue that further decline would allow foreigners to "buy up the United States on the cheap" and that dollar decline is inflationary. These arguments are often advanced by those who want to maintain the status quo, by foreign competitors who do not want to make the adjustments that further dollar depreciation will force on them. Understandably, they want to postpone the adjustments they must make when their trade surpluses shrink.

But the reality is that the relatively modest gains in U.S. trade balances of the late 1980s do not signal that exchange rate adjustment has failed or that it will not work. Indeed, it has been working. A 1989 study estimated that, had the dollar remained at its early 1985 peak level, the current account deficit would have reached an astronomical $400 billion in 1992, compared with the $150 billion deficit projected in light of the depreciation that did occur.[1]

The beneficial effects of earlier declines in the dollar were, however, exhausted by the beginning of the new decade. Further significant improvement without further dollar decline or lagging U.S. economic growth is unlikely. The dollar decline that occurred was simply not adequate to increase exports and cut imports enough to eliminate the deficits. By the beginning of 1990, foreign producers had, through new cost-cutting and investment efforts, "adjusted" to the new dollar exchange rate. The ability of foreign producers to adjust to declines in the dollar has been impressive, but their ability to cut prices, shrink profits, and achieve productivity gains is not unlimited. Moreover, the willingness of foreign populations to continue to pay high prices for domestic goods compared to foreign imports is also limited. The dollar must decline to levels at which foreign producers can no longer run large trade surpluses. The dollar exchange rate must be one that will both cut total U.S. expenditures for goods and switch much of remaining expenditures from foreign-based to U.S.-based production.

Further dollar declines, it is true, will offer better terms for individual purchases of U.S. assets by foreigners. But it will also be part of a process that will more quickly halt the accumulation of additional foreign debt. Halting the growth of foreign debt that must be serviced—not the exchange rate that determines how cheap or dear U.S. assets may appear to foreigners—should be the primary concern of policy actions.

Additional devaluation will, it is true, add to inflationary pressures. Unfortunately, a rise in the price of foreign imports will be necessary both to lower total U.S. consumption and to switch purchases from foreign goods to domestic goods. Cutting the U.S. budget deficit is not an alternative to further dollar decline. It lowers total demand, but only a small fraction of that reduction falls on imports. Both deficit reduction and additional dollar devaluation will be required for a smooth, gradual reduction of U.S. trade deficits. Additional devaluation will also be necessary to give U.S. trading partners stronger incentives to make adjustments in their economies. In the United States' current situation there simply are no viable policy alternatives that do not have significant negative effects. No painless exits from the large trade deficits of the 1980s are available. Instead, the problem is to select the mix of policies that is least undesirable.

While additional dollar decline will almost certainly be an important and necessary factor in eliminating large current account deficits during the 1990s, it is not an acceptable long-term route to improved U.S. international competitiveness. Policies to improve U.S. competitiveness should focus on generating the saving and investment required to ensure that balancing trade in future years will not require continuing dollar devaluation.

More Realistic Exchange Rates Vis-à-Vis
LDC Surplus Countries

The current account surpluses of Taiwan and Korea have declined but remain large relative to their GNPs. Both economies face difficult adjustments in order to shrink their surpluses. Both must raise consumption and lower saving, and a disruption of some of their industries is likely. As long as their large trade surpluses continue, both countries are unlikely to make these necessary changes quickly enough. The Taiwanese and South Korean currencies are pegged to the dollar at exchange rates unlikely to facilitate an adequate decline in their surpluses. Both countries must be pressured to appreciate their currencies further and to speed changes in their economies. This will be a difficult, sensitive process. It will, however, be less inflammatory than high-profile individual sector negotiations or "reciprocity" mandated under the trade act of 1988.

Deemphasize Foreign Trade Barriers

Foreign trade barriers are an important problem but not a significant factor in the growth of global trade imbalances. Blaming U.S. deficits on foreign actions and focusing too much attention on bilateral negotiations in individual product areas unrealistically raises the public's expectations. It gives the impression that our problems can be solved by foreign rather than U.S. initiatives, diverts public attention from more fundamental problems, and contributes to protectionist pressures when expectations are not met. It also diverts the attention of U.S. and foreign policymakers from more fundamental and important issues. Bilateral microeconomic negotiations on individual product and sector problems should continue but with reduced visibility and expectations. More emphasis should be given to top-level negotiations on macroeconomic issues. They include lowering the implicit macroeconomic barriers to increased consumption and increased imports in major trade surplus countries. That is, there should be more emphasis on decreasing saving and increasing consumption in the surplus countries. Without such changes, a more painful, delayed adjustment via significant currency appreciation in the surplus countries is ensured. The Structural Impediment Initiative (SII) negotiations of 1990 are an important beginning in directing more attention to macroeconomic factors.

U.S. INTERNATIONAL COMPETITIVENESS

Declining U.S. international competitiveness is a complex problem. Improving U.S. competitiveness will require action on many fronts. No actions will likely be more important than those dealing with the improvement of human capital—the U.S. work force. The focus of this book—and the thrust of the recommendations that follow in this section—is, however, on steps to improve productivity through additional investment in physical capital.

Define and Address U.S. International Competitiveness

Unless it is identified as an issue separate from the trade deficits, U.S. international competitiveness is unlikely to be given the attention it deserves. Indeed, the wrong actions—policies that impair competitiveness—may be taken. Competitiveness should be defined and discussed in the terms presented in the report of the President's Commission on Industrial Competitiveness—in terms of productivity and living standards. The nature of the competitiveness race, the key role of advances in productivity, and the fundamental factors that determine competitiveness should be identified. There is a need to examine thoroughly U.S. attitudes, laws, and regulations to determine if changes are required to maintain the economic strength that is the basis of U.S. political, economic, and military leadership.

Tax, Regulatory, and Other Policies Focus on Manufacturing

A 1990 report of the Office of Technology Assessment (OTA) begins with "U.S. manufacturing is in trouble. That spells trouble for the Nation, because manufacturing provides well-paid jobs, pays for most privately funded research and development, and dominates international trade.''[2] The OTA diagnosis is correct. In fact, it understates the problem.

The concept of a "post-industrial" society—espoused by some—in which the United States becomes a nation of corporations performing information and other services with manufacturing done principally in less sophisticated economies is naive and dangerous. The United States cannot pay its way in the world economy and run large deficits in manufactured goods. In fact, to balance its external accounts it will have to have substantial manufactures trade surpluses. No modern nation can be politically, militarily, and economically strong without a strong, vibrant manufacturing sector developing and using the latest technologies to produce a full spectrum of goods ranging from basic products that are inputs to the production process to final products for delivery to consumers and industry.

Newly integrated international capital markets have led to large and rapid changes in the size and direction of international capital flows. This new phenomenon requires added consideration in tax and other policies. Manufactures trade is the primary interface of the U.S. economy with the world economy. The manufacturing sector must inevitably bear the brunt of significant changes in the direction and volume of net capital flows to and from the United States. Some tax and other policies that generate large net capital inflows may help other sectors but impair the performance of and investment in U.S.-based manufacturing.

Tax, regulatory and other policies can significantly affect the international competitiveness of U.S.-based production of tradeable goods and services in other ways. U.S. technology and U.S.-based production seldom have unique advantages. Most goods can be and are produced at many locations around the globe. In a more competitive world, prices are an increasingly important competitive factor. Tax, regulatory, and other policies that disadvantage U.S.-based production simply drive production outside of the United States. The resulting negative effects on the trade balance then put additional downward pressures on U.S. wage rates and the dollar exchange rate, negatively affecting U.S. living standards in the long term. Taxes, regulatory actions, and other policies that disadvantage U.S.-based production of goods are not in the best interests of the U.S. economy unless their benefits outweigh the costs of impaired U.S. competitiveness.

There is no single reason for manufacturing's current difficulties and no single or simple policy solution. Nevertheless, correct macroeconomic policies are a necessary, if not a sufficient, condition to major improvement. During the 1980s, U.S. manufacturing did not fare well in an often hostile environment of foreign competition and domestic policies with unfavorable consequences. Moving into the 1990s, policymakers and the public should see the manufacturing sector as an asset to be enhanced and nurtured, not as an adversary. Public policy should, if not cosset the goods-production sector, at least not handicap it.

Examine the Long-Term versus the Short-Term Phenomenon

A high-wage country such as the United States will be unable to compete successfully in world markets if its planning horizon is shorter than those of its major competitors. The planning horizons of Japanese business, for example, appear much longer than those of U.S. business. Japanese investment plans seem motivated more to long-term objectives than do those of U.S. business.

U.S. business has been chastised for taking a short-term approach to its investment decisions. Businesses, however, are usually not irrational. Their investment decisions are shaped by the incentive systems they face. Investment incentives are determined in large measure by the cost of capital—by interest rates and tax laws. After-dinner speeches that exhort U.S. business to take a longer term view will not change a short-term orientation that is rational under existing incentive systems. Behavior will be changed by altering incentive systems, not by rhetoric. A comprehensive examination of the effects of current laws, policies, and regulations on investment time horizons should be undertaken and necessary changes made.[3]

Avoid "Tailored" or "Managed" Trade

A slow, irregular decline in U.S. current account deficits, intensified competition for world and U.S. markets, and increased structural change will probably escalate calls for "tailored" or "managed" trade and for creation of a U.S. "industrial policy." The methods used by Japan and some Asian newly industrializing countries may be recommended as models for the United States to emulate. But even if government management in Japan and some other countries has been instrumental in their success—an arguable issue—it does not follow that the United States can successfully use the same strategy.

Managed trade proposals typically advocate bilateral export and import levels set by negotiation or U.S. mandate, with attempts to enhance selected U.S. industries. The "free market" approach—letting the market sort out winners and losers—may have its costs and inefficiencies, but the alternatives for the United States are undoubtedly much worse. The United States' ability to "manage" trade would be handicapped by many factors, including the constant turnover of political appointees in key U.S. policy making positions, lack of an elite civil service, superficial media treatment of complex issues, the short-term orientation of both legislators and executive branch political appointees, the adversarial nature of business-government relations, the similarly adversarial nature of legislative and executive branch relations, and the existence of thousands of highly effective special interest groups whose function it is to make their particular case to the government. These and other factors make it apparent that effective U.S. government management of trade or industrial policy would be a first-order miracle.

Increased U.S. government involvement in managing trade (a large portion of U.S. trade is already managed in some way) or some form of industrial policy would be a recipe for disaster. Those who advocate various forms of managed trade should be asked to spell out in detail just *how* the process would work and *who* would do the managing. Clearly, in the open U.S. society every element of trade issues would become a tugging match, with various interest groups pressing their cases on executive and legislative branch officials. Policy would too often be driven by the relative power of conflicting interest groups and short-term political expediencies, infrequently by correct appraisals of long-term merit.

Moreover, some managed trade proposals would, in effect, mandate increased involvement of foreign governments in the management of their trade with the United States. In the end, U.S. endorsement of managed trade implicit in U.S. actions could lead to the demise of the current global trading system.

With all of its faults and problems, the best U.S. industrial policy in the long term is likely to be one of keeping government intervention in microeconomic, individual industry issues to a minimum. Instead, the government should focus on providing a general environment in which U.S.-based production can compete with foreign-based production. The government's role should be one of ensuring that laws and regulatory policies encourage saving and investment and do not disadvantage U.S.-based production. It should then let the dollar exchange rate and other macroeconomic factors sort out which industries will thrive, which manufacturing industries now located abroad will move to the United States, and which businesses and industries will decline.

Also, maximum pressure should be exerted on trading partners—particularly those with large global current account surpluses—to adopt policies that will lead to diminished surpluses. U.S. and international actions that would progressively reduce the current account surpluses of some countries relative to their GNPs should be considered. U.S. pressures will be much more effective if the United States takes steps to increase its saving and decrease its consumption relative to production. Even so, substantial further dollar decline will probably be essential to motivate needed trading partner actions.

Conduct a Serious Reexamination of Tax Policy

If U.S. competitiveness is to be maintained and enhanced, the U.S. saving rate must be raised to levels that compare more favorably with those of major competitors. The increase will be necessary to lower interest rates and the cost of capital sufficiently to raise U.S. investment—particularly in the tradeable goods sectors. How the current structure of taxes influences U.S. saving and investment and international capital and trade flows in a newly interdependent world must be thoroughly examined.

Eliminating government dissaving (eliminating the federal budget deficit) alone will not adequately increase U.S. saving rates. Increased private-sector saving (personal and business saving) will also be needed to achieve investment capital costs that compare more favorably with those of major competitors. Private-sector saving is determined by many economic, demographic, and social factors. The key policy tool for affecting saving, however, is tax policy. Wide differences in saving rates among countries stem in part from wide differences in tax policies. It will be difficult, probably impossible, for the United States to remain competitive while relying on tax policies that do not encourage a higher rate of saving and investment.

The major tax policy changes necessary to increase saving relative to consumption will require politically difficult philosophical changes. In today's more competitive world, tax policy making must shift attention from initial incidence—who appears to bear the burden of the tax initially—to its effect on capital formation, which in turn affects innovation, productivity, and investment in the tradeable goods and services sector. New attention must be given to the fact that taxes and other costs that disadvantage U.S.-based production relative to foreign production are borne by the economy as a whole. Tax policy making needs to increase its emphasis on policies that make the pie grow, rather than concentrate on how the pie will be divided among members of the economy.

Those reassessing the effects of U.S. tax policy on the international competitiveness of U.S.-based production should focus on the long term. U.S. industry's ''ability to pay,'' implied by profits in the manufacturing sector in the late 1980s, is transient. As international competition for world markets in manufactured items continues to intensify and global supplies of such items continue to increase, profit levels in many industries will come under heavy pressure and will inevitably decline. As industries become more globalized and international competition increases, even factors that only marginally influence the costs of production and rates of return on investment will become increasingly important in determining investment and production locations. Moreover, even though manufacturing profits in the late 1980s rose well above earlier levels, they were not adequate to stimulate a broad-based revitalization of the manufacturing sector in the face of uncertainty and increased foreign competition.

There should also be a reexamination of the effects of tax laws on rates of return and investment in research and development and new plants and equipment. In an integrated world economy these factors are increasingly important in determining the pace of technological advance and where research and production will be located.

Examine the Merits of Consumption Taxes

The value-added tax or other forms of consumption taxes deserve careful consideration. Current U.S. tax structure disadvantages U.S.-based production compared to production in foreign countries that use a value-added tax or other forms of consumption taxes to produce major portions of their tax revenues.

Most importantly, however, a value-added tax should be examined as an alternative to income and other taxes that discourage saving and encourage consumption. The consumption tax should be considered as a potential means of altering the private-sector consumption-saving relationship.

Always Consider the Competitiveness Factor

International competitiveness should always be considered in legislative, regulatory, and other policy initiatives and decisions. The international competitiveness of U.S.-based production can be influenced and disadvantaged by many forms of legislative, regulatory, environmental, and policy actions. The U.S. position is no longer strong enough to absorb the burden of added costs without significantly affecting competitiveness. Actions that have greater costs than benefits unnecessarily disadvantage U.S.-based production without providing adequate compensation.

Look Seriously at Job Retraining Schemes

Government-assisted job-retraining programs have never met with much success. The years ahead, however, promise an escalation in the pace of technological change and an increasing need for retraining and mobility in the labor force. Actions that improve labor mobility—steps to facilitate learning new skills and moving to new jobs—will increase the efficiency of the economy and reduce pressures to shut off imports. A reexamination of the retraining needs and alternatives is merited.

ORGANIZATION FOR INTERNATIONAL ECONOMIC POLICY

During the 1990s and beyond, international economic competition will likely supplant the military competition that has prevailed most of this century. Many steps need to be taken to "refit" the executive branch of the U.S. government to deal with these new realities. A few recommendations follow.

White House Coordination

Issues of international economic policy are more important than ever before, and their importance will doubtless continue to grow. Establishment of a White House coordination organization—the international economic policy equivalent of the National Security Council—offers the best chance of harnessing government and other national resources to deal effectively with the many complex and important international economic problems.

Increase the Analytical Capabilities of the Executive Branch

Each of the several federal government agencies involved in international economic issues should have some analytical capability to assess the big picture. These analytical units should report to high levels within their agencies to facilitate access to the agency head and to lower the likelihood that controversial, or "bad news," assessments will be filtered out by numerous layers of administrators before reaching the agency head.

Increased Attention to Collecting Statistics

Correctly assessing and effectively dealing with international economic issues requires valid statistical information. The collection and analysis of statistical data are frequent budget-cut targets. Many believe the quality and quantity of U.S. economic statistics are inadequate and have deteriorated compared to those of several competitor countries in recent years. The resources applied to developing many key statistics used to guide the economy are woefully thin. A major review of U.S. government statistical needs and resources should be conducted and desirable resource and organizational changes undertaken. The merits of consolidating data collection and dissemination resources in a national statistical office should be assessed.

RAISING VISIBILITY AND UNDERSTANDING

The legislative and other actions that will be required to deal effectively with the trade and competitiveness problems will be controversial and difficult. Public support will require a better informed electorate. Some recommendations for raising the visibility and understanding of international economic issues follow.

Initiate a Major Assessment of the Problems of the 1990s

U.S. political and military leadership of the West rests in large measure on the strength of the U.S. economy, which in turn is increasingly dependent on U.S. international economic policies and performance. There has been little examination by recent administrations of longer term international economic issues facing the nation. There has been no recent comprehensive, systematic review of the effects of U.S. international economic policies and performance on the nation's broader economic, political, and national security interests. The last presidential commission to address a broad spectrum of international economic issues was the Commission on International Trade and Investment Policy—popularly known as "the Williams Commission"—which rendered its report to President Richard Nixon in 1971. To harness both government and private-sector resources and focus public attention, the administration should initiate a major review by a presidential commission of the directions and problems of the United States in the world economy. Although presidential commissions are an imperfect means of such a review, there is no better alternative. No government or private-sector organization has the resources and credibility for a wide-ranging public examination with a long-term focus. If the administration does not initiate such a comprehensive examination, the Congress should do so.

Regular International Economic Assessments

Comprehensive periodic reviews of the international economic environment that include the use of resources outside of the executive branch should be conducted on a regular basis and set by tradition or mandate. Recurring use of presidential commissions could be useful, preferably timed to submit reports at the beginning of each new administration.

Reinstitute the International Economic Report of the President

The Council on International Economic Policy published for several years an annual International Economic Report of the President. The tradition of an annual review of the full spectrum of international economic issues should be reestablished and, if necessary, mandated. The mandate could specify both the general topic areas to be covered and whether the assessment is to be retrospective or prospective. The report could serve multiple purposes and aid in focusing attention on important issues. Hearings in connection with submission of the report should be considered.

Change the Policy Orientation

There is a need to shift public attention from microeconomic, industry-oriented issues to broader, more important problems. International economic policy making oriented to longer term national interests will require difficult, controversial changes that probably will not be accomplished without the support of an informed public. A new administration has an opportunity to shift public attention from the narrower, more politically oriented issues such as job lost, unfair foreign trade practices, and the effects of trade on individual industries to more basic determinants of trade performance and international competitiveness. Policymakers should strive to increase the visibility and understanding of international economic issues in speeches, statements, and publications and by other appropriate means.

The legislative branch also has analytical resources that could be applied to macroeconomic assessments of international economic problems. These resources include the International Trade Commission, the Joint Economic Committee, the Joint Committee on Taxation, the General Accounting Office, the Congressional Research Service, and the Office of Technology Assessment.

NOTES

1. William R. Cline, "American Trade Adjustment: The Global Impact," in *Policy Analyses in International Economics* (Washington, D.C.: Institute for International Economics, 1989), 43.

2. Office of Technology Assessment, Congress of the United States, *Making Things Better: Competing in Manufacturing* (Washington, D.C., 1990), iii.

3. For a very insightful examination of why U.S. business has a short time frame in its investment decisions, see George Hatsopoulos, Paul Krugman, and Lawrence Summers, "U.S. Competitiveness: Beyond the Trade Deficit," *Science*, 15 July 1988, 299.

Bibliography

The American Banker. U.S. Daily Banking and Financial Services Newspaper. New York. 25 July 1989, 23.

Balassa, Bela, and John Williamson. *Adjusting to Success: Balance of Payments Policy in the East Asian NICs*. Washington, D.C.: Institute for International Economics, June 1987.

Bank for International Settlements. *58th Annual Report*. Basle, Switz., 13 June 1988.

Barfield, Claude E., and John H. Makin, eds. *Trade Policy and U.S. Competitiveness*. Washington, D.C.: American Enterprise Institute, 1987.

Behrman, Jack N. *The Rise of the Phoenix: The United States in a Restructured World Economy*. Boulder, Colo., and London: Westview Press, 1987.

Bergsten, C. Fred, and William R. Cline. "Trade Policy in the 1980s." In *Policy Analyses in International Economics 3*. Washington, D.C.: Institute for International Economics, November 1982.

———. "The United States–Japan Economic Problem." In *Policy Analyses in International Economics 13*. Washington, D.C.: Institute for International Economics, October 1985.

Bergsten, C. Fred, William R. Cline, and John Williamson. "Bank Lending to Developing Countries: The Policy Alternatives." In *Policy Analyses in International Economics 10*. Washington, D.C.: Institute for International Economics, April 1985.

Broderick, Nancy. "Consumer Electronics." In *1988 U.S. Industrial Outlook*. Washington, D.C.: U.S. Department of Commerce, January 1988, 47–1 to 47–12.

Christian, James W. "Prospects and Policies for Higher Personal Saving Rates in the 1990s." Paper delivered at "Saving: The Challenge for the U.S. Economy," a Public Policy Symposium sponsored by the American Council on Capital Formation, Washington, D.C., 12 October 1989.

Cline, William R. "American Trade Adjustment: The Global Impact." In *Policy Analyses in International Economics 26*. Washington, D.C.: Institute for International Economics, 1989.

———. "International Debt and the Stability of the World Economy." In *Policy Analyses in International Economics 4.* Washington, D.C.: Institute for International Economics, September 1983.

Commission of International Trade and Investment Policy. "Administering International Economic Policy." In *U.S. International Economic Policy in an Interdependent World.* Report to the President. Washington, D.C., July 1971, 299.

Competitiveness Index. Washington, D.C.: Council on Competitiveness, June 1989.

Corporate Taxes: A World Wide Summary, 1989 Edition. New York: Price Waterhouse, 1989.

Dertouzos, Michael L., Richard K. Lester, and Robert M. Solow. *Made in America: Regaining the Productivity Edge.* Cambridge, Mass.: MIT Press and MIT Commission on Industrial Productivity, 1989.

Destler, I. M., and C. Randall Henning. *Dollar Politics: Exchange Rate Policymaking in the United States.* Washington, D.C.: Institute for International Economics, 1989.

Destler, I. M., and John S. Odell. "Anti-Protection: Changing Forces in United States Trade Politics." In *Policy Analyses in International Economics 21.* Washington, D.C.: Institute for International Economics, September 1987.

Dornbusch, Rudiger, James Poterba, and Lawrence Summers. *The Case for Manufacturing in America's Future.* Rochester: Eastman Kodak Co., 1988.

Drucker, Peter F. "Japan's Choices," *Foreign Affairs,* Summer 1987, 923–941.

———. "Japan's Not-So-Secret Weapon," *Wall Street Journal,* 9 January 1990.

Economic Perspectives. Morgan Stanley & Co. New York. 14 July 1988 and 11 May 1989.

Economic Report of the President. Washington, D.C.: U.S. Government Printing Office, January 1989.

Economic Report of the President. Washington, D.C.: U.S. Government Printing Office, February 1990.

Emmot, William. "The Limits to Japanese Power." *International Economics and Financial Markets.* AMEX Bank Review Prize Essays, New York: Oxford University Press 1989, 6–24.

Feldstein, Martin, Herve de Carmoy, Koei Narusawa, and Paul R. Krugman. *Restoring Growth in the Debt-Laden Third World.* New York: Trilateral Commission, 1987.

Frankel, Jeffrey A. "The Yen/Dollar Agreement: Japanese Capital Markets." In *Policy Analyses in International Economics 9.* Washington, D.C.: Institute for International Economics, December 1984.

"Global Implications of Japan's Changing Financial Structure and an International Yen: What's Ahead for Asia? A Two-Conference Series." *Summary Report.* New York: Japan Society and Asia Society, October, November 1984.

Graham, Ellen. "The Pleasure Dome." *Wall Street Journal,* 13 May 1988.

Greenberg, Daniel S. "A Hidden Cost of Military Research: Less National Security." *Discover,* January 1987, 94–101.

Hale, David D. "The World's Largest Debtor: The Risks of America's New Role as a Capital Importer," *Policy Review,* Fall 1986, 28–39.

Hale, David D. "Tax Reform in the U.S. and Japan: The Movement Towards International Tax Convergence." Paper delivered to U.S.–Japan Consultative Group on International Monetary Affairs, San Diego, February 1987.

Hatsopoulos, George, Paul Krugman, and Lawrence Summers. "U.S. Competitiveness: Beyond the Trade Deficit," *Science,* 15 July 1988, 299.

"The Hollow Corporation," *Business Week*, 3 March 1986, 57–85.

Hufbauer, Gary Clyde, Diane T. Berliner, and Kimberly Ann Elliot. *Trade Protection in the United States: 31 Case Studies*. Washington, D.C.: Institute for International Economics, 1986.

Hufbauer, Gary Clyde, and Jeffrey J. Schott, "Trading for Growth: The Next Round of Trade Negotiations." In *Policy Analyses in International Economics 11*. Washington, D.C.: Institute for International Economics, September 1985.

Institute for International Economics. *Resolving the Global Economic Crisis: After Wall Street*. Washington, D.C., December 1987.

Institutional Investor Fact Book, 1990. New York: New York Stock Exchange, January 1990.

International Monetary Fund. *World Economic Outlook*. Washington, D.C., October 1989.

International Trade Administration, U.S. Department of Commerce. *Foreign Direct Investment in the United States Transactions, 1987*. Washington, D.C.: U.S. Government Printing Office, 1988.

————. *Improving U.S. Competitiveness*. Conference Proceedings. Washington, D.C.: U.S. Department of Commerce, 22 September 1987.

————. *International Direct Investment: Global Trends and the U.S. Role*. Washington, D.C.: U.S. Government Printing Office, 1988.

————. *U.S. Foreign Trade Highlights, 1988*. Washington, D.C.: U.S. Government Printing Office, June 1988.

————. "U.S. Trade Facts," *Business America*, 28 March 1984, 40.

————. *U.S. Trade Performance in 1985 and Outlook*. Washington, D.C.: U.S. Government Printing Office, October 1986.

————. *U.S. Trade Performance in 1987*. Washington, D.C.: U.S. Government Printing Office, June 1988.

————. *U.S. Trade Performance in 1988*. Washington, D.C.: U.S. Government Printing Office, September 1989.

Joint Economic Committee, Congress of the United States. *Restoring International Balance: The Federal Republic of Germany and World Economic Growth*. Staff study. Washington, D.C., June 1988.

————. *Restoring International Balance: Japan's Trade and Investment Patterns*. Staff study. Washington, D.C., July 1988.

————. *Restoring International Balance: The Taiwan Economy and International Trade*. Staff study. Washington, D.C., 30 October 1987.

Kaldor, Mary, Margaret Sharp, and William Walker. "Industrial Competitiveness and Britain's Defense." *Lloyds Bank Review*, October 1986, 31–49.

Kirschten, Dick. "Going for the Breakthrough." *National Journal*, 18 November 1989, 2805.

Kolarik, William F. *Exports of Financially Distressed LDC Debtors to the United States and Industrial West: Trends, Outlook, Implications*. Washington, D.C.: International Trade Administration, U.S. Department of Commerce, 1988.

Kuttner, Robert. "U.S. Industry Is Wasting Away—But Official Figures Don't Show It." *Business Week*, 16 May 1988, 26.

Lawrence, Robert Z. "The International Dimension." In Robert Litan, Robert Lawrence, Charles Schultz, eds., *American Living Standards: Threats and Challenges*. Washington, D.C.: The Brookings Institution, 1988, 23–65.

"LDC Capital Flight." *World Financial Markets*. Morgan Guaranty Bank. New York City. March 1986, 13.

"LDC Debt Reduction: A Critical Appraisal." *World Financial Markets*. Morgan Guaranty Bank. New York City. December 1988, 9.

Lenz, Allen J. "Narrowing the U.S. Trade and Current Account Deficits: How It Will Occur." Paper. April 1988.

———. "Slimming the U.S. Trade and Current Account Deficits." In *International Economics and Financial Markets*. AMEX Bank Review Prize Essays. New York: Oxford University Press, 1989, 19–41.

Lessard, Donald R., and John Williamson. "Financial Intermediation Beyond the Debt Crisis." In *Policy Analyses in International Economics 12*. Washington, D.C.: Institute for International Economics, September 1985.

Life Insurance Fact Book Update, 1989. Washington, D.C.: American Council of Life Insurance, 1989.

Litan, Robert E., Robert Z. Lawrence, and Charles L. Schultz. "American Living Standards, Threats, and Standards." *The Brookings Review*, Winter 1988/89, 23–31.

Little, Jane Sneddon. "Foreign Investment in the United States: A Cause for Concern?" *New England Economic Review*, July–August 1988, 55–71.

Marris, Stephen. "Deficits and the Dollar Revisited." In *Policy Analyses in International Economics 14*. Washington, D.C.: Institute for International Economics, August 1987.

Morici, Peter. *Meeting the Competitive Challenge: Canada and the United States in the Global Economy*. Washington, D.C.: Canadian–American Committee, February 1988.

———. *Reassessing American Competitiveness*. Washington, D.C.: National Planning Association, 1988.

Niskanen, William A. *Reaganomics: An Insider's View*. New York: Oxford University Press, 1988.

Obey, David, and Paul Sarbanes, ed. *The Changing American Economy*. New York: Basil Blackwell, 1986.

Office of Technology Assessment, Congress of the United States. *Making Things Better: Competing in Manufacturing*. Washington, D.C., 1990.

Office of Trade and Investment Analysis, U.S. Department of Commerce. *Technology Intensity of U.S. Output and Trade*. Washington, D.C.: U.S. Government Printing Office, July 1982.

———. *Weekly Exchange Rate Developments*. Washington, D.C., January 26, 1990.

Organization for Economic Cooperation and Development. *Economic Outlook*. Paris, December 1989.

———. *Facing the Future: Mastering the Probable and Managing the Unpredictable*. Paris: Interfutures Project, 1979.

"Overseas Investments by Japan Seen Soaring." *Journal of Commerce*, 26 March 1986, 5A.

Ozawa, Terutomo. *Multinationalism, Japanese Style: The Political Economy of Outward Dependency*. Princeton, N.J.: Princeton University Press, 1979.

Pechman, Joseph A., ed. "Comparative Tax Systems: Europe, Canada, and Japan." Arlington, VA: Tax Analysts, 1987.

President's Commission on Industrial Competitiveness. *Global Competition: The New*

Reality. Vol. 1. Commission Report. Washington, D.C.: U.S. Government Printing Office, 1985.

President's Export Council. *U.S. Trade in Transition: Maintaining the Gains.* Vols. 1 and 2. Commission Report. Washington, D.C.: U.S. Government Printing Office, 1988.

Rutledge, John, and Deborah Allen. *Rust to Riches: The Coming of the Second Industrial Revolution.* New York: Harper and Row, 1989.

Tax Notes. Arlington, VA: Tax Analysts, 23 October 1989.

Thurow, Lester C. *The Zero Sum Solution: An Economic and Political Agenda for the '80s.* New York: Simon & Schuster, 1985.

Tolchin, Martin, and Susan Tolchin. *Buying into America.* New York: Times Books, 1988.

van der Voort, A. B. *Trends and Prospects for U.S. Manufacturing in World Markets.* Washington, D.C.: Machinery and Allied Products Institute, August 1985.

Veeger, Martin R., and James W. Fatheree. *Exchange Rate Management in the East Asian NICs: Issues and Prospects.* Washington, D.C.: International Trade Administration, U.S. Department of Commerce, August 1988.

Velz, Orawin. "Concerned About Saving? Why Not Stop Taxing It!" U.S. Chamber of Commerce. Policy Working Papers. No. 21 (August 1989).

Volcker, Paul A. *Public Service: The Quiet Crisis.* Washington, D.C.: American Enterprise Institute for Public Policy Research, 1988.

"West Germany's Export Irritate Its Trading Partners." *New York Times*, 19 September 1988.

"Will the Baby Boomers Bail Out America?" *Business Week*, 9 October 1989, 20.

Williamson, John, and Donald R. Lessard. "Capital Flight: The Problem and Policy Responses." In *Policy Analyses in International Economics 23.* Washington, D.C.: Institute for International Economics, November 1987.

World Debt Tables, 1987–88. Washington, D.C.: World Bank, 1988.

World Debt Tables, 1989–90. Washington, D.C.: World Bank, 1989, Vol. 1.

Index

260 Index

About the Author

ALLEN J. LENZ is director, trade and economics, for the Chemical Manufacturers Association in Washington, D.C. Previously, he served as director of the Office of Trade and Investment Analysis, International Trade Administration, U.S. Department of Commerce, staff director of the National Security Council, and director of the Office of East-West Policy and Planning, International Trade Administration, U.S. Department of Commerce.

Dr. Lenz holds a B.S. from the University of Pennsylvania, an M.B.A. from the University of Colorado, and a Ph.D. from Stanford University Graduate School of Business.